D0392109

*Mass Political Violence*

*Comparative Studies in Behavioral Science:*
A WILEY SERIES

Robert T. Holt and John E. Turner, *Editors*
Department of Political Science
University of Minnesota

# Mass Political Violence: A Cross-National Causal Analysis

**DOUGLAS A. HIBBS, JR.**
*Massachusetts Institute of Technology*

A WILEY-INTERSCIENCE PUBLICATION

**JOHN WILEY & SONS,** New York · London · Sydney · Toronto

**Library of Congress Cataloging in Publication Data**

Hibbs, Douglas A     1944–
    Mass political violence.

    (Comparative studies in behavioral science)
    "A Wiley-Interscience publication."
    1. Violence. 2. Riots. 3. Government,
Resistance to. I. Title.

JC328.6.H5          301.6'33          72-14185

ISBN 0-471-38600-6

Printed in the United States of America

10 9 8 7 6 5 4 3 2 1

To G. M. H. AND C. C. H.

The last decade has witnessed the burgeoning of comparative studies in the behavioral sciences. Scholars in specific disciplines have come to realize that they share much with experts in other fields who face similar theoretical and methodological problems and whose research findings are often related. Moreover, specialists in a given geographic area have felt the need to look beyond the limited confines of their region and to seek new meaning in their research results by comparing them with studies that have been made elsewhere.

This series is designed to meet the needs of the growing cadre of scholars in comparative research. The emphasis is on cross-disciplinary studies, although works within the perspective of a single discipline are included. In its scope, the series includes books of theoretical and methodological interest, as well as studies that are based on empirical research. The books in the series are addressed to scholars in the various behavioral science disciplines, to graduate students, and to undergraduates in advanced standing.

*Robert T. Holt*
*John E. Turner*

*University of Minnesota*
*Minneapolis, Minnesota*

# *Preface*

This book reports the quantitative empirical research I have been engaged in over the past few years on the casual processes underlying differences across nations in levels of mass political violence during the post-World War II period. Since I have been concerned with domestic violence at the macropolitical level, the specificity and the richness of detail that characterize micropolitical analyses or the study of particular cases have been sacrificed in favor of the potential for generalization made possible by a more global and aggregate investigation.

The book is divided into three parts. Chapter 1 of Part I discusses the constraints imposed in the macroquantitative study of mass political violence and thereby defines the context within which the research was undertaken. The empirical base for the study is a recently compiled multiple cross-section of aggregate data on more than 100 nations. As the title of the book implies, my interest centered on events of domestic violence that had an antisystem character, were of immediate political significance, and directly involved or were sponsored by collectivities. Six of the available domestic violence variables satisfied these conditions: riots, armed attacks, political strikes, political assassinations, deaths from political violence, and antigovernment demonstrations. Dimensional analysis of these variables uncovered two clearly defined clusters. Riots, antigovernment demonstrations, and political strikes distinguished the first cluster, which I have denoted as Collective Protest. The second, denoted as Internal War, is indexed by armed attacks, deaths from political violence, and political assassinations. Chapter 2 of Part I describes these dimensional analyses and develops the method by which I create the composite measures of Collective Protest and Internal War that are used as the operational indicators of mass political violence throughout the rest of the book.

Part II, Chapters 3 to 7, is devoted to an exploratory examination of "single equation" hypotheses and "partial" theories derived from the relevant literature. These analyses are designed to provide an empirical foundation for the specification of a more comprehensive model of mass political violence in Part III. Hence Part II represents an incremental and eclectic approach to the task of model specification and causal inference and reflects my unwillingness to rely exclusively on any single prior theoretical formulation.

The factors examined in Part II include levels and rates of change in socioeconomic development; social structural imbalances and systemic frustration and satisfaction; cultural differentiation and national integration; the behavior of political elites, especially repression and coups; and finally some important features of domestic political structure, in particular, political democracy, Communist totalitarianism, and left party strength. Many of the hypotheses investigated in these chapters are rejected as empirically unsound, some are retained, and others are reformulated as recursive and nonrecursive partial causal systems.

The final section of the book, Part III, integrates and elaborates on the provisional conclusions and formulations of Part II by specifying a more complete multiequation, block recursive, causal model of mass political violence. The core of the model is a block or sector of simultaneous equations which articulates mathematically the causal interdependencies inferred on the basis of prior theory and initial estimation results to be operative among mass violence, elite repression, coups, and the rate of economic change. Other sectors of the model specify equations for variables hypothesized to exert predetermined causal influence on these core endogenous variables. Simultaneous equations estimation techniques and ordinary least-squares regression are employed as appropriate to estimate the model. After a number of revisions in the model's structure, the implications of the final parameter estimates for a dynamic theory of mass political violence are pursued.

I have assumed throughout that the reader is familiar with the logic of cross-national, quantitative research and has some knowledge of regression analysis and multiequation causal modeling. Appendix 3 provides an introduction to the more difficult and less widely known problems associated with the estimation and identification of simultaneous equations models and block recursive causal systems.

I am indebted to many people who read all or parts of the book in one version or another during the past year. They include Hayward Alker, Nazli Choucri, and Franklin Fisher of the Massachusetts Institute of Technology, Charles Cnudde, Arthur Goldberger, and Robert Jackman, of the University of Wisconsin, and Ted Gurr of Northwestern University.

I am also grateful to Lester Warner and his associates at the Center for Research on Conflict Resolution at the University of Michigan for making available to me most of the data used in the research and for providing the funds and assistance necessary to prepare the data for analysis. Financial support was also received from the Ford Foundation, the Vilas

Foundation, the University of Wisconsin Graduate Research Committee, and the Center for International Studies at the Massachusetts Institute of Technology.

Naturally, all errors of fact and judgment are my own.

DOUGLAS A. HIBBS, JR.

*Cambridge, Massachusetts*
*December 1972*

# CONTENTS

*Mass Political Violence*

# PART ONE

# The Quantitative Study of Mass Political Violence

CHAPTER ONE

# Introduction

The purpose of this study is to advance our knowledge of the causal structures that underlie mass political violence within nations. Stated most briefly, we have attempted to answer the question: What produces differences across nations in the magnitude of domestic political violence? In pursuing this goal we have tried to capture *causal relationships* and not simply to explain variance in mass violence in a purely statistical way.[1] Such an effort is constrained in at least three ways. A discussion of these constraints serves to outline the setting within which the research reported in the chapters that follow was conducted.

First there are *theoretical* constraints. This book would have been a great deal shorter and the investigation it records a much less demanding exercise if there had been available to us a single, compelling theory that specified, even crudely, a comprehensive causal model of mass political violence.[2] The task would then have been simply to obtain the relevant data, estimate the model as specified, and, on the basis of the results, perhaps make a few modifications in the original theoretical structure. Unfortunately, the research process is rarely so straightforward. There is an enormous body of qualitative and quantitative literature that deals in no particularly unified way with the many facets of domestic violence,

---

[1] The best introduction to the causal perspective in social science is undoubtedly Hubert M. Blalock, *Causal Inferences in Nonexperimental Research* (Chapel Hill: University of North Carolina Press, 1964). A seminal essay on the causal modeling of political phenomena that presaged much of the subsequent work in the field is Hayward R. Alker, Jr., "Causal Inference and Political Analysis," in J.L. Bernd, (ed.) *Mathematical Applications in Political Science, II* (Dallas: Southern Methodist University Press, 1966).

[2] This does not mean that there are no attempts at large-scale models of mass violence in the existing literature; however, we find no single attempt, qualitative or quantitative, persuasive enough to rely on completely. Instead, an eclectic and incremental model specification and causal inference procedure is preferred. This is outlined more fully below.

conflict, instability, and the like. In addition to the absence of theoretical convergence in the literature, its usefulness to this study was limited in a number of other ways.

The qualitative research has two principal deficiencies. First, qualitative case studies are often concerned primarily with the idiosyncrasies of the particular instance. As a result, factors that may have general relevance tend to become obscured. A problem that characterizes the qualitative work more generally is an ambiguity and circumlocution in style that makes the extraction of testable hypotheses difficult and, at times, impossible.[3] Much of Part II is devoted to ferreting out testable propositions from the most useful studies in this literature.

The quantitative literature also has limitations. Many of these studies are almost entirely atheoretical in the sense that they are exclusively concerned with determining the "dimensions" of domestic conflict through the factor analysis of quantitative data. This has been useful for conceptual clarification, but it does not advance causal understanding in any direct way. Other quantitative studies predict (or postdict!) variance in measures of domestic conflict by means of regression and correlation analyses but ignore issues concerning the underlying causal linkages among the variables involved.[4]

Investigations that have dealt explicitly with causal relationships have often done so badly. Some employ dubious techniques of parameter estimation and causal inference, and others are ambiguous about the way that final causal structures are derived. Frequently, analysis is confined to very limited subsamples of the potential data universe, or only one indicator of the many possible mass violence measures is utilized. The former practice is suspect given the instability of parameter estimates that are based on a small number of observations, whereas the latter procedure is risky because of the unreliability that results from using a single indicator for a multifaceted phenomenon. Finally, all the quantitative studies to date have looked only at models that incorporate linear, additive, and hierarchical relationships. Exclusive reliance on models of this kind is overly (and unnecessarily) restrictive, since the theories we wish to test and the real-world processes we seek to capture are clearly not entirely linear, additive, and unidirectional in causes and effects.

[3] Again, Blalock has given the most attention to this important issue in quantitative social research. See Hubert M. Blalock, *Theory Construction, from Verbal to Mathematical Formulations* (Englewood Cliffs, N.J. : Prentice-Hall, Inc., 1969).
[4] An insightful treatment of the causal models implicit in commonly used regression algorithms is provided by Hayward R. Alker, Jr., "Statistics and Politics: The Need for Causal Data Analysis," in S. M. Lipset (ed.). *Politics and the Social Sciences* (London: Oxford University Press, 1969).

These last observations bear on the *methodological* constraints that affected this research. Even the most sophisticated techniques of non-experimental causal inference cannot overcome the lack of sound, prior theoretical thinking. Although the existing literature suggests hypotheses that deserve further testing with new data and aids in the development of richer causal models, it does not, in our view, provide a persuasive and comprehensive theoretical structure. Given our unwillingness to rely exclusively on any single line of theorizing, one of the major methodological concerns was to proceed in a way that allowed rigorous and systematic investigation of hypotheses that had theoretical merit, without degenerating into a gross fishing operation posing as "empirical" research.[5]

Our effort to achieve this trade-off between exploratory empiricism and theoretically grounded hypothesis testing is represented in Part II, Chapters 3 to 7. In these chapters numerous "single equation" hypotheses and "partial" theories dealing with potential causal determinants of mass political violence are evaluated. Independent variables suggested by such hypotheses and partial theories that are estimated to have coefficients at least twice their respective standard errors are provisionally retained as significant direct causal influences on mass violence. This is not a particularly demanding standard, but it is appropriate to the exploratory purpose of Chapters 3 to 7. We also have anticipated that the causal processes which are at the root of cross-national differences in levels of violence are much too complex to be adequately captured by a single equation formulation. Thus the analyses in Part II are geared to the sequential development of a more realistic multiequation model. Hence, where it is meaningful theoretically and fits preliminary estimation results, what initially are unrelated single equation models are reformulated as multiequation (partial) causal sequences. The result of this incremental hypothesis-testing, model-building process is found in Chapter 8 of Part III, where the provisional results of Part II are integrated as a fully specified causal model of mass political violence.[6]

The third factor that constrained the investigation was *data availability*. Since the focus of inquiry is mass political violence across nations, the research was confined to the macro, systemic level of analysis for which aggregate data are appropriate. As the principal source of data, we were fortunate to obtain the most comprehensive cross-national aggregate data file now in existence. It represents several years of collection effort by a

---

[5] This is especially important for studies that include very large numbers of variables. The importance of theory in multivariate quantitative research is developed well by Robert A. Gordon, "Issues in Multiple Regression," *American Journal of Sociology*, Vol. 73, March 1968, pp. 592–616.

[6] This method of model specification is reviewed in the final chapter.

large team of investigators headed by Charles Taylor and Michael Hudson of the World Data Analysis Program at Yale University, in cooperation with Robert Hefner and Lester Warner of the Center for Research on Conflict Resolution at the University of Michigan.[7] The data file includes numerous measures of domestic conflict as well as dozens of socioeconomic and political variables for a very large number of nations. The next chapter describes the mass violence variables used and the strategy employed for constructing composite violence measures. The socioeconomic and political variables are introduced throughout Part II, Chapters 3 to 7, as they become relevant to the hypothesis-testing, model-building effort.

Although the primary data source is the most complete single file of its kind, we were determined to sacrifice a minimum number of cases because of missing data. Hence a good deal of effort was spent updating as well as supplementing and cross-validating the primary file from other available data sources.[8] As a result of these additional data collection efforts, complete data were obtained on variables of interest for a cross-section of 108 nations. The countries are listed in Appendix 1. This is a very large sample, and it insures that the analyses described here are based on the widest possible range of observations.

---

[7] The data are described at length in Charles L. Taylor and Michael C. Hudson (eds.), *World Handbook of Political and Social Indicators*, 2nd edition (New Haven: Yale University Press, 1972).

[8] For reasons made clear later, we were interested in a 1960 time point for most of the independent variables. If a 1960 value for a particular variable could not be obtained and adjacent time points were available, we interpolated. "Event" variables, such as the violence indicators and others introduced in the chapters ahead, come exclusively from the primary data source. A few variables were obtained entirely from alternative sources. Where this is the case, it is noted in the appropriate chapter.

# CHAPTER TWO

# Mass Political Violence—Its Scope and Measurement

This chapter delineates exactly what is meant by mass political violence and describes how the available quantitative data can most effectively be employed to measure it. A discussion of these issues serves to define more sharply the focus of the research and to prepare the way for the quantitative analyses presented in Parts II and III.

Quite a number of variables have been included in one study or another of domestic violence, conflict, and instability. Our choice of domestic violence event variables from those available in the principal data file was governed by the following, somewhat overlapping, criteria. First, the behavior or "event" in question must on the whole have had an *antisystem* character, in the sense of being at odds with existing political authority. For example, antigovernment demonstrations would meet this criterion, but progovernment demonstrations would not. Second, it must have direct and fairly immediate *political significance*; that is, it must pose a threat of at least severe inconvenience to the normal operation of the political elite. Hence ordinary labor strikes would not satisfy this condition, but strikes with at least mildly threatening political objectives would. Finally, the event must involve *collective* or *"mass" activity*. Therefore, phenomena such as murder, armed robbery, and similar criminal acts are not relevant here, although they may have important second-order political implications by becoming "public" issues, and sometimes stem from widespread alienation from existing socioeconomic and political arrangements.

An exception of sorts to the last constraint is the inclusion of assassinations, which typically are not actually carried out by collectivities, but frequently are sponsored by disaffected groups. Note also that this condition excludes elite actions of various kinds—for example, military coups or government repression—which usually have been included in analyses of domestic violence.[1] It does not exclude, however, deaths that result from clashes of elites and masses in insurgent or protest situations.

Given these prior theoretical constraints, the following six event variables were selected for study:[2]

1. *Riots.* Any violent demonstration or clash of a large group of citizens. "Violence" implies the use of physical force and is generally evinced by the destruction of property, the killing or wounding of people, or the use of riot control equipment. They are distinguished from armed attack events on the basis of whether the event seems to have been organized, whether it is goal directed, and whether it involves all or most of the participants acting purposefully.

2. *Armed Attack Events.* Acts of violence committed by or involving organized groups with weapons of any kind, when these acts are intended as protests, or acts of revolt or rebellion against a government, its members, policies, intended policies, and the like.

3. *Political Strikes.* Any strike by industrial or service workers, or students, for the purpose of protesting against a government, its leaders, or a government policy or action.

4. *Assassinations.* Any politically motivated murder or attempted

---

[1] Many quantitative analyses of domestic violence and instability, especially the dimensional studies, do not distinguish between mass and elite event variables. They are of course correlated. We think it is important, however, to differentiate these theoretically and explore the interdependencies causally. The dimensional studies include: Rudolph J. Rummel, "A Field Theory of Social Action with Application to Conflict Within Nations," *Yearbook of the Society for General Systems Research*, Vol. 10, 1965, pp. 183–211; *idem.*, "Dimensions of Conflict Behavior Within and Between Nations," *ibid.*, Vol. 8, 1963, pp. 1–49; Douglas P. Bwy, "Dimensions of Social Conflict in Latin America," *American Behavioral Scientist*, Vol. 11, No. 4, March–April, 1968, pp. 39–50; *idem.*, "Correlates of Political Instability in Latin America: Over-Time Comparisons from Brazil, Cuba, the Dominican Republic, and Panama," American Political Science Association paper, Washington, D.C., September 1968; Raymond Tanter, "Dimensions of Conflict Behavior Within Nations, 1955–60: Turmoil and Internal War," *Peace Research Society Papers*, III, Chicago Conference, 1965, pp. 159–183; *idem.*, "Dimensions of Conflict Behavior Within and Between Nations, 1958–60," *Journal of Conflict Resolution*, Vol. 10, No. 1, March 1966, pp. 41–64.

[2] The short description of each event variable that follows is paraphrased from "Political Indicators Definitions," November 21, 1966 (no author listed), obtained with the raw data from the Center for Research on Conflict Resolution, University of Michigan. More complete definitions and instructions to coders may be obtained from this source. Riots, armed attacks, demonstrations, and strikes are frequencies crudely weighted for magnitude. Deaths and assassinations (including assassination attempts) are the numbers involved. A detailed description of a slightly revised version of the data can be found in Charles L. Taylor and Michael C. Hudson (eds.), *World Handbook of Political and Social Indicators*, 2nd edition (New Haven: Yale University Press, 1972).

murder of a high government official or politician. Included in addition to national leaders are state and provincial leaders, mayors of large cities, members of the cabinet and national legislature, members of the inner core of the ruling party or group, leaders of the opposition, and newspaper editors.

5. *Deaths from Political Violence.* The number killed in conjunction with any domestic intergroup violence in the nature of armed attacks, riots, demonstrations, and the like. Assassinations are excluded.

6. *Antigovernment Demonstrations.* Organized, nonviolent gatherings of a large number of people for the purpose of protesting against a government, its actions or policies, or one or more of its leaders. Demonstrations that become riots are excluded.

Data on each of these variables were collected by the Yale World Data Analysis Program research team for the 20-year time period January 1, 1948 to December 31, 1967. We aggregated the data into two 10-year periods: *decade 1* (D1) = January 1, 1948 to December 31, 1957; *decade 2* (D2) = January 1, 1958 to December 31, 1967. These decade aggregations provide a summary assessment of the magnitude of the various kinds of violence that are not too severely affected by the specific events of a particular year. They also are compatible with the time point of the available data on potential explanatory variables in the 108-nation cross-section. Moreover, they allow for the consideration of models that posit "past" violence (decade 1) as having a causal influence on the magnitude of "current" violence (decade 2).

## The Dimensions of Mass Political Violence

Previous empirical research suggests that indicators of domestic violence similar to those in this study should not be conceived as distinct phenomena but, rather, are best analyzed in terms of a smaller number of underlying dimensions.[3] Factor analyses of a number of cross-national data sets of varying sample sizes and time frames have typically uncovered two dimensions of domestic conflict. One, usually denoted as "Turmoil" or "Anomic Violence," is indexed by riots, general strikes, antigovernment demonstrations, and the like; the other, typically referred to as an "Internal War" or "Revolutionary" dimension, is characterized by such variables as guerrilla attacks, deaths, and assassinations.[4] This research, then,

[3] See the sources cited in footnote 1.
[4] See Tanter, "Dimensions of Conflict Behavior . . . 1955–60," and "Dimensions of Conflict Behavior . . . 1958–60" for a comparison of the results from a number of dimensional analyses. The convergence of findings is quite convincing evidence of the reliability of the dimensions.

argues for a factor analysis of the political violence indicators in order to ascertain the underlying dimensions and provide a basis for the construction of composite measures that more effectively "tap" these basic dimensions than any particular indicator would.

Factor analysis, like analysis of variance, analysis of covariance, and regression analysis, is a linear mathematical model.[5] All too frequently, practitioners of factor analysis simply input the results of one linear model —the correlation or covariance matrix of the variables under investigation —into another—the factor analysis algorithm—without attention to the assumptions that are (implicitly) made.[6] The strategy should be, however, to *first* take steps to achieve linear relationships between variables and a reduction in the distorting effect of outliers. Accordingly, a distributional plot (histogram) of each event variable in each time period was examined in order to detect the presence of potentially distorting outliers. A scatterplot of each event variable against each of the others was also inspected to ascertain the form of the relationships. The upshot of this tedious but necessary process was the determination that a logarithmic transformation of each variable best stabilized variances and, more important, maximized linear relationships.[7]

The transformed data for each decade were then factor analyzed as a preliminary step to the generation of a smaller number of composite measures or scores. It is important to note that the dimensional analysis was employed here as a descriptive, data reduction device, and *not* as a

[5] This is often overlooked in social science treatments of statistical analysis procedures. The point that the general linear model underlies all conventionally used statistical techniques is especially well developed in Jacob Cohen, "Multiple Regression as a General Data-Analytic System," *Psychological Bulletin*, Vol. 70, No. 6, 1968, pp. 426–433; James Fennessey, "The General Linear Model: A New Perspective on Some Familiar Topics," *American Journal of Sociology*, Vol. 72, No. 1, July 1968, pp. 1–27; and William Mendenhall, *Introduction to Linear Models and the Design and Analysis of Experiments* (Belmont, Calif.: Wadsworth Publishing Co., Inc., 1968). A solid treatment of the various methods of factor analysis and factor score generation is found in Harry H. Harmon, *Modern Factor Analysis*, 2nd edition, revised (Chicago: University of Chicago Press, 1967). A very useful exposition of the relationship of statistical developments generally in psychometrics and econometrics is provided by Arthur S. Goldberger, "Econometrics and Psychometrics: A Survey of Communalities," *Psychometrika*, Vol. 36, No. 2, June 1971, pp. 83–107.

[6] This crucial point is well developed by John M. Digman, "Interaction and Non-linearity in Multivariate Experiments," in Raymond B. Cattell (ed.), *Handbook of Multivariate Experimental Psychology* (Chicago: Rand McNally, & Co., Inc. 1966), Chapter 15, pp. 459–475. See also Rudolph J. Rummel: *Applied Factor Analysis* (Evanston, Ill.: Northwestern University Press, 1970), Chapter 11.

[7] On transformations, the following are instructive: J. W. Richards, *Interpretation of Technical Data* (Princeton N.J.: D. Van Nostrand Co., Inc., 1967); J. B. Kruskal, "Transformations of Data," in David L. Sills (ed.), *International Encyclopedia of the Social Sciences*, Vol. 15 (New York: Macmillan and Co., 1968), pp. 182–192; F. J. Anscombe, "Outliers," in *ibid.*, pp. 178–181; and Rummel, *Applied Factor Analysis*, Chapter 11.

causal model.[8] Given this limited objective, there is still no consensus in the relevant literature on the optimum technique, although a number of investigators have persuasively argued for a principal components solution in such a context.[9] In any case, two methods of factor analysis were employed at this exploratory stage: principal components, and principal factor with squared multiple correlations in the diagonal. Factors were orthogonally rotated by means of the varimax method.

The results are displayed in Tables 2.1 to 2.4. Two quite distinct dimensions are present in the data, and these converge across factor methods and time periods, thus generating a good deal of confidence in the stability of the results. The first factor in each solution and time period is distinguished by the high loadings of riots, antigovernment demonstrations, and political strikes. It parallels, as we noted earlier, what has been referred to as an "Anomic Violence" or "Turmoil" dimension in previous analyses of similar data. *Collective Protest* is probably a more appropriate label for such a cluster of political violence event variables. Armed attacks, assassinations, and deaths from political violence characterize the second factor, which resembles what elsewhere has been denoted as a "Revolutionary," or "Internal War" dimension. *Internal War* is perhaps the best way to describe a cluster of events involving insurgent armed attacks, actual and attempted assassinations of political authorities, and large numbers of people being killed in antistate or intergroup conflict situations.[10]

## Constructing Composite Measures of Mass Political Violence

The factor analysis results can be used in several ways. Bwy, for example, has argued for the computation of factor scores from a second

[8] Hence, it is not maintained that the resulting factors or dimensions necessarily *cause* the interrelationships among the inputted variables, but only that they are useful in the generation of composite measures, which are presumably less idiosyncratic in cross-national variation than any individual variable.

[9] See Jack E. Vincent, "Factor Analysis as a Research Tool in International Relations: Some Problem Areas, Some Suggestions and an Application." American Political Science Association paper, New York, September 2–6, 1969; and Carl-Gunnar Janson, "Some Problems of Ecological Factor Analysis," in Mattei Dogan and Stein Rokkan (eds.), *Quantitative Ecological Analysis in the Social Sciences* (Cambridge, Mass.: M.I.T. Press, 1969). Note that Janson argues for a principal factor solution with 1's in the diagonal, which is identical to a principal components solution!

[10] Note that a relatively small proportion of the variance in Assassinations is accounted for by the dimensions in the principal factor analyses (Tables 2.2 and 2.4), which do not assume perfect reliabilities. This underscores the ambiguity frequently surrounding the political motivation, antisystem character, or collective significance of particular assassinations. Hence more "noise" is introduced by the inclusion of this variable in a composite measure than is introduced by the inclusion of others. I am grateful to Hayward Alker for the substantive comment that led to this observation.

Table 2.1 Principal Components Analysis: Decade 1 Mass Violence Event Variables

| Variables[a] | Factors[b] | | Variance Reproduced |
|---|---|---|---|
| | I | II | $h^2$ |
| Riots | .712 | .531 | .789 |
| Antigovernment Demonstrations | .942 | .212 | .900 |
| Political Strikes | .906 | .261 | .890 |
| Assassinations | .135 | .835 | .716 |
| Armed Attacks | .454 | .803 | .851 |
| Deaths | .323 | .868 | .858 |
| % Factor Variance | 50.2 | 49.8 | 100 |
| % Total Variance | 41.9 | 41.5 | 83.4 |

[a] All variables have been logarithmically transformed.
[b] Orthogonally rotated, varimax method; blocked loadings > .600.

Table 2.2 Principal Factor Analysis:[a] Decade 1 Mass Violence Event Variables

| Variables[b] | Factors[c] | | Variance Reproduced |
|---|---|---|---|
| | I | II | $h^2$ |
| Riots | .629 | .564 | .714 |
| Antigovernment Demonstrations | .855 | .274 | .806 |
| Political Strikes | .833 | .324 | .799 |
| Assassinations | .229 | .616 | .432 |
| Armed Attacks | .401 | .822 | .836 |
| Deaths | .279 | .866 | .828 |
| % Factor Variance | 52.2 | 47.8 | 100 |
| % Total Variance | 38.4 | 35.2 | 73.6 |

[a] Squared multiple correlations in the diagonal.
[b] All variables have been logarithmically transformed.
[c] Orthogonally rotated, varimax method; blocked loadings > .600.

Table 2.3   Principal Components Analysis: Decade 2 Mass Violence
Event Variables

| Variables[a] | Factors[b] | | Variance Reproduced |
|---|---|---|---|
| | I | II | h$^2$ |
| Riots | .884 | .227 | .834 |
| Antigovernment | | | |
|   Demonstrations | .898 | .189 | .842 |
| Political Strikes | .842 | .258 | .776 |
| Assassinations | .088 | .893 | .806 |
| Armed Attacks | .666 | .607 | .813 |
| Deaths | .477 | .757 | .801 |
| % Factor Variance | 58.8 | 41.2 | 100 |
| % Total Variance | 49.3 | 34.5 | 83.8 |

[a] All variables have been logarithmically transformed.
[b] Orthogonally rotated, varimax method; blocked loadings >.600 *or* are
the highest shown.

Table 2.4   Principal Factor Analysis:[a] Decade 2 Mass Violence
Event Variables

| Variables[b] | Factors[c] | | Variance Reproduced |
|---|---|---|---|
| | I | II | h$^2$ |
| Riots | .783 | .363 | .745 |
| Antigovernment | | | |
|   Demonstrations | .842 | .285 | .791 |
| Political Strikes | .738 | .363 | .676 |
| Assassinations | .189 | .546 | .335 |
| Armed Attacks | .529 | .731 | .814 |
| Deaths | .339 | .831 | .806 |
| % Factor Variance | 55.1 | 44.9 | 100 |
| % Total Variance | 38.1 | 31.0 | 69.1 |

[a] Squared multiple correlations in the diagonal.
[b] All variables have been logarithmically transformed.
[c] Orthogonally rotated, varimax method; blocked loadings >.600 *or* are
the highest shown.

unrotated principal components analysis of only the variables that are found to distinguish each dimension on the first exploratory analysis. The result is a composite scale created by the (linear) combination of variables identified as common to the dimension and hence not "contaminated" by secondary loadings from variables common to other dimensions.[11] Tanter, in contrast, has advocated using "representative" variables—that is, variables that load most highly on each dimension—rather than factor scores whose substantive meaning is less readily apparent.[12] Obvious candidates here would be antigovernment demonstrations to "represent" the *Collective Protest* dimension, and deaths from political violence to "represent" the *Internal War* dimension. Another possibility, which is less elegant mathematically than the generation of factor scores but has the advantage of clear substantive interpretation without the loss of information entailed in choosing particular representative variables, is simply to sum the event variables that index a particular dimension. Given the distributions of the component variables, the logarithms of these sums would provide the most appropriate composite index of this type.

Tables 2.5 to 2.6 and 2.7 to 2.8 show the intercorrelations of the three potential measures of Collective Protest and Internal War within each time period. The measures clearly are highly collinear, although as we might expect, the "representative" variables manifest slightly lower intercorrelations because they contain less information than either the factor scores or logarithmically transformed summed scores. The principal disadvantage of factor scores is that in (single or multiequation) causal

Table 2.5   Correlation Matrix of Collective Protest Measures: Decade 1

|     | (1)<br>Factor Scores[a] | (2)<br>ln Summed Index[b] | (3)<br>Representative Variable[c] |
|-----|-------------------------|---------------------------|-----------------------------------|
| (1) | 1.0                     | .938                      | .936                              |
| (2) |                         | 1.0                       | .828                              |
| (3) |                         |                           | 1.0                               |

[a] Created by unrotated principal components analysis of log transformed Riots, Antigovernment Demonstrations, Political Strikes.

[b] ln (Riots + Antigovernment Demonstrations + Political Strikes).

[c] ln (Antigovernment Demonstrations).

[11] Bwy, "Dimensions of Social Conflict in Latin America"; and *idem., Political Instability in Latin America: A Comparative Study,* Ph.D. dissertation, Northwestern University, Evanston, Ill., August 1968. Edward Muller proceeded in the same fashion in "Cross-National Dimensions of Political Competence," *American Political Science Review,* Vol. 64, No. 3, September 1970, pp. 792–809.

[12] Tanter, "Dimensions of Conflict Behavior . . . 1958–60."

Table 2.6    Correlation Matrix of Collective Protest Measures: Decade 2

|  | (1)<br>Factor Scores[a] | (2)<br>ln Summed Index[b] | (3)<br>Representative Variable[c] |
|---|---|---|---|
| (1) | 1.0 | .970 | .933 |
| (2) |  | 1.0 | .913 |
| (3) |  |  | 1.0 |

[a] Created by unrotated principal components analysis of log transformed Riots, Antigovernment Demonstrations, Political Strikes.
[b] ln (Riots + Antigovernment Demonstrations + Political Strikes).
[c] ln (Antigovernment Demonstrations).


Table 2.7    Correlation Matrix of Internal War Measures: Decade 1

|  | (1)<br>Factor Scores[a] | (2)<br>ln Summed Index[b] | (3)<br>Representative Variable[c] |
|---|---|---|---|
| (1) | 1.0 | .943 | .933 |
| (2) |  | 1.0 | .976 |
| (3) |  |  | 1.0 |

[a] Created by unrotated principal components analysis of log transformed Assassinations, Armed Attacks, Deaths.
[b] ln (Assassinations + Armed Attacks + Deaths).
[c] ln (Deaths).


Table 2.8    Correlation Matrix of Internal War Measures: Decade 2

|  | (1)<br>Factor Scores[a] | (2)<br>ln Summed Index[b] | (3)<br>Representative Variable[c] |
|---|---|---|---|
| (1) | 1.0 | .947 | .931 |
| (2) |  | 1.0 | .969 |
| (3) |  |  | 1.0 |

[a] Created by unrotated principal components analysis of log transformed Assassinations, Armed Attacks, Deaths.
[b] ln (Assassinations + Armed Attacks + Deaths).
[c] ln (Deaths).

models, the interpretation of regression parameter estimates, unlike correlation coefficients, is problematic. The metric has no clear substantive or intuitive meaning. The logged, summed indices, however, take greater advantage of the information provided by the dimensional analyses than do the representative variables and, unlike factor scores, do not create an uninterpretable metric.[13] Hence the (natural) logarithm of the sum of the events distinguishing each dimension is used as the operational measure of Collective Protest and Internal War throughout the study.

## Summary

In this chapter we defined the foci of the investigation as events of domestic violence that have an antisystem character, have direct and immediate political significance, and involve collective or mass actions. The variables that satisfied these theoretical constraints are Riots, Armed Attacks, Political Strikes, Assassinations, Deaths from Political Violence, and Antigovernment Demonstrations. Dimensional analysis of these variables disclosed two clearly defined underlying clusters that are analogous to those uncovered in parallel analyses of other civil conflict data files. These were denoted as *Collective Protest*—indexed by riots, antigovernment demonstrations, and political strikes—and *Internal War*—indexed by deaths from political violence, armed attacks, and assassinations. It was determined that the most useful way to take advantage of the information generated by the dimensional analysis was to construct a composite measure of Collective Protest as the (natural) logarithm of the sum of the variables indexing this dimension, and a composite measure of Internal War in

---

[13] In many ways, log transformed variables or indices have a more appealing interpretation in regression models than do raw metric variables, which is hardly the case with factor scores. Double log models, for example, are particularly revealing because the coefficients are estimates of constant elasticities. Such models require somewhat different assumptions about the behavior of disturbances, however. Good treatments of this topic are provided by John Johnston, *Econometric Methods, 2nd edition* (New York: McGraw-Hill Book Co., 1972), Chapter 2; and Richards, *Interpretation of Technical Data*. Recent work on more technical points can be found in Arthur S. Goldberger, "The Interpretation and Estimation of Cobb–Douglas Functions." *Econometrica*, Vol. 35, Nos. 3–4, July–October 1968, pp. 464–472; and Dale M. Heien, "A Note on Log-Linear Regression," *Journal of the American Statistical Association*, Vol. 63, September 1968, pp. 1034–1038.

A feature of additive indices which should be noted is that the means and variances of component variables are not standardized; thus one of the components (which are all weighted equally) may dominate the index. But we view this as more acceptable than the disadvantages of alternative multivariable indices. Psychometricians have apparently reached a similar conclusion, that is, the most sensible way to measure psychological attributes of people is simply to sum scores on items. See J. M. Nunnally, *Psychometric Theory* (New York: McGraw-Hill Book Co., 1967), Chapter 2.

the same manner. These composite variables comprise the operational measures of mass political violence that are used throughout Parts II and III.

# PART TWO

# Single Equation Hypotheses and Partial Theories

# CHAPTER THREE

# Levels and Rates of Change in Socioeconomic Development

We begin the evaluation of single equation hypotheses and partial theories with an investigation of economic development, which surely is among the most frequently cited factors in the literature dealing with cross-sectional and longitudinal variation in mass political violence and domestic instability. The existing work suggests that economic development is best considered from at least two perspectives: statically, as a structural condition of society—the level of economic well-being—and dynamically, as a feature of structural change—the process of economic development. Also considered are such related features of socioeconomic change as the rate of urbanization and population growth.

This exploratory analysis of the potential causal influence of the level of economic development and rates of socioeconomic growth confronts some of the most hotly disputed issues in the literature on mass violence. What most sharply differentiates our treatment of these topics from those in many previous studies is that the propositions involved are unambiguously specified as stochastic equations and then systematically evaluated against the available quantitative data. The various single equation analyses are reviewed in the last section of the chapter, which explores the implications of the results for a larger and more persuasive multiequation model of political violence.

## Economic Development and Mass Violence

Many observers have commented on the stabilizing impact of "postindustrial" affluence. The most common argument is that the high level of economic development achieved by some nations, largely in Western Europe and North America, has produced societies without the severe conflicts and instabilities generated by the initial process of modernization and industrialization. Typical of such conventional sociological thinking are the observations of Lipset, Dahrendorf, and others about the "new" Europe, where the growth of affluence is seen to produce social systems in which class conflict is minimized as all classes are integrated into society and polity. So large a proportion of the population is now feeling the advantageous effects of economic development that the age-old obsession with the distribution of profits is weakened and the "modern" concern with development is reinforced. The formerly aliented working class, in the view of these theorists, is now at peace with the industrial system, and ideology has lost its former relevance as the absence of a suppressed class leaves little hope for radicalism. Rational calculation has come to replace ideology and dogma, permanent negotiation and occasional conciliation have supplanted active confrontation and class warfare, and compulsory arbitration rather than the general strike becomes the norm.[1]

A similar theme was reflected by Clark Kerr et al., in their assessment of the impact of industrialization on social stability:

"The discontent of workers, reflected in the disruptive forms of protest, tends to be greatest in the early stages of industrialization and tends to decline as workers become more accustomed to industrialization. The partially committed industrial worker, with strong ties to the extended family and village, unaccustomed to urban life and to the discipline and mores of the factory, is more likely to reflect open revolt against industrial life than the seasoned worker more familiar with the ways of the factory, more understanding of the reasons for the web of factory rules, more reconciled to factory life, . . . . The worker in the process of the early stages of industrialization is more prone to . . . prolonged and sporadic withdrawal from industrial work, wildcat stoppages, naked violence, and destruction of machines and property. In later periods, industrial workers tend to be more disciplined in their withdrawal of effort and in the use of the strike."[2]

Accounts such as the foregoing suggest that cross-nationally we should observe a curvilinear relationship between mass violence and the level of

[1] See the essays by Lipset, Dahrendorf, and others, in Stephen R. Graubard (ed.), *A New Europe?* (Boston: Houghton Mifflin, 1964).
[2] Clark Kerr et al., *Industrialism and Industrial Man* (Cambridge, Mass.: Harvard University Press, 1960), p. 30. Note that this also speaks to the impact of urbanization on domestic stability, which is discussed in some detail below. For additional surveys of the points developed here and below, see Samuel P. Huntington, *Political Order in Changing Societies* (New Haven: Yale University Press, 1968), especially Chapter 1; and Douglas P. Bwy, "Political Instability in Latin America: The Cross-Cultural Test of a Causal Model," *Latin American Research Review*, Vol. 3, No. 2, 1968, pp. 17–66.

economic development; that is, violence should increase across societies from low to middle ranges of economic development but then decline at the highest levels—thereby reflecting the stabilizing effect of postindustrial affluence.[3] There are a great many cases that even the most casual observer might cite to deny this line of argument. They include such events as the "May Revolution" in France in 1968; similar outbreaks of political strikes by students and workers in Italy during the following year; the often violent demonstrations and riots by West German students in recent years; and, in the most "postindustrial" society of them all—the United States —a militant movement for fundamental social change, and violent ghetto uprisings by racial minorities.[4] This is hardly indicative of postindustrial quiescence, yet there is some quantitative evidence supporting the cross-national curvilinearity hypothesis and, hence, the notion that highly developed societies are somewhat less violent than those at middle ranges of development. For example, Feierabend et al. reported that their cross-tabular analyses revealed a moderate curvilinear relationship between ordinally scored measures of political instability and level of economic development across 84 nations.[5] On the basis of a more rigorous regression analysis of data on some 74 nations, Russett similarly concluded that a curvilinear model best captures the relationship of ln Deaths from Domestic Group Violence per million population (1950–62) and ln Gross National Product per capita (1957)[6]

---

[3] The hypotheses in this literature suggest not only relationships of this kind across societies, but also across individuals within societies, as well as aggregate patterns through time within societies. Only the former can be examined directly with aggregate cross-sectional data, although we hope to draw valid inferences about macrodevelopmental relationships within societies—a practice for which there is considerable precedent and justification. There is little basis for inferring anything about subnational (e.g., individual) relationships, however. We discuss these issues at some length in Chapter 10.

[4] Although the decline of ideology, radicalism, and direct concern here, conflict is a persistent theme in contemporary sociology, the ideas are by no means universally shared. See Joseph La Palombara, "Decline of Ideology: A Dissent and an Interpretation," *American Political Science Review*, Vol. 60, No. 1, March 1966, pp. 5–16; Richard F. Hamilton, *Affluence and the French Worker in the Fourth Republic* (Princeton, N.J.: Princeton University Press, 1967); and John H. Goldthorpe et al., *The Affluent Worker: Political Attitudes and Behaviour* (London: Cambridge University Press, 1968) for discussions on Italy, France, and Great Britain, respectively.

[5] Ivo D. Feierabend et al., "Social Change and Political Violence: Cross-National Patterns," in Hugh D. Graham and Ted R. Gurr (eds.), *Violence in America: Historical and Comparative Perspectives*, A Report to the National Commission on the Causes and Prevention of Violence, June 1969 (New York: Signet Books, 1969). The instability measure is an aggregation for the 1948–1965 period of annual ordinal ratings of the intensity of domestic instability, including elite behavior—for example, coups.

[6] Bruce M. Russett et al., *World Handbook of Political and Social Indicators* (New Haven: Yale University Press, 1964), pp. 306–307.

However, other quantitative studies provide evidence indicating that the relationship of economic development and domestic violence is linear and negative rather than curvilinear. Flanigan and Fogelman's scatterplot analysis of longitudinal data on a diverse sample of nations for the period from 1800 to 1960 led them to infer that domestic violence (as measured by crude rating scores) is inversely and linearly related through time to such indices of economic development as percentage of the labor force in agriculture and Gross National Product per capita.[7] Rubin and Schainblatt reached a similar conclusion in their analysis of Internal War events across nations. They reported energy consumption per capita to be a consistently good (negative and linear) predictor in the numerous equations they examined.[8]

Yet other researchers, employing different data sets and analysis techniques, have found no meaningful relation at all between economic development and domestic instability. Rummel has argued that since mass violence variables and economic development variables load on separate dimensions when jointly factor analyzed, they are unrelated causally.[9] Hudson drew the same inference from his regression analysis of "Civil Order" factor scores (derived from logged aggregates of a number of violence variables over the 1948–1965 period) and energy consumption per capita across a 63-nation sample.[10]

[7] William H. Flanigan and Edwin Fogelman, "Patterns of Political Violence in Comparative Historical Perspective," *Comparative Politics*, Vol. 3, No. 1, October 1970, pp. 1–20.

[8] Theodore J. Rubin and A.H. Schainblatt, *Empirical Development of the Prototype Environmental Information System, Phase I,* Volume I, Interim Research Report, August, 1969 (Santa Barbara, Calif.: Technical Military Planning Operation, General Electric Company, 1969). It is interesting to note that this study, sponsored by the Air Force, was exclusively concerned with "the future likelihood of occurrence in a nation of any of a small class of violent events, intense enough to portend a fundamental governmental change." It is pointed out by the authors that the Air Force "has a continuing interest in forecasts of the future international environment which bear on its long range planning responsibilities."

[9] See Rudolph J. Rummel, "Some Empirical Findings on Nations and Their Behavior," *World Politics*, Vol. 21, No. 2, January 1969, pp. 226–241, and the studies cited. Rummel's use of factor analysis, unlike that in Chapter 2 of this study, was designed to draw causal inferences and not simply to serve as a useful data reduction mechanism. This requires severe assumptions, and most of them are probably not met in his case. For a discussion of the relevant issues, see Jack E. Vincent, "Factor Analysis as a Research Tool in International Relations: Some Problem Areas, Some Suggestions and an Application." American Political Science Association paper, New York, September 1969; and Arthur S. Goldberger, "Econometrics and Psychometrics: A Survey of Communalities," *Psychometrika,* Vol. 36, No. 2, June 1971, pp. 83–107.

[10] Michael C. Hudson, "Conditions of Political Violence and Instability: A Preliminary Test of Three Hypotheses," *Sage Professional Papers in Comparative Politics*, Series Number 01–005, 1971.

The adequacy of the curvilinear, linear, and null hypotheses concerning the relation of political violence to the level of economic development can be rigorously evaluated by comparing the regression results for models such as (3.1) and (3.2).

(3.1) $\quad Y = \alpha + \beta_1 \ln \text{Pop.} + \beta_2 X + \varepsilon$ $\qquad$ Linear model

(3.2) $\quad Y = \alpha + \beta_1 \ln \text{Pop.} + \beta_2 X + \beta_3 (X)^2 + \varepsilon$ $\qquad$ Curvilinear model

where $\quad Y = $ Mass Violence D2

$\quad \ln \text{Pop.} = \ln$ Population 1960 (in thousands)

$\quad X = $ Economic Development 1960

$\quad \varepsilon = $ stochastic disturbance

These equations were estimated for both Internal War and Collective Protest in the 108-nation cross-section. Recall that the six domestic violence variables were not per capitized when the Collective Protest and Internal War indices were created in Chapter 2. We proceeded in this way in order to avoid the spurious correlation that may arise when independent and dependent variables are deflated by a common variable, such as population.[11] Other things being equal, however, we might expect, the magnitude of Collective Protest, and perhaps Internal War, to be partly a function of the size of a nation's population. Since the natural logarithm of population best maximizes its linear effect, this term is included in each violence equation *throughout the study.*[12] This allows a judgment about the impact of variables of central importance in the presence of the logically prior but theoretically uninteresting size variable.

Equations 3.1 and 3.2 were each estimated with three different indicators of the level of economic development: Gross National Product per capita, Energy Consumption per capita, and Percentage of Economi-

[11] That two variables with no correlation may show a quite high relationship when expressed as ratios to a common third variable was first pointed out by Karl Pearson, "On a Form of Spurious Correlation Which May Arise When Indices are Used in the Measurement of Organs," *Proceedings of the Royal Society of London*, 1897. The topic has been more extensively analyzed by Edwin Kuh and John R. Meyer, "Correlation and Regression Estimates When the Data Are Ratios," *Econometrica*, Vol. 23, No. 4, October 1955, pp. 400–416; and Adam Przeworski and Fernando Cortés, "Per Capita or Sin Capita: A Note of Caution," American Political Science Association paper, Chicago, September 1971. Additional complications arise when variables are subject to error. See F.E.A. Briggs, "The Influence of Errors on the Correlation of Ratios," *Econometrica*, Vol. 30, No. 1, January 1962, pp. 162–177. The strategy here is to allow for the (linear) effect of population by including it in all equations for Internal War and Collective Protest.

[12] The bivariate correlations of Population and ln Population with Internal War were .19 versus .28; with Collective Protest, .37 versus .42. Also, examination of scatterplots indicated that ln Population has a linear relationship with each of the mass violence measures.

cally Active Males in Nonagricultural Occupations.[13] Again, the logarithm of each of these variables best captured relationships.[14] Internal War displayed a significant negative linear relationship with each of the economic indicators and for two, Energy Consumption and Nonagricultural Employment, the curvilinear model produced a moderate yet significant improvement in fit. Collective Protest did not bear a linear relationship to any of the development variables, but the curvilinear model again proved significant for Energy Consumption and Nonagricultural Employment. Recall that by "significant" we mean that the regression coefficient associated with a particular variable is at least twice its respective standard error.[15] Actual regression results for the linear and curvilinear models with Energy Consumption per capita as the economic development indicator are reported in Tables 3.1 to 3.4.

A clearer indication of the nature of the curvilinearity is provided by the scatter diagrams in Figures 3.1 and 3.2, which are presented for illustrative purposes only. They assume (3.2) to be the correct model and depict the relationship of ln Energy Consumption per capita (1960) and

[13] They are, of course, high related.  The intercorrelations are:

|     | ln (1) GNP per capita | ln (2) Energy Consumption per capita | ln % in (3) NonAgricultural Occupations |
|-----|-----|-----|-----|
| (1) | 1.0 | .91 | .79 |
| (2) |     | 1.0 | .73 |
| (3) |     |     | 1.0 |

Note that these independent variables are for the year 1960. Since the mass violence measures are for decade 2 (January 1, 1958–December 31, 1967), they are for the most part lagged, which insures unambiguous temporal status vis á vis Internal War and Collective Protest. This is essential, but of course not sufficient, for causal arguments. Therefore, *throughout the study a 1960 time point is used for independent variables unless data availability does not permit it.*

[14] Log-transformed variables are used here purely on the basis of goodness-of-fit criteria and not for theoretical reasons. Naturally, logged independent variables have much larger regression coefficients than their unlogged counterparts, since a "unit" increase in the former denotes an order of magnitude change (in this case, base $e$). See the sources cited in Chapter 2, footnote 13, for further discussion of logged variables in regression analysis.

[15] As was pointed out in Chapter 1, this not very demanding "significance" condition is used throughout the exploratory analyses of Part II as a criterion for provisionally retaining variables for further investigation. It, of course, does not conform to the strict usage of significance tests, since we do not have a random sample from which we wish to generalize to a population. It is appropriate, however, as a general decision rule for accepting and rejecting hypotheses in the sense that similar decisions would likely obtain in another body of data. We return to this point in Chapter 10.

Table 3.1 Linear Regression of Collective Protest D2 on ln Energy Consumption per Capita 1960 ($N = 108$)

| Independent Variable | Parameter Estimate[a] | $t$ Statistic |
|---|---|---|
| ln Energy Consumption per capita 1960 | 0.087 | 0.95 |
| ln Population 1960 | 0.571* | 4.40 |
| Constant | $-2.345$ | |

| $R^2$ | Regression Standard Error | $F$ |
|---|---|---|
| .187 | 1.62 | 2,105   12.1 |

[a] Starred (*) estimate is more than twice its standard error.

Table 3.2 Linear Regression of Internal War D2 on ln Energy Consumption per Capita 1960 ($N = 108$)

| Independent Variable | Parameter Estimate[a] | $t$ Statistic |
|---|---|---|
| ln Energy Consumption per capita 1960 | $-0.484$* | $-3.06$ |
| ln Population 1960 | 0.844* | 3.93 |
| Constant | $-0.408$ | |

| $R^2$ | Regression Standard Error | $F$ |
|---|---|---|
| .159 | 2.67 | 2,105   9.9 |

[a] Starred (*) estimates are more than twice their standard error.

Table 3.3 Curvilinear Regression of Collective Protest D2 on ln Energy Consumption per Capita 1960 ($N = 108$)

| Independent Variable | Parameter Estimate[a] | $t$ Statistic |
|---|---|---|
| ln Energy Consumption per capita 1960 | 1.760* | 3.29 |
| ln Energy Consumption per capita Squared | $-0.151$* | $-3.16$ |
| ln Population 1960 | 0.627* | 4.98 |
| Constant | $-7.060$ | |

| $R^2$ | Regression Standard Error | $F$ |
|---|---|---|
| .258 | 1.55 | 3,104   12.0 |

[a] Starred (*) estimates are more than twice their standard error.

Table 3.4    Curvilinear Regression of Internal War D2 on ln Energy Consumption per Capita 1960 ($N = 108$)

| Independent Variable | Parameter Estimate[a] | $t$ Statistic |
|---|---|---|
| ln Energy Consumption per capita 1960 | 2.390* | 2.74 |
| ln Energy Consumption per capita Squared | −0.259* | −3.35 |
| ln Population 1960 | 0.941* | 4.55 |
| Constant | −8.52 | |

| $R^2$ | Regression Standard Error | $F$ | |
|---|---|---|---|
| .239 | 2.56 | 3,104 | 10.9 |

[a] Starred (*) estimates are more than twice their standard error.

each type of mass violence with ln Population held at its mean value.[16] In conjunction with the regression results, the scatter diagrams reveal a tendency for Internal War to increase somewhat with initial increases in economic development as one looks across nations, but on the whole it declines with industrialization. Collective Protest, in contrast, is more broadly curvilinear in its relation to economic development; but the character of the response surface or curve is quite flat, indicating a less than dramatic increase and especially decrease in such violence at the appropriate economic development levels. Moreover, the magnitudes of the $R$ squareds are very modest, accentuating the stochastic nature of these models.

In any case, these relationships are more *descriptive* than *causal* in suggesting that societies at middle ranges of economic development typi-

[16] Hence, the observations for Collective Protest (CP) and Internal War (IW) were generated by the following equations:

CP $= -7.06 + 0.627 \overline{\text{ln Population}} + 1.76 \text{ ln Energy Consumption per capita}$
$-0.151 (\text{ln Energy Consumption per capita})^2 + e$

IW $= -8.52 + 0.941 \overline{\text{ln Population}} + 2.39 \text{ ln Energy Consumption per capita}$
$-0.259 (\text{ln Energy Consumption per capita})^2 + e$

The bars denote means; $e$ is the residual. The method was suggested by Edward J. Mitchell, "Land Tenure and Rebellion: A Statistical Analysis of Factors Affecting Government Control in South Vietnam," Memorandum RM-5181-ARPA (Abridged), June 1967 (Santa Monica, Calif.: The RAND Corporation); and *idem.*, "Inequality and Insurgency: A Statistical Study of South Vietnam," *World Politics*, Vol. 20, April 1968, pp. 421–438. It is a neat way of plotting the relationship of two variables in a multivariate equation. It is, however, a heuristic device and should not be literally interpreted. In particular, the extreme values generated are often not possible empirically; for example, the negative values for Internal War and Collective Protest in Figures 3.1 and 3.2.

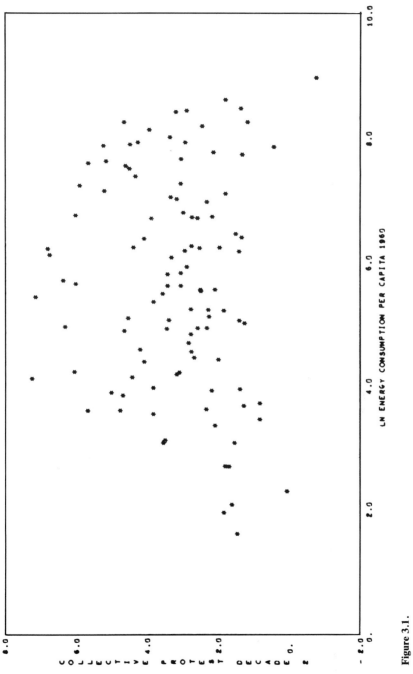

**Figure 3.1.**

29

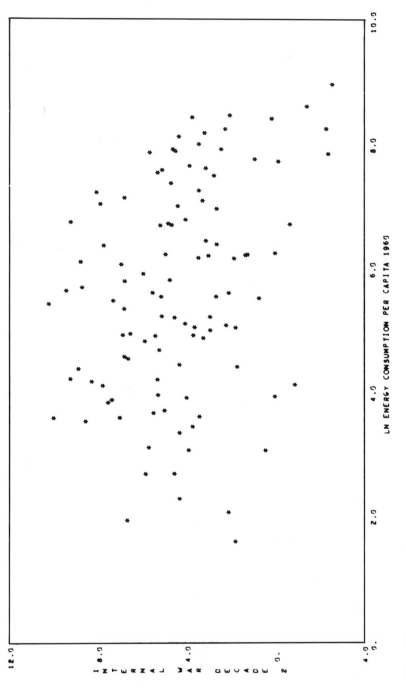

LN ENERGY CONSUMPTION PER CAPITA 1960

Figure 3.2.

30

cally experience slightly greater magnitudes of Collective Protest and Internal War than those at low or high development levels. As we demonstrate in the next section and in Part III, where factors are examined to which direct causal influence is attributed, the causal impact of economic development is multifaceted but indirect. At that point we will have identified more explicitly the reasons for the moderate curvilinearity apparent in Figures 3.1 and 3.2.

## Socioeconomic Change and Mass Violence

The previous hypotheses and equations deal with the level of economic development, but much of the theorizing about the determinants of mass violence focuses not on levels but on rates of change in socioeconomic development. A classic example is the work of Sorokin. Sorokin collected data on "most of the recorded internal disturbances of importance, from the relatively small disorders to the biggest revolutions, which [had] taken place in the life history of Greece, Rome, France, Germany, England, Italy, Spain, the Netherlands, Byzantium, Poland, Lithuania, and Russia."[17] His extensive qualitative examination of this data led him to observe that

"The hypothesis of transition accounts for these tidal waves of disturbances. It means that, other conditions being equal, during the periods when existing culture, or the system of social relationships, or both, undergo a rapid transformation, the internal disturbances in the respective societies increase . . . . "[18]

Hence, Sorokin concluded:

" . . . the main and indispensable condition for an eruption of internal disturbances is that the social system or cultural system or both be unsettled. This datum seems to fit the facts much better than most of the popular theories . . . that ascribe internal disturbances either to growing poverty and the "hard material conditions" or, on the contrary, to material progress . . . . "[19]

Sorokin, then, argued that long-term, secular changes in cultural and socioeconomic systems should have relatively little impact on the incidence of internal disturbances. Rather than looking to developmental changes in levels for explanations, the investigator should concentrate on rapid transformations of socioeconomic structure and cultural systems. Only

---

[17] Pitirim A. Sorokin, *Social and Cultural Dynamics* (Boston: Horizon Books, 1957), p. 573.
[18] *Ibid.*, p. 602. Note that Sorokin had little quantitative data on causal variables, nor was the technology that now makes large-scale quantitative data analysis then available to him.
[19] *Ibid.*

the former is even crudely testable with the data at hand, since there is no adequate measure of cultural change. However, Sorokin had to rely on instances of internal disorder prominent enough to be recorded in historical sources; therefore, our Internal War and Collective Protest measures are much more sensitive to degrees of domestic instability than his data are. Hence, a test of the thrust of Sorokin's theory that would not be overly simplified might involve looking at relatively short-term magnitudes of change in an indicator of socioeconomic structure, such as Gross National Product, in relation to magnitudes of mass violence across societies.

Mancur Olson made a case quite similar to that of Sorokin when he wrote that rapid economic change, whether "upswing" or "downswing," frequently produces severe social instability, conflict, and the potential for revolution.[20] Contrary to the common notion that economic growth promotes political stability and even stable democracy, Olson maintained that it produces severe social dislocations, loosening the caste and class ties that bind men to the existing social order. Those separated in the historical process of rapid economic growth from their villages, manors, and extended families, Olson argued, are not apt to acquire comparable social connections in the city and thus are prone to join destabilizing mass movements. Furthermore, economic growth frequently increases the number of social "losers," since although the national product increases, it often becomes concentrated in fewer hands so that large segments of society experience a net loss in economic well-being.[21]

Moreover, societies experiencing rapid growth rarely have the institutions for mitigating the adversities that the losers suffer, unlike the situation in static, traditional societies (where tribe, manor, or extended family provides a cushion against adversity), or the case in modern industrial nations (where formal welfare programs and agencies serve the same function). Likewise, Olson contended that a rapid *decrease* in the level of economic development of a society can produce similar destabilizing effects. This is true because such a decrease usually involves changes in the relative economic positions of large numbers of people, thus setting up contradictions between the structure of economic power and the distribution of social and political power.[22]

---

[20] Mancur Olson, Jr., "Rapid Growth as a Destabilizing Force," *Journal of Economic History*, Vol. 23, No. 4, December 1963, pp. 529–552.

[21] It is not possible to incorporate the impact of inequality on mass violence in the models because the relevant data exist for only a small number of nations. See the discussion in Chapter 10.

[22] Here Olson took a theoretical tack somewhat different from the argument just outlined, namely, that rapid change produces social dislocation and adversity, and then violence. Brinton made a similar case: Crane Brinton, *The Anatomy of Revolution* (New York: Vintage Books, 1965).

The proposition that discontinuities attendant to rapid and wide-spread socioeconomic change are conducive to social instability and violence appears also in the work of Kornhauser.[23] Kornhauser was interested in explaining the phenomena of "mass politics," which occurs "when large numbers of people engage in political activity outside of the procedures and rules instituted by a society to govern action."[24] Although he confined his attention largely to mass movements, such as Nazism in Germany of the 1930s, and most of his evidence consist of examples of extremist electoral behavior, Kornhauser's research is nevertheless useful for developing explanations of the kinds of mass violence and instability of direct concern here. He viewed major discontinuities in the social process, as indexed by the rate, scope, and mode of social change, as the principal cause of mass society and political violence. The social disruption that accompanies rapid urbanization and industrialization is destabilizing because it uproots and atomizes large numbers of people by vitiating or entirely destroying intermediate organizations and institutions that align them with the larger society.[25]

The theme that social discontinuity creates "available" masses prone to extremism and violence figures not only in the work of Olson and Kornhauser, but is pervasive in the literature, particularly as it relates to urbanization. For example, Smelser saw high rates of internal migration as a source of the kind of "strain" in society that lies behind such manifestations of collective behavior as the "hostile outburst" and the "value oriented [revolutionary] movement."[26] Writing of South Asia, Myron Weiner remarked that rapid urbanization results in

". . . large numbers of rootless, crowded, and often unmarried urban workers [who] are easily prodded to violence and readily organized by political groups."[27]

In a similar vein, Hauser observed:

[23] William Kornhauser, *The Politics of Mass Society* (New York: The Free Press, 1959). See also Kerr et al., *Industrialism and Industrial Man.*

[24] Kornhauser, *Politics of Mass Society*, p. 37.

[25] The importance of organizational and institutional development for extremist politics, which figure as important intervening variables in Kornhauser's work and in that of many others, is dealt with in subsequent chapters. Here we assess only the direct effects of rapid change.

[26] Neil J. Smelser, *Theory of Collective Behavior* (New York: The Free Press, 1963).

[27] Myron Weiner, "The Politics of South Asia," in G. A. Almond and J. S. Coleman (eds.), *The Politics of the Developing Areas* (Princeton, N.J.: Princeton University Press, 1960), p. 173. A similar theme is found in Shanti Tangri, "Urbanization, Political Stability, and Economic Growth," reprinted in Jason L. Finkle and Richard W. Gable (eds.), *Political Development and Social Change* (New York: John Wiley & Sons, Inc., 1966) pp. 305–319.

"Another group of serious problems created or augmented by rapid rates of urbanization are those of internal disorder, political unrest, and government instability fed by mass misery and frustration in the urban setting. The facts that the differences between the 'have' and 'have not' peoples within nations, have become 'felt differences,' and that we are experiencing a 'revolution in expectations', have given huge urban popula- tion agglomerations an especially incendiary and explosive character."[28]

The predominant view, then, is that the process of rapid urbanization in general makes for social instability and that recent migrants caught up in this process are especially likely to engage in political violence. Only the rate of urbanization hypothesis can be examined with the cross-national aggregate data employed in this study, although growing evidence based on the analysis of survey data belies the conventional supposition that migrant populations are responsible for urban political extremism and violence.[29] Indeed, Tilly's examination of collective violence in the European experience led him to reject both the conventional, macro-level process of urbanization thesis as well as its micro-level, recent migrant corollary.

"In the short run, growth of large cities and rapid migration from rural to urban areas in Western Europe probably acted as a damper on violent protest rather than a spur to it. That is for two reasons: (1) The process withdrew discontented men from communities in which they already had the means for collective action and placed them in communities where they had neither the collective identity nor the means necessary

[28] Phillip M. Hauser, "The Social, Economic, and Technological Problems of Rapid Urban- ization," in Bert F. Hoselitz and Wilbert F. Moore (eds.), *Industrialization and Society* (The Hague: UNESCO and Mouton, 1963), p. 212. The implications here for societies that have large urbanized or mobilized populations with high expectations or feelings of relative deprivation is systematically examined in the next chapter.

[29] For a survey of the conventional theorizing and disconfirming evidence based on Mexican data, see Wayne A. Cornelius, Jr., "Urbanization as an Agent in Latin American Political Instability: The Case of Mexico," *American Political Science Review*, Vol. 63, No. 3, September 1969, pp. 833–857. A useful critical appraisal is also provided by Anthony Oberschall, "Group Violence: Some Hypotheses and Empirical Uniformities," American Sociological Association paper, San Francisco, September 1969. Weiner has abandoned the thesis in the light of empirical evidence from his Indian research. See Myron Weiner, "Urbanization and Political Protest," *Civilisations Trimestrial Quarterly*, Vol. 17, 1967, pp. 44–52. Considerable data on ghetto rioters in the United States also deny the recent migrant theory. See R. M. Fogelson and R. B. Hill, "Who Riots?: A Study of Participation in the 1967 Riots" in *Supplemental Studies for The National Advisory Commission on Civil Disorders* (Washington, D.C., 1968). The most devastating critique of the thesis, which came to my attention after this section was first written, is Joan M. Nelson's "Migrants, Urban Poverty, and Instability in Developing Nations," *Occasional Papers in International Affairs,* No. 22 (Harvard University, Center for International Affairs, September 1969).

to strike together. (2) It took considerable time and effort both for the individual migrant to assimilate to the large city, and thus to join the political strivings of his fellows, and for new forms of organization for collective action to grow up in the cities."[30]

Thus, Tilly concludes, "There is, if anything, a negative correlation over time and space between the pace of urban growth and the intensity of collective violence."[31] He therefore viewed the process of rapid urbanization as serving to dampen political violence for the very reasons that many theorists have asserted that it promotes such violence—large numbers of people become atomized, or unhinged from the ties of neighborhood and community. Only when the newly urbanized become reintegrated into the social structure by "forming or joining associations—trade unions, mutual-aid societies, political clubs, conspiratorial groups—devoted to the collective pursuit of their interests" does the probability of collective violence increase.[32]

The quantitative evidence on the impact of socioeconomic change on domestic conflict is much thinner than the qualitative research, but it yields results that are no less conflicting. Feierabend et al. report a linear positive correlation between their political instability index and a six-variable composite measure of "societal change."[33] Tanter and Midlarsky found that for the subset of 14 nations that experienced "successful revolutions" during the period from 1955 to 1960, there is a moderate yet positive correlation between $\log_{10}$ Deaths from Domestic Group Violence and the slope of growth for Gross National Product per capita during 1955 to 1962.[34]

In contrast, Alker and Russett's "multifactor explanation" of the same phenomenon across 33 nations for the period from 1950 to 1962 showed that the rate of change in Gross National Product (1950–1960) had the strongest negative effect of any independent variable in their equations.[35] Similarly, Bwy reports a negative relationship between the 1950 to 1959 rate of change in GNP per capita and "Anomic Violence"

---

[30] Charles Tilly, "Collective Violence in European Perspective," in Graham and Gurr, *Violence in America*, p. 10.

[31] *Ibid.*, p. 32.

[32] *Ibid.*, pp. 33–34.

[33] Feierabend et al., "Social Change and Political Violence." They found, however, that the rate of change in *national income* is *negatively* related to political instability (pp. 647ff.).

[34] Raymond Tanter and Manus Midlarsky, "A Theory of Revolution," *Journal of Conflict Resolution*, Vol. 11, No. 3, September 1967, pp. 264–280. "Revolutions" in this study included military coups, that is, "palace revolutions."

[35] Hayward R. Alker, Jr., and Bruce M. Russett, "Multifactor Explanations of Social Change," in Russett et al., *World Handbook of Political and Social Indicators*, p. 321.

and "Organized Violence" factor scores for a cross-section of Latin American countries.[36] Finally, Flanigan and Fogelman also concluded on the basis of their longitudinal analyses that domestic political violence seems to decrease as the rate of economic growth increases.[37]

The literature surveyed in this section suggests a number of single-equation models which, when estimated, should provide fresh evidence about the adequacy of conflicting hypotheses and prove useful as well in the specification of a more elaborate, multiequation causal model.[38] The work of Sorokin, Olson, Kornhauser, Tanter and Midlarsky, and Feierabend et al. leads us to expect that estimation of the model represented in (3.3) will yield a positive coefficient for economic change. That is, as the rate of economic growth increases, magnitudes of mass political violence across societies should also increase. In contrast, the research of Alker and Russett, Bwy, and Flanigan and Fogelman indicates that a negative coefficient is likely.

Note that (3.3) includes a term for the rate of population growth in addition to the term for the rate of economic growth. This was introduced initially because in some of the economic change models we examined, the growth rate variables—Gross National Product and Energy Consumption—were not percapitized, and these of course tend to increase with population growth alone. (As it turned out, these models produced results not very different from the percapitized versions, and so we report only the latter.) The rate of population growth variable is retained here, however, because the pressure of increasing population is in itself an interesting facet of social change that has usually been ignored in studies of domestic violence.

$$(3.3) \qquad Y = \alpha + \beta_1 \ln \text{Pop.} + \beta_2 \, \Delta \text{Pop.} + \beta_3 \, \Delta \text{Econ.} + \varepsilon$$

where      $Y$ = Mass Violence D2

ln Pop. = ln Population 1960 (in thousands)

$\Delta$ Pop. = Average Annual % Change in Population 1955–1965

$\Delta$ Econ. = Average Annual % Change in GNP per capita or Energy Consumption per capita 1955–1965

$\varepsilon$ = stochastic disturbance

---

[36] Douglas P. Bwy, "Correlates of Political Instability in Latin America: Over-Time Comparisons from Brazil, Cuba, The Dominican Republic, and Panama," American Political Science Association paper, Washington, D.C., September 1968; *idem., Political Instability in Latin America.* Bwy's Anomic Violence and Organized Violence closely parallel our measures of Collective Protest and Internal War, respectively.

[37] Flanigan and Fogelman, "Patterns of Political Violence."

[38] The literature here, as elsewhere, is often ambiguous about the kind of violence involved; therefore, we routinely test the hypothesized relationships for both dimensions of violence.

(3.4) $\qquad Y = \alpha + \beta_1 \ln \text{Pop.} + \beta_2 \Delta \text{Urban.} + \varepsilon$

where $\Delta$ Urban. = % Change in Population in Cities of 20,000 or more
Residents per 1000 Population 1955–1960; and other terms are as
in (3.3).

Equation 3.4 is designed to assess the singular effect of the rate of
urbanization. Unfortunately, lack of data reduced the $N$ to 58 observations
and restricted the change period to 1955 to 1960. Thus the regression
estimation results for (3.4) are not comparable to those of all the other
equations in the study, which are based on the 108-nation cross-section.[39]
Again, the literature provides conflicting expectations about the results.
We would anticipate from the analyses of Smelser, Hauser, and others
a positive relationship between the rate of urbanization and political
violence, whereas the work of Tilly and others suggests a probable negative
relationship.

The estimation results of each equation for Internal War and Collective Protest are presented in Tables 3.5 to 3.8. As Tables 3.7 and 3.8
reveal, urbanization displays a positive effect on both Internal War and
Collective Protest, but the estimated parameters are not significant. Thus,
at the marco-level, at least, there is no strong, systematic relationship
between the pace of urbanization and the magnitude of mass violence
across the 58 nations for which data were obtainable.[40] The rate of population growth, in contrast, demonstrates a positive and significant impact
on both dimensions of violence (Tables 3.5 and 3.6). At this stage in our
analysis, then, the pressure of rapidly increasing population, a factor overlooked in much of the previous research, appears to be an important determinant of cross-national variation in Internal War and Collective Protest.

As was the case with the rate of urbanization, the impact of the rate
of economic growth, about which so much has been written, is less than
dramatic. Two measures of economic change were available: average
annual percentage change in Gross National Product per capita and Energy
Consumption per capita (1955–1965). The former had the strongest relation
to Internal War, the latter with Collective Protest. Energy Consumption
per capita change shows a negative association with Collective Protest
(Table 3.5), but the parameter estimate is quite small in relation to its

---

[39] As noted at the outset, the investigation is geared to the 108-nation sample in order to
obtain results based on the widest possible sample of observations.
[40] A variety of conditional or interaction rate of urbanization models were also examined.
One of the more interesting is a model, implicit in much of the literature, that sees
rapid urbanization in societies with low levels of economic development as especially likely
to produce instability and violence. Equations incorporating this hypothesis did not produce
significant results.

Table 3.5  Regression of Collective Protest D2 on the Rate of Economic and
Population Change 1955–1965 ($N = 108$)

| Independent Variable | Parameter Estimate[a] | $t$ Statistic |
|---|---|---|
| Average Annual % Change in Energy Consumption per capita 1955–1965 | −0.048 | −1.16 |
| Average Annual % Change in Population 1955–1965 | 0.312* | 2.43 |
| ln Population 1960 | 0.658* | 5.15 |
| Constant | −3.248 | |

| $R^2$ | Regression Standard Error | $F$ |
|---|---|---|
| .236 | 1.58 | 3,104  10.7 |

[a] Starred (*) estimates are more than twice their standard error.

Table 3.6  Regression of Internal War D2 on the Rate of Economic and
Population Change 1955–1965 ($N = 108$)

| Independent Variable | Parameter Estimate[a] | $t$ Statistic |
|---|---|---|
| Average Annual % Change in GNP per capita 1955–1965 | −0.149 | −1.48 |
| Average Annual % Change in Population 1955–1965 | 0.868* | 4.14 |
| ln Population 1960 | 0.828* | 3.97 |
| Constant | −4.940 | |

| $R^2$ | Regression Standard Error | $F$ |
|---|---|---|
| .225 | 2.58 | 3,104  10.0 |

[a] Starred (*) estimates are more than twice their standard error.

Table 3.7  Regression of Collective Protest D2 on the Rate of Urbanization 1955–1960 ($N = 58$)

| Independent Variable | Parameter Estimate[a] | $t$ Statistic |
|---|---|---|
| Average Annual % Change in Urbanization 1955–1960 | 0.012 | 1.48 |
| ln Population 1960 | 0.599* | 3.69 |
| Constant | −1.780 | |

| $R^2$ | Regression Standard Error | $F$ |
|---|---|---|
| .218 | 1.64 | 2,55  7.6 |

[a] Starred (*) estimate is more than twice its standard error.

Table 3.8  Regression of Internal War D2 on the Rate of Urbanization 1955–1960 ($N = 58$)

| Independent Variable | Parameter Estimate[a] | $t$ Statistic |
|---|---|---|
| Average Annual % Change in Urbanization 1955–1960 | 0.024 | 1.76 |
| ln Population 1960 | 0.688* | 2.74 |
| Constant | −1.890 | |

| $R^2$ | Regression Standard Error | $F$ |
|---|---|---|
| .156 | 2.70 | 2,55  5.1 |

[a] Starred (*) estimate is more than twice its standard error.

standard error. The estimated effect of the rate of GNP change on Internal War is similarly negative, and although somewhat larger vis à vis its standard error than is the case in the Collective Protest equation, it also fails to reach significance.[41]

Despite the lack of a strong relationship between the rate of economic growth and political violence in these single equation results, perhaps we should not be too hasty in eliminating the economic growth variables from further consideration. Although economic processes more often than not are best cast as first movers with respect to sociopolitical phenomena, there is good theoretical reason to believe that the natural inclination of sociologists and political scientists to specify such variables as unidirectional causal influences on mass violence is inappropriate here. In this case it is more likely that the political violence, rate of economic growth causal relationship is reciprocal rather than unidirectional. Consider the following observation by one of the most prominent contemporary analysts of economic growth, Simon Kuznets:

" . . . clearly some minimum political stability is necessary if members of the economic society are to plan ahead and be assured of a relatively stable relation between their contribution to economic activity and their rewards. *One could hardly expect much economic growth under conditions of political turmoil, riots, and unpredictable changes in regimes.*"[42]

Kuznets thus suggests that domestic disorder hinders the rate of economic growth, whereas a number of the theorists cited earlier in this section argued that such growth produces low levels of domestic violence. Perhaps, then, the specification of one-way causation between growth and mass violence in either "direction" is incorrect. It would seem that the true causal relation, if any, is most likely to be approximated by a nearly instantaneous or immediate feedback model, especially since the change period for the rate of economic growth variables (1955–1965) and the aggregation period for decade 2 mass violence variables (1958–1967) are nearly coterminous.[43] A respecification of the model and a somewhat different estimation technique are necessary in order to capture such interdependence, but we postpone dealing with this until Part III. At this point

---

[41] Olson's observation that either "upswing" *or* "downswing" in the rate of economic growth is conducive to social instability and violence was tested by using the absolute value of the rate of Gross National Product and Energy Consumption change in (3.3), but this formulation did not yield significant results.

[42] Simon Kuznets, *Modern Economic Growth* (New Haven: Yale University Press, 1966), p. 451. Emphasis added.

[43] Lagged effects may be incorporated as well, and it is argued in Part III that this should be done in order to properly capture this relationship.

let us try to formulate what has been developed thus far into an integrated set of relationships.

## Summary and Implications for a Larger Model

What are the implications of the results of this chapter for the specification of a theoretically more appealing multiequation model? Recall that we found a moderately curvilinear association between the level of economic development and both dimensions of mass political violence, although the nature of the response surface was somewhat different for each. We also saw that the rate of population growth demonstrated a rather strong positive effect on both modes of violence, and, contrary to much that has been written, the impact of rapid urbanization was insignificant. Finally, we noted a very moderate negative relationship between the rate of economic change and each dimension of violence but concluded that economic growth and violence, if related causally at all, are jointly dependent and therefore must be estimated as a system of simultaneous or interdependent equations.

These results are perhaps best integrated in the following manner. The curvilinear association of economic development level and the dimensions of mass violence is due in part to the levels at which nations typically experience certain rates of population and economic growth. Thus it may be that societies at low to middle levels of economic development, where violence increases across nations, are precisely those with the highest rates of population growth and relatively low rates of economic

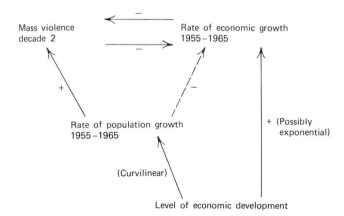

**Figure 3.3**

growth. This incorporates the proposition, which is virtually axiomatic in development economics, that rapid population growth is, *ceteris paribus*, incompatible with high economic growth. Conversely, nations at middle to high levels of economic development, where violence (especially Internal War) tends to decline across nations, may be the societies with decreasing rates of population growth and increasing rates of economic growth.[44] This assumes, of course, that economic growth has a negative effect on violence (and thus far there is only limited evidence for this). In any event, we can investigate these propositions by specifying and estimating a system of equations that incorporates the functional form and direction of effects of the implied development level, rate of change sequence, as well as the jointly dependent nature of the domestic violence, rate of economic growth relationship. Figure 3.3 depicts this possible sequence of relationships. However, the causal structure underlying the variance across nations in levels of mass political violence is unlikely to be this simple. So we return to these possibilities in Part III, after considering in the chapters that follow additional single equation hypotheses and partial theories.

---

[44] Rostow, for example, has suggested that this is the case. He notes that, historically, disruptive population pressure has occurred in "pre-take-off" societies, that is, in those which have not yet begun to generate self-sustaining economic growth. (W. W. Rostow, "The Take-Off Into Self-Sustained Growth," *The Economic Journal*, Vol. 66, March 1956, pp. 25–48.) This may be even more true in recent times, since external agents, such as the United Nations, bring public health and the "green revolution" to nations with relatively low levels of economic development and slow rates of change. In many of these nations, which have not developed the cultural constraints or the governmental capacity and willingness to effectively diminish the birthrate, infant mortality and starvation drop off and the rate of population growth skyrockets.

# CHAPTER FOUR

# Social Structural Imbalances and Systemic Frustration and Satisfaction

A large body of research, particularly micro, individual level studies by social psychologists, deals with the impact of frustration, relative deprivation, alienation, and the like, on the propensity of individuals and social strata to engage in collective violence.[1] Although cross-national, aggregate data necessarily restrict the investigator to macro, social structural modes of theory testing and explanation, the social psychological literature has proved to be suggestive of structural hypotheses.[2] Indeed, many cross-national researchers resort to systemic analogs of psychological concepts in order to explain or interpret their results. For example, Feierabend et al. anticipated the curvilinear relation between economic development and political instability in their data by postulating:

" ... the peak discrepancy between systemic goals and their satisfaction, and hence maximum systemic frustration, is likely to occur during the transitional phase. Highly modern and fully traditional nations should experience less systemic frustration—in modern nations, because of their

---

[1] See, for example, Leonard Berkowitz, *Aggression: A Social Psychological Analysis* (New York: McGraw-Hill Book Company, Inc., 1962)

[2] Gurr's work illustrates the possibilities here. See Ted R. Gurr, "The Genesis of Violence: A Multivariate Theory of the Preconditions for Civil Strife," Ph.D Dissertation, New York University, 1965; "Psychological Factors in Civil Violence," *World Politics*, Vol. 20, January 1968, pp. 245–278; and *Why Men Rebel* (Princeton, N.J.: Princeton University Press, 1970). A major problem in Gurr's work is the arbitrary way by which he develops his various "deprivation" measures. See especially Gurr, "A Causal Model of Civil Strife: A Comparative Analysis Using New Indices," *American Political Science Review*, Vol. 62, No. 4, December 1968, pp. 1104–1124.

ability to provide a high level of attainment commensurate with modern aspirations; in the traditional nations, unexposed to modernity, because modern aspirations are still lacking."[3]

Feierabend et al. have suggested that systemic frustration is most likely in "transitional" societies because in such nations aspirations characteristically outrun satisfactions. Is this in fact the case? And, more importantly, does it produce relatively high levels of mass political violence? We confront these questions in this chapter by investigating a number of prominent systemic frustration–deprivation theories that are amenable to direct and rigorous testing with cross-national, aggregate data. These include a variety of social structural "imbalance" hypotheses—in particular those which speak to the consequences of imbalances in education and economic development and in urbanization and economic development, as well as some related propositions that derive from Deutsch's work on the relationship of social mobilization to government performance and social welfare.

After evaluating the adequacy of these imbalance hypotheses by estimating the single equation models that they imply, we pursue the usefulness of the results for the development of a more elaborate multi-equation sequence of causes and effects.

## Imbalances in Education and Economic Development

Perhaps the most prolific of those who have attempted to employ aggregate data to examine social psychological causes of mass violence is Ted Gurr,[4] Gurr sees relative deprivation as the basic determinant of civil violence:

"The fundamental cause of civil strife is deprivation-induced discontent: the greater the discrepancy between what men believe they deserve and what they think they are capable of attaining, the greater their discontent.

---

[3] Ivo D. Feierabend et al., "Social Change and Political Violence: Cross-National Patterns," in Hugh D. Graham and Ted R. Gurr (eds.), *Violence in America: Historical and Comparative Perspectives*, A Report to the National Commission on the Causes and Prevention of Violence, June 1969 (New York: Signet Books, 1969), p. 620.
[4] See Gurr, "A Causal Model of Civil Strife;" and Ted R. Gurr and Charles Ruttenberg, *The Conditions of Civil Strife; First Tests of a Causal Model*, Research Monograph No. 28, Center of International Studies, Princeton University, April 1967.

The more intense and widespread discontents are in society, the more intense and widespread strife is likely to be."[5]

One test of the deprivation hypothesis undertaken by Gurr involved an examination of the relation between the magnitude of civil strife and the ratio of educational level to economic development across nations. The assumptions were that educational level is indicative of the level of aspirations and expectations in society, and that economic development taps the ability of society to satisfy such expectations. Hence Gurr anticipated that societies with high levels of education and low levels of economic development would have high deprivation-induced discontent and thus relatively high civil strife, whereas those with low educational levels in relation to the level of economic development would have low discontent and commensurately less violence.

The statistical relationship hypothesized by Gurr is implied in the observations of numerous scholars in the political development field. In a volume entitled *Education and Political Development*, James Coleman wrote:

" . . . a gross imbalance has tended to develop between the great expansion in the educational system and the comparatively limited growth in the economy and in the occupational structure. The result, now a commonplace, is a vast and nearly uncontrollable increase in the number of unemployed and underemployed school leavers, whose political orientation toward the polity is marked by disaffection and alienation, and whose behavioral disposition is basically anomic."[6]

[5] Ted R. Gurr, "A Comparative Study of Civil Strife," in Graham and Gurr, *Violence in America*, p. 590. A similar conceptualization was proposed by Lerner: "The spread of frustration . . . can be seen as the outcome of a deep imbalance between achievement and aspiration. In simple terms, this situation arises when many people in a society want far more than they can hope to get . . . . The relationship we here propose for study can be expressed by the following equation: Satisfaction = Achievement/Aspiration," Daniel Lerner, "Toward a Communication Theory of Modernization: A Set of Considerations," in Lucien W. Pye (ed.), *Communications and Political Development* (Princeton, N.J.: Princeton University Press, 1963), p. 333. Lerner also notes that such frustration often produces aggression (*ibid.*, p. 349). A parallel argument is made by Galtung. See Johan Galtung, "A Structural Theory of Aggression," *Journal of Peace Research*, Vol. 1, No. 2, 1964, pp. 94–119. For an evaluation of this and related propositions vis á vis the "Negro revolt" in the United States, see James A. Geschwender, "Social Structure and the Negro Revolt: An Examination of Some Hypotheses," *Social Forces*, Vol. 43, No. 2, December 1964, pp. 248–256.

[6] James S. Coleman (ed.), *Education and Political Development* (Princeton, N.J.: Princeton University Press, 1968), p. 29.

Not only is a social–structural imbalance between educational level and economic development seen as producing candidates for "anomic" or unorganized expressions of discontent, but as promoting organized or "revolutionary" violence as well. In the same volume, Hoselitz assessed the possible impact of educational development:

"Rather than a tool for an economic breakthrough, the excessive dispensation of elementary education may be a hindrance through its adverse impact upon political stability. For as I have pointed out earlier, in a society with large pockets of illiteracy the acquisition of primary education has chiefly an impact on consumption and aspirations for higher levels of consumption by those who receive an education. They congregate in cities and there form a pool of relatively unskilled labor. They experience long periods of unemployment and some remain permanently without regular jobs. These basically hopeless educated unemployed become the members of the cadres of various messianic or revolutionary political movements."[7]

Despite the appeal of the hypothesis in the qualitative literature, Gurr's quantitative data indicated that the conjunction of increasing educational development in the face of relatively low economic development was associated with comparatively low, rather than high, domestic violence in the 1961 to 1963 period across 119 nations. In contrast, Feierabend *et al* reported results contrary to those in the Gurr study lending support to the hypothesis.[8]

A rigorous test of the education–economic development "imbalance" hypothesis requires the specification of a well-defined statistical model that takes full advantage of the interval scale quality of the available data. One appropriate macro-level specification would be a ratio interaction model of the following form:

$$(4.1) \qquad Y = \alpha + \beta_1 \ln \text{Pop.} + \beta_2 X + \beta_3 Z + \beta_4 \frac{X}{Z} + \varepsilon$$

where 
$Y$ = Mass Violence D2
$\ln \text{Pop.}$ = ln Population 1960 (in thousands)
$X$ = Educational Level 1960
$Z$ = Economic Development Level 1960

---

[7] Bert F. Hoselitz, "Investment in Education and its Political Impact," in James S. Coleman, (ed.,), *Education and Political Development* (Princeton, N.J.: Princeton University Press, 1968), p. 561. We examine urbanization–economic development imbalance theories in the next section.

[8] Gurr and Ruttenberg, *The Conditions of Civil Strife*; Feierabend *et al*, "Social Change and Political Violence."

$\dfrac{X}{Z}$ = Ratio (interaction term) of Educational Level to Economic Development Level

$\varepsilon$ = stochastic disturbance

If the hypothesis has merit, then the ratio term of education to economic development should have a significant (positive) parameter estimate. This would indicate that the conjunction of high education and low economic development, low education and high economic development, and so on, has an impact on domestic violence *beyond that attributable to the additive effects of these variables.*

An alternative to the ratio interaction specification of the imbalance hypothesis is a logarithmic formulation of the form:

(4.2a)       $Y = \alpha + \beta_1 \ln \text{Pop.} + \beta_2 \ln X + \beta_3 \ln Z + \varepsilon$

where           all terms are as in (4.1).

Equation 4.2a provides a test of the hypothesis which is less susceptible to the problem of multicollinearity than the straightforward ratio interaction model of (4.1), and thus allows for sharper estimates of effects.[9] Multicollinearity is a less vexing problem because there is no additional explicit interaction term. Only the main effects terms, ln $X$ and ln $Z$, need to be estimated. Yet the model still captures the thrust of the imbalance hypothesis. Recall that the measures of Collective Protest and Internal War ("$Y$") are the (natural) logs of the sum of the events indexing each dimension. Hence (4.2a) is actually:

(4.2b)       $\ln Y = \alpha + \beta_1 \ln \text{Pop.} + \beta_2 \ln X + \beta_3 \ln Z + \varepsilon$

which implies

(4.2c)               $Y = \alpha^* \cdot \text{Pop.}^{\beta_1} \cdot X^{\beta_2} \cdot Z^{\beta_3} \cdot \varepsilon^*$

---

[9] Multicollinearity refers to the intercorrelation of independent variables. It produces high variances (and thus standard errors) for parameter estimates. Thus, although $R^2$ may be high, the estimated effects of individual independent variables are not sharp, and it is impossible to reject hypotheses concerning them. In matrix terms, it means that one or more of the vectors in the matrix of independent variables X is too closely a linear combination of others; hence the variance–covariance coefficient matrix, $\sigma^2 (X'X)^{-1}$ has very large elements. See Arthur S. Goldberger, *Econometric Theory* (New York: John Wiley & Sons, Inc., 1964), pp. 192–194; and Donald E. Farrar and Robert R. Glauber, "Multicollinearity in Regression Analysis: The Problem Revisited," *Review of Economics and Statistics*, Vol. 49, 1967, pp. 92–107.

which, when $\beta_3$ is negative, implies[10]

(4.2d)
$$Y = \alpha^* \cdot \text{Pop.}^{\beta_1} \cdot \frac{X^{\beta_2}}{Z^{\beta_3}} \cdot \varepsilon^*$$

where   $\ln \alpha^* = \alpha$
        $\ln \varepsilon^* = \varepsilon$

Therefore, if societies with high educational levels in relation to economic development in fact have greater violence than those with a more "balanced" ratio of education to economic development, and this relationship is a systematic one, then the regression estimate of the coefficient $\beta_2$ should be significantly positive and the estimate of the coefficient $\beta_3$ should be significantly negative.

Each of the alternative formulations of the education–economic imbalance thesis represented by (4.1) and (4.2) was estimated for Internal War and for Collective Protest. A number of measures of educational development and economic development were tried, and all produced essentially the same results.[11] Tables 4.1 to 4.4 report the findings where Literacy per 1000 Adults 1960 is the indicator of educational level, and GNP per capita 1960 (in millions of U.S. dollars) is the indicator of economic development. Clearly, neither the ratio interaction nor the natural log multiplicative formulation yields outcomes that substantiate this widely held hypothesis, since the estimates shown in Tables 4.1 to 4.4 do not satisfy our minimal significance condition that the relevant coefficients be at least twice their standard errors.[12]

Thus, although the proposition has great theoretical and intuitive appeal, the imbalance of education and economic development appears to have little value for explaining actual variation across nations in either dimension of mass political violence. The theory may of course be valid for particular cases; however it does not aid the formulation of a broadly applicable explanatory model at the macro or systemic level of analysis.

---

[10] Recall the law of exponents: $Z^{-n} = 1/Z^n$.

[11] An interesting variant of the education–economic development hypothesis focusing on elites is a model that examines the effects of an imbalance between university students or graduates and professional–technical employment opportunities. Where the former substantially outruns the latter, the consequence may be the "alienation of the intellectuals" phenomenon which Brinton and many others have suggested is an important determinant of revolutionary or protest situations [Crane Briton, *The Anatomy of Revolution* (New York: Vintage Books, 1965)]. We tested this hypothesis across 70 nations for which the appropriate data were available, but the results were not significant.

[12] Recall that when this is the case the $t$ statistic associated with each parameter estimate in the Tables will be 2 or greater.

Table 4.1   Regression of Collective Protest D2 on Education and Economic Development: Ratio Interaction Model ($N = 108$)

| Independent Variable | Parameter Estimate[a] | $t$ Statistic |
|---|---|---|
| Literacy per 1000 Adults 1960 | −0.00003 | −0.03 |
| GNP per capita 1960 (millions US dollars) | −0.0002 | −0.48 |
| Literacy/GNP per capita | −0.078 | −0.55 |
| ln Population 1960 | 0.643* | 4.82 |
| Constant | −2.237 | |

| $R^2$ | Regression Standard Error | $F$ | |
|---|---|---|---|
| .187 | 1.63 | 4,103 | 5.9 |

[a] Starred (*) estimate is more than twice its standard error.

Table 4.2   Regression of Internal War D2 on Education and Economic Development: Ratio Interaction Model ($N = 108$)

| Independent Variable | Parameter Estimate[a] | $t$ Statistic |
|---|---|---|
| Literacy per 1000 Adults 1960 | −0.002* | −2.32 |
| GNP per capita 1960 (millions of US dollars) | −0.0003 | −0.46 |
| Literacy/GNP per capita | 0.325 | 1.46 |
| ln Population 1960 | 0.819* | 3.94 |
| Constant | −1.854 | |

| $R^2$ | Regression Standard Error | $F$ | |
|---|---|---|---|
| .250 | 2.55 | 4,103 | 8.5 |

[a] Starred (*) estimates are twice their standard error.

Table 4.3   Regression of Collective Protest D2 on Education and Economic Development: ln Multiplicative Model ($N = 108$)

| Independent Variable | Parameter Estimate[a] | $t$ Statistic |
|---|---|---|
| ln Literacy per 1000 Adults 1960 | 0.164 | 0.78 |
| ln GNP per capita 1960 | −0.114 | −0.52 |
| ln Population 1960 | 0.580* | 4.47 |
| Constant | −2.258 | |

| $R^2$ | Regression Standard Error | $F$ |
|---|---|---|
| .186 | 1.63 | 3,104   7.9 |

[a] Starred (*) estimate is more than twice its standard error.

Table 4.4   Regression of Internal War D2 on Education and Economic Development: ln Multiplicative Model ($N = 108$)

| Independent Variable | Parameter Estimate[a] | $t$ Statistic |
|---|---|---|
| ln Literacy per 1000 Adults 1960 | 0.318 | 0.93 |
| ln GNP per capita 1960 | −1.247* | −3.53 |
| ln Population 1960 | 0.736* | 3.56 |
| Constant | 3.010 | |

| $R^2$ | Regression Standard Error | $F$ |
|---|---|---|
| .216 | 2.59 | 3,104   9.5 |

[a] Starred (*) estimates are more than twice their standard error.

We consider now another "imbalance" thesis which parallels the one analyzed in this section but nevertheless merits separate investigation.

## Imbalances in Urbanization and Economic Development

A second proposition that bears on the systemic frustration and satisfaction theme, which was implied in much of the theorizing on the consequences of rapid social change surveyed in the last chapter, is an urbanization analog of the education–economic development imbalance hypothesis. The line of reasoning in this version of the thesis is that when the level of urbanization outruns the level of economic development, satisfaction tends to lage behind aspirations, and frustration-induced discontent is a probable consequence. Like education, urbanization is viewed in such theories as stimulating aspirations in formerly "quiescent" segments of the population who encounter, in the urban setting, modern life styles and patterns of consumption. But unlike the rate of urbanization or recent migrant propositions considered in Chapter 3, what is crucial here is the *balance* between such urban-generated aspirations and society's ability to satisfy them by providing economic opportunities, high standards of living, and so on.[13] This is seen as particularly troublesome in developing nations since, as Hauser tells us, it is "the underdeveloped nations of the world [that] are 'over-urbanized' in that larger proportions of their population live in urban places than their degree of economic development justifies."[14]

This variant of the imbalance hypothesis can be evaluated in the same manner as was its education counterpart. Again, the level of economic development is taken to be the best cross-national index of systemic satisfaction capability. The ratio interaction model for the urbanization case is

$$(4.3) \qquad Y = \alpha + \beta_1 \ln \text{Pop.} + \beta_2 X + \beta_3 Z + \beta_4 \frac{X}{Z} + \varepsilon$$

where $\quad Y$ = Mass Violence D2

$\ln \text{Pop.}$ = ln Population 1960 (in thousands)

$X$ = Urbanization

$Z$ = Economic Development Level

$\frac{X}{Z}$ = Ratio (interaction term) of Urbanization to Economic Development Level

$\varepsilon$ = stochastic disturbance

The natural log multiplicative formulation is

$$(4.4) \qquad Y = \alpha + \beta_1 \ln \text{Pop.} + \beta_2 \ln X + \beta_3 \ln Z + \varepsilon$$

where $\qquad$ all terms are as in (4.3).

---

[13] For a good survey and discussion of the literature here, see Wayne A. Cornelius, Jr., "Urbanization as an Agent in Latin American Political Instability: The Case of Mexico," *American Political Science Review*, Vol. 63, No. 3, September, 1969, pp. 833–857; and Joan M. Nelson, "Migrants, Urban Poverty, and Instability in Developing Nations," *Occasional Papers in International Affairs*, No. 22 (Harvard University, Center for International Affairs, September 1969).

[14] Phillip M. Hauser, "The Social, Economic, and Technological Problems of Rapid Urbanization," in Bert F. Hoselitz and Wilbert F. Moore (eds.), *Industrialization and Society* (The Hague, UNESCO, and Mouton, 1963), p. 203.

The regression outcomes for these alternative formulations are displayed in Tables 4.5 to 4.8, where GNP per capita 1960 is the measure of economic development, and population in cities of 100,000 or more residents per 1000 population 1965 is the urbanization indicator.[15] The ratio interaction specification of this imbalance hypothesis has no explanatory power for Collective Protest cross-nationally, but it has some utility for Internal War, since the interaction term has a (barely) significant parameter estimate (Tables 4.5 and 4.6). The log multiplicative model does better for both dimensions of mass violence, as is evident in Tables 4.7 and 4.8. In the Internal War equation the coefficients have the "correct" sign (positive for urbanization, negative for economic development) and are more than twice their respective standard errors. The estimates also have the proper sign in the log multiplicative equation for Collective Protest; however, the coefficient of GNP per capita does not reach significance.

These results, therefore, provide some limited supporting evidence for the urbanization–economic development formulation of the aspirations–satisfaction hypothesis, insofar as it applies to the Internal War dimension of mass political violence. But the explanatory power is weak indeed. A multiequation respecification that includes the key variables and their likely causal linkages might perform much better when put to the empirical test. We take this up at the end of the chapter, after examining one more group of single equation imbalance hypotheses.

Table 4.5   Regression of Collective Protest D2 on Urbanization and Economic Development: Ratio Interaction Model ($N = 108$)

| Independent Variable | Parameter Estimate[a] | $t$ Statistic |
|---|---|---|
| Population in Cities of 100,000 + Residents per 1000 Population 1965 | 0.002 | 1.36 |
| GNP per capita 1960 | −0.0004 | −0.88 |
| Urbanization/GNP per capita | 0.339 | 0.74 |
| ln Population 1960 | 0.589* | 4.62 |
| Constant | −2.431 | |

| $R^2$ | Regression Standard Error | $F$ |
|---|---|---|
| .228 | 1.59 | 4,103   7.6 |

[a] Starred (*) estimate is more than twice its standard error.

[15] The urbanization indicator was available across a large number of nations for the year 1965 only. Thus it is not lagged relative to decade 2 Violence measures, as are the other variables.

Table 4.6  Regression of Internal War D2 on Urbanization and Economic
Development:  Ratio Interaction Model ($N = 108$)

| Independent<br>Variable | Parameter<br>Estimate[a] | $t$<br>Statistic |
|---|---|---|
| Population in Cities of 100,000 +<br>    Residents per 1000 Population 1965 | −0.002 | −0.86 |
| GNP per capita 1960 | −0.001 | −1.34 |
| Urbanization/GNP per capita | 1.576* | 2.14 |
| ln Population 1960 | 0.748* | 3.66 |
| Constant | −2.348 | |

| $R^2$ | Regression Standard Error | $F$ |
|---|---|---|
| .246 | 2.56 | 4,103   8.4 |

[a] Starred (*) estimates are more than twice their standard error.

Table 4.7  Regression of Collective Protest D2 on Urbanization and
Economic Development:  ln Multiplicative Model ($N = 108$)

| Independent<br>Variable | Parameter<br>Estimate[a] | $t$<br>Statistic |
|---|---|---|
| ln Population in Cities of 100,000 +<br>    Residents per 1000 Population 1965 | 0.473* | 3.10 |
| ln GNP per capita 1960 | −0.375 | −1.94 |
| ln Population 1960 | 0.527* | 4.26 |
| Constant | 1.615 | |

| $R^2$ | Regression Standard Error | $F$ |
|---|---|---|
| .250 | 1.56 | 3,104   11.5 |

[a] Starred (*) estimates are more than twice their standard error.

Table 4.8  Regression of Internal War D2 on Urbanization and Economic Development: ln Multiplicative Model ($N = 108$)

| Independent Variable | Parameter Estimate[a] | $t$ Statistic |
|---|---|---|
| ln Population in Cities of 100,000+ Residents per 1000 Population 1965 | 0.858* | 3.57 |
| ln GNP per capita 1960 | −1.708* | −5.60 |
| ln Population 1960 | 0.643* | 3.30 |
| Constant | 4.160 | |

| $R^2$ | Regression Standard Error | $F$ |
|---|---|---|
| .295 | 2.46 | 3,104  14.5 |

[a] Starred (*) estimates are more than twice their standard error.

## *Further Imbalance Theories: Social Mobilization, and Government Performance and Social Welfare*

Another class of models comparable in theoretical orientation to those considered so far derive from Karl Deutsch's work on the process and consequences of "social mobilization." Deutsch conceives of social mobilization as:

" . . . the process by which major clusters of old social, economic, and psychological commitments are eroded or broken and people become available for new patterns of socialization and behavior."[16]

The process involves two distinct stages:

"(1) the stage of uprooting or breaking away from old settings, habits and commitments; and (2) the induction of the mobilized persons into some relatively stable new patterns of group membership, organization and commitment."[17]

Thus Deutsch distinguishes between the initial uprooting of formerly quiescent or "traditional" people through the process of urbanization and industrialization, and their induction into new patterns of social and political interaction. It is the incidence and consequences of the latter stage that concern us here. Deutsch indicates these are as follows:

[16] Karl W. Deutsch, "Social Mobilization and Political Development," *American Political Science Review*, Vol. 55, September 1961, p. 494.
[17] *Ibid.*

"Social Mobilization . . . brings about a change in the quality of politics by changing the range of human needs that impinge upon the political process. As people are uprooted from their physical and intellectual isolation in their immediate localities, . . . they experience drastic changes in their needs. They may now come to need provisions for housing and employment, for social security, . . . for risks of cyclical or seasonal unemployment, . . . instruction for themselves and their children. They need, in short, a wide range and large amounts of new government services."[18]

In this way, the mobilization of large sectors of society generates increased pressure for the expansion of governmental services and the improvement of social welfare. If the needs and expectations of the mobilized population outrun the capacity or responsiveness of government, the consequence, Deutsch argues, is likely to be the disaffection of a large proportion of the population and hence the breakdown of domestic stability.

This line of theorizing clearly has much in common with that of previous sections, although the variables involved are somewhat different. It suggests that in nations where the ratio of social mobilization to the effort or performance of government in meeting human needs is relatively high, domestic violence will be comparatively high. For where the social mobilization–government performance ratio is large, the pressures generated by mobilization probably have exceeded government performance in meeting civilian needs, and widespread domestic instability is the likely consequence. By the same logic, we might hypothesize on the basis of Deutsch's work that nations with high social mobilization relative to the level of *actual* mass social welfare would also have commensurately high levels of mass violence.

Appropriate specifications of these propositions have the same functional form as previous "imbalance" hypotheses: the straightforward ratio interaction model of (4.5) and the alternative log multiplicative formulation of (4.6).

$$(4.5) \qquad Y = \alpha + \beta_1 \ln \text{Pop.} + \beta_2 X + \beta_3 Z + \beta_4 \frac{X}{Z} + \varepsilon$$

where      $Y$ = Mass Violence D2
          $\ln$ Pop. = ln Population 1960 (in thousands)
          $X$ = Social Mobilization 1960

---

[18] *Ibid.*, p. 498. For a similar conceptualization, see Gabriel A. Almond, "A Developmental Approach to Political Systems," *World Politics*, Vol. 17, January 1965, pp. 183–214. Also relevant is Ernest A. Duff and John F. McCamant, "Measuring Social and Political Requirements for System Stability in Latin America," *American Political Science Review*, Vol. 62, No. 4, December 1968, pp. 1125–1143.

$Z$ = Government Performance or Actual Social Welfare 1960

$\dfrac{X}{Z}$ = Ratio (interaction term) of Social Mobilization to Government Performance or Social Welfare

$\varepsilon$ = stochastic disturbance

(4.6)         $Y = \alpha + \beta_1 \ln \text{Pop.} + \beta_2 \ln X + \beta_3 \ln Z + \varepsilon$

where                all terms are as in (4.5).

Before the validity of these models can be evaluated, the key concepts must be operationally defined. Deutsch has suggested that the size of the mobilized population is delimited by the following "yardsticks of measurement":

" . . . the set of persons who live in towns, the set of persons engaged in occupations other than agriculture, forestry, and fishing; the set of persons who read a newspaper at least once a week; the set of persons who pay direct taxes to a central government, or who are directly subject to military conscription; the set of persons who have attended public or private schools for at least four years; the set of persons attending markets at least once a month; the set of persons sending or receiving a letter at least once a month; the set of literate adults, or moviegoers, or radio listeners, of registered voters for elections, or of insured persons under social security schemes; or all persons working for money wages in units of five or more employees; and many more."[19]

Data were available on five of the indicators that Deutsch proposed to delimit the extent of social mobilization, which is more than sufficient to devise a solid measure of the concept. Rather than create a composite index by way of factor analysis (scores) or rely on particular "representative" variables, a simple additive index was constructed. This seemed to be the best way to capture as full a range of the concept as the available data permitted and at the same time to retain an interpretable metric in order that parameter estimates would have a meaningful empirical referent.[20]

Accordingly, a social mobilization index was created by taking the arithmetic mean of the sum of the following variables: Population in Cities of 100,000 or more residents per 1000 population (1965); Economically Active Males in Nonagricultural Occupations per 1000 population (1960); News-

[19]  Karl W. Deutsch, *Nationalism and Social Communication: An Inquiry into the Foundations of Nationality, 2nd edition,* (Cambridge, Mass.: M.I.T. Press, 1966), p. 126.
[20]  See the discussion on this point in Chapter 2.

paper Circulation per 1000 population (1960); Radios per 1000 population (1960); and Literacy per 1000 adults (1960).

The measure employed for the performance or effort of government in meeting social needs is straightforward: General Government Expenditures for Civilian (nondefense) Activities as a percentage of Gross Domestic Product (1960).[21] Construction of a measure of mass social welfare posed a more difficult problem. It had to incorporate indicators that unambiguously appraised the state of actual human welfare. Three variables for which data were obtainable seemed to be appropriate: Infant Live Births per 1000 births (1960); Calories per capita per 10 days (1960); and Physicians per million Population (1960). These variables by no means cover all the facets of the concept, but at least they assess in an unmistakable fashion important features of human welfare.[22] A Social Welfare Index was created by taking the arithmetic mean of the sum of these indicators.

We are now able to determine the adequacy of (4.5) and (4.6) against data for the 108-nation cross-section. The regression estimation results for the ratio interaction and log multiplicative formulations of the social mobilization–government performance version of these "imbalance" hypotheses appear in Tables 4.9 to 4.12. As Tables 4.9 and 4.10 demonstrate, the ratio interaction test of Equation 4.5 did not produce significant results for either Collective Protest or Internal War. In the log multiplicative specification, the parameter estimates have the proper sign in the Collective Protest regression (Table 4.11); that is, Social Mobilization is positive and nondefense General Government Expenditures as a percentage of Gross Domestic Product is negative, but only the latter is significant. In the Internal War regression (Table 4.12), the parameter of nondefense General Government Expenditures is negative and highly significant, but the Social Mobilization coefficient has the "wrong" sign and is, in any case, not significant.

Tables 4.13 to 4.16 report the results for the social mobilization–social welfare models. The interaction term in the regression equation for Collective Protest (Table 4.13) has a barely significant parameter estimate,

[21] "General Government" refers to all levels: local, state or provincial, and national. Military expenditures, which often constitute a large proportion of government expenditure, are excluded because they seldom are used to meet social needs.

[22] By "unmistakable" we mean the following: It is possible (and frequently the case) that aggregate indicators such as national income per capita, although potentially measuring general human welfare, are nevertheless concentrated in relatively narrow strata. This is much less likely of the variables in the Social Welfare Index. It is difficult to imagine infant live births, physicians, and caloric consumption being effectively monopolized by a narrow group —after all, a privileged elite can eat only so much, produce so many children, or make use of so many physicians. Elites are frequently able, however, to effectively control a huge proportion of the national income and wealth.

Table 4.9 Regression of Collective Protest D2 on Social Mobilization and Government Performance: Ratio Interaction Model ($N = 108$)

| Independent Variable | Parameter Estimate[a] | $t$ Statistic |
|---|---|---|
| Social Mobilization 1960 | −0.001 | −0.71 |
| Nondefense General Government Expenditures as a % of GDP 1960 | −0.010 | −0.44 |
| Social Mobilization/Nondefense General Government Expenditures | 0.038 | 1.29 |
| ln Population 1960 | 0.605* | 4.83 |
| Constant | −2.189 | |

| $R^2$ | Regression Standard Error | $F$ |
|---|---|---|
| .239 | 1.58 | 4,103  8.12 |

[a] Starred (*) estimate is more than twice its standard error.


Table 4.10 Regression of Internal War D2 on Social Mobilization and Government Performance: Ratio Interaction Model ($N = 108$)

| Independent Variable | Parameter Estimate[a] | $t$ Statistic |
|---|---|---|
| Social Mobilization 1960 | −0.007* | −2.33 |
| Nondefense General Government Expenditures as a % of GDP 1960 | −0.040 | −1.04 |
| Social Mobilization/Nondefense General Government Expenditures | 0.045 | 0.96 |
| ln Population 1960 | 0.864* | 4.39 |
| Constant | −1.278 | |

| $R^2$ | Regression Standard Error | $F$ |
|---|---|---|
| .289 | 2.48 | 4,103   10.5 |

[a] Starred (*) estimates are more than twice their standard error.

Table 4.11   Regression of Collective Protest D2 on Social Mobilization and Government Performance: ln Multiplicative Model ($N = 108$)

| Independent Variable | Parameter Estimate[a] | $t$ Statistic |
|---|---|---|
| ln Social Mobilization 1960 | 0.382 | 1.88 |
| ln Nondefense General Government Expenditures as a % of GDP 1960 | −0.877* | −2.55 |
| ln Population 1960 | 0.558* | 4.47 |
| Constant | −1.230 | |

| $R^2$ | Regression Standard Error | $F$ | |
|---|---|---|---|
| .238 | 1.57 | 3,104 | 10.8 |

[a] Starred (*) estimates are more than twice their standard error.

Table 4.12   Regression of Internal War D2 on Social Mobilization and Government Performance: ln Multiplicative Model ($N = 108$)

| Independent Variable | Parameter Estimate[a] | $t$ Statistic |
|---|---|---|
| ln Social Mobilization 1960 | −0.529 | −1.59 |
| ln Nondefense General Government Expenditures as a % of GDP 1960 | −2.040* | −3.71 |
| ln Population 1960 | 0.770* | 3.82 |
| Constant | 6.300 | |

| $R^2$ | Regression Standard Error | $F$ | |
|---|---|---|---|
| .247 | 2.54 | 3,104 | 11.3 |

[a] Starred (*) estimates are more than twice their standard error.

Table 4.13 Regression of Collective Protest D2 on Social Mobilization and Social Welfare: Ratio Interaction Model ($N = 108$)

| Independent Variable | Parameter Estimate[a] | $t$ Statistic |
|---|---|---|
| Social Mobilization 1960 | −0.010 | −1.92 |
| Social Welfare 1960 | 0.003 | 1.42 |
| Social Mobilization/Social Welfare | 6.760* | 2.29 |
| ln Population 1960 | 0.647* | 5.06 |
| Constant | −4.950 | |

| $R^2$ | Regression Standard Error | $F$ |
|---|---|---|
| .230 | 1.59 | 4,103   7.6 |

[a] Starred (*) estimates are more than twice their standard error.

Table 4.14 Regression of Internal War D2 on Social Mobilization and Social Welfare: Ratio Interaction Model ($N = 108$)

| Independent Variable | Parameter Estimate[a] | $t$ Statistic |
|---|---|---|
| Social Mobilization 1960 | −0.017* | −2.01 |
| Social Welfare 1960 | 0.003 | 0.78 |
| Social Mobilization/Social Welfare | 7.800 | 1.69 |
| ln Population | 0.933* | 4.57 |
| Constant | −4.670 | |

| $R^2$ | Regression Standard Error | $F$ |
|---|---|---|
| .251 | 2.55 | 4,103   8.6 |

[a] Starred (*) estimates are more than half their standard error.

Table 4.15 Regression of Collective Protest D2 on Social Mobilization and Social Welfare: ln Multiplicative Model ($N = 108$)

| Independent Variable | Parameter Estimate[a] | $t$ Statistic |
|---|---|---|
| ln Social Mobilization 1960 | 0.645* | 2.02 |
| ln Social Welfare 1960 | $-1.310$ | $-1.71$ |
| ln Population 1960 | 0.606* | 4.72 |
| Constant | 2.590 | |

| $R^2$ | Regression Standard Error | $F$ |
|---|---|---|
| .212 | 1.60 | 3,104   9.3 |

[a] Starred (*) estimates are more than twice their standard error.

Table 4.16 Regression of Internal War D2 on Social Mobilization and Social Welfare: ln Multiplicative Model ($N = 108$)

| Independent Variable | Parameter Estimate[a] | $t$ Statistic |
|---|---|---|
| ln Social Mobilization 1960 | 0.197 | 0.39 |
| ln Social Welfare 1960 | $-3.410*$ | $-2.75$ |
| ln Population 1960 | 0.892* | 4.26 |
| Constant | 16.697 | |

| $R^2$ | Regression Standard Error | $F$ |
|---|---|---|
| .204 | 2.62 | 3,104   8.9 |

[a] Starred (*) estimates are more than twice their standard error.

indicating that the ratio interaction formulation of the hypothesis has a degree of validity for this dimension of political violence. This is not true, however, in the Internal War ratio interaction regression, as is evident from Table 4.14. In the log multiplicative equations (Tables 4.15 and 4.16), the variables in each regression have the correct sign, but neither for Collective Protest nor Internal War are the estimates of both variables significant; hence the equations do not support the social mobilization–social welfare imbalance thesis.

One clear message emerges from all these results. Like the imbalance theories considered in earlier sections of the chapter, the social mobilization–

government performance and social mobilization–social welfare hypotheses do not provide powerful explanations of differences across nations in levels of mass political violence. Yet the imbalance propositions are very appealing theoretically. Why is there a discrepancy between seemingly sound theory and our empirical observations and causal inferences? Let us pursue this question after briefly summarizing the findings developed thus far.

## Summary and Interpretation

In this chapter we examined a variety of social structural "imbalance" hypotheses that were derived from systemic analogs of propositions in deprivation and frustration theory and from Deutsch's work on the political consequences of social mobilization. On the whole, they did poorly when put to the empirical test within the framework of clearly specified statistical models, although a ratio interaction formulation of the social mobilization–social welfare hypothesis, and both the ratio interaction and the log multiplicative specifications of the urbanization–economic development hypothesis, demonstrated a limited ability to explain Collective Protest and Internal War, respectively. Again, this is not to say that imbalance models might not furnish powerful explanatory mechanisms in the case of particular nations or for different units of analysis, but only that they have very little utility as general explanations at the cross-national level.

Why did these models do so badly, given the impressive theoretical base from which they are derived? The reason is undoubtedly the high collinearity that exists between the independent variables involved. Collinearity in a nonexperimental setting means that there are not many instances where variables such as social mobilization and social welfare diverge markedly; thus there is little opportunity for theoretically postulated interactive effects, or even additive effects, to "show up" in regression results. This underlies the discrepancy we noted earlier between interaction hypotheses that are repeatedly advanced in the theoretical work and the empirical, data-based regression results.

We can conclude from all this that the various imbalance theories are probably not valid as *descriptive* propositions. However, this does not mean that *theoretically*, taken in the abstract sense, such theories are unsound. If it were possible experimentally to manipulate nations so that, for example, there was little correlation between social mobilization and social welfare, then we could observe more satisfactorily the (interactive) effects of the conjunction of high social mobilization, low social welfare, and so on, and thereby draw definitive theoretical conclusions. Yet collinearity is in itself produced by some causal process that is responsible for variables "moving together." Therefore, unless these causal processes were to be disrupted in some fundamental and improbable way, such that the variables became no longer highly correlated, we never need to know the potential consequences of such interaction effects.[23] What might these causal processes be for the case at hand? This brings us to the question of the multiequation implications of the results.

## *Implications for a Multiequation Causal Sequence*

A formulation that is likely to approximate the true causal structure more closely than any of the single equation imbalance theories is the multiequation model depicted in Figure 4.1, where solid and dotted lines indicate probable and possible causal paths, respectively. Recall that in the regression results of this chapter, the parameter estimates of Social Welfare and civilian General Government Expenditures as a percentage of Gross Domestic Product were often highly significant (negative) although the overall results did not support in any systematic way the various imbalance hypotheses. Hence the model in Figure 4.1 depicts Social Welfare as having a direct, negative causal influence on mass political violence. The assumption is that populations enjoying comparatively high social welfare are relatively less likely to engage in collective violence. Social Welfare is in itself hypothesized to be a function of governmental efforts in the civilian sphere (civilian General Government Expenditures as a percentage of GDP) as well as of the nation's level of Economic Development.

Civilian General Government Expenditures is also expected to have a direct (negative) impact on violence, since the stabilizing effects of high civilian government spending are likely to be only partially captured by the Social Welfare Index, which has a rather limited scope. Government Expenditures are depicted in Figure 4.1 to be caused in part by the pres-

---

[23] It is not generally realized that "rejecting" hypotheses on the basis of nonexperimental analyses when independent variables are moderately to highly intercorrelated (which is often the case in social science) does not necessarily reject the theory at hand, but only denies its usefulness in describing existing causal relations. Only true experimentation can definitively determine whether a theory is valid, since the investigator is able to manipulate the situation in such a way that the effects predicted by the theory have maximum opportunity to manifest themselves. Such manipulation constitutes the fundamental disruption that is unlikely to occur naturally—hence the comment that we really never need to know its consequences, at least if the purpose is to model existing processes. The experimental perspective, in the context of the general linear model, is presented well by William Mendenhall, *Introduction to Linear Models and the Design and Analysis of Experiments* (Belmont, Calif.: Wadsworth Publishing Co., 1968).

sures generated by Social Mobilization (as Deutsch hypothesized) and also by the level of Economic Development, since highly developed nations are typically able to devote a larger proportion of their resources for the provision of governmental services than are less developed ones.

It would be premature to evaluate here the adequacy of the partial model diagrammed in Figure 4.1. A considerably more elaborate model, which includes the causal relationships and sequences that have been proposed in this chapter, is examined in Part III.

We turn now to an investigation of some possible causal influences on mass political violence that are a good deal different from those considered thus far.

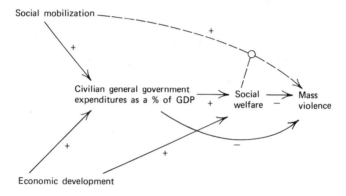

**Figure 4.1.**

# CHAPTER FIVE

# Sociocultural Differentiation and National Integration

Among the foremost problems that face transitional or developing societies —or at least one that has loomed very large in the literature on socio-economic and political development—is the achievement of national integration.[1] Considerable attention has been devoted to the obstacles to national unity and development posed by what Geertz has called the "primordial" attachments to race, language, religion, and custom of differentiated population subgroups.[2] However, the disintegrative con-sequences of subnational loyalties and attachments by large segments of the population are by no means confined to "developing" nations, as evidenced by the French separatist movement in Canada, persisting ethnic and racial identification and conflict in the United States, the insurgency of the Irish Catholic minority in northern Ireland, and the pressing issue of unassimilated minorities in the Soviet Union. This chapter considers some of the direct and possible second-order effects of sociocultural differentiation on mass political violence.

---

[1] For an overview of the topic, see Myron Weiner, "Political Integration and Political Development," reprinted in Claude Welch (ed.), *Political Modernization* (Belmont, Calif.: Wadsworth Publishing Co., Inc., 1967), pp. 150–166. Also see Arend Lijphart, "Cultural Diversity and Theories of Political Integration," *Canadian Journal of Political Science*, Vol. 4, March 1971, pp. 1–14; and Leonard Binder, "National Integration and Political Development," *American Political Science Review*, Vol. 58, No. 3, September 1964, pp. 622–631.

[2] Clifford Geertz, "The Integrative Revolution: Primordial Sentiments and Civil Politics in the New States," reprinted in Welch, *Political Modernization*, pp. 167–187.

*Differentiation and Mass Violence: Single Equation Models*

A frequent observation by analysts of comparative political violence is that organized insurrections and rebellions (or what we have denoted as Internal War) hinge in part on the presence of the primordial cleavages delineated previously. Pye, for example, has written:

"The possibility of an insurrectionary movement arising and then employing organized violence depends upon the existence of sharp divisions within society created by regional, ethnic, linguistic, class, religious, and other communal differences that may provide the necessary social and demographic basis for supporting the movement . . . ."[3]

Pye notes further that it is not the most highly industrialized nor the most traditional societies that typically experience rebellions or insurgencies based on such divisions, but rather those where the "process of social and psychological disruption that accompanies the downfall of traditional societies *opens the way* to a host of sharp cleavages within such societies."[4] But why is it that the "sharp cleavages" attendant to the absence of national integration become politically salient—in the sense of creating the potential for rebellion or insurgency—after the breakdown of traditional society? Geertz has suggested two reasons: First, ex-colonial or recently independent states undergo the "process of the formation of a sovereign civil state that, among other things, stimulates sentiments of parochialism, communalism, racialism, and so on, because it introduces into society a valuable new prize over which to fight . . . ."[5] And, second, the processes of industrialization and urbanization produce the "aggregation of independently defined, specifically outlined traditional primordial groups into larger, more diffuse units whose implicit frame of reference is not the local scene but the 'nation'—in the sense of the whole society encompassed by the . . . civil state . . . The process . . . is a progressive extension of the sense of primordial similarity and difference generated from the direct and protracted encounter of culturally diverse groups in local contexts to more broadly defined groups of a similar sort interacting within the framework of the entire national society . . . ."[6] The consequence of this encounter of culturally differentiated groups, according to Geertz, is the concentration

---

[3] Lucian W. Pye, *Aspects of Political Development* (Boston: Little, Brown and Co., 1966), p. 136.

[4] *Ibid.* Emphasis added.

[5] Geertz, "The Integrative Revolution," p. 177.

[6] *Ibid.*, p. 184. See also Robert Melson and Howard Wolpe, "Modernization and the Politics of Communalism: A Theoretical Perspective," *American Political Science Review*, Vol. 64, December 1970, pp. 1112–1130.

of group antagonisms, communal clashes, and the potential for separatist movements.

Perhaps the best conceptualization of the line of reasoning used by Geertz is provided by Karl Deutsch. Deutsch's theoretical framework is quite elaborate, but only its bare essentials and operational implications are developed here.[7] In order to assess the impact of sociocultural differentiation on the prospects for national integration and stability versus national disintegration and conflict, Deutch proposes what amounts to a fourfold classification of the total national population. The categorization is generated by two key (dichotomous) variables. The first is social mobilization, which was introduced in a much different context in the previous chapter. The size of the population mobilized for relatively more intense social communication is designated simply as the *mobilized population*; that which is not mobilized for intensive communication forms the inactive *underlying population*. The second component of Deutsch's theoretical scheme involves the concept of assimilation—where the *assimilated population* is that proportion integrated into the predominant cultural community, and the *differentiated population* is the segment that is culturally distinct. Of the four population types generated by the interface of these two key variables, the mobilized *and* differentiated group is the most crucial for assessing the likelihood of domestic conflict and violence. Deutsch put it this way:

"... [the mobilized and differentiated] have been mobilized for intensive communication but have not been assimilated to the predominant language and culture. These persons have remained culturally or linguistically different from the members of [the mobilized and assimilated] group and they are frequently and acutely reminded of this difference by the intensity of social communications in which they must take part. *The share of the mobilized but differentiated persons among the total population ... is the first crude indicator of the probable incidence and strength of national conflict.*"[8]

---

[7] The best single source of Deutsch's relevant work is: Karl W. Deutsch, *Nationalism and Social Communication: An Inquiry into the Foundations of Nationality*, 2nd edition (Cambridge, Mass.: M.I.T. Press, 1966). But see also Karl W. Deutsch, "Communication Theory and Political Integration," in P. E. Jacob and J. V. Toscano (eds.), *The Integration of Political Communities* (Philadelphia: J. B. Lippincott, 1964), pp. 46–74.

[8] Deutsch, *Nationalism and Social Communication,* pp. 129–130. Emphasis added. The probabilistic nature of Deutsch's statement should be carefully noted, for as he remarks elsewhere, differentiated minorities may continue "to express their particular concerns of social cohesion and political preference within the framework of a common state without necessarily threatening its continued existence." Deutsch, "Communication Theory and Political Integration," p. 9.

Deutsch developed these ideal types based on dichotomous variables for heuristic purposes. The variables involved are, of course, continuous. In Chapter 4, a continuous, quantitative measure of the size of the socially mobilized population was developed on the basis of the "yardsticks of measurement" that Deutsch proposed. Fortunately, a very good quantitative measure of the degree of sociocultural differentiation is also available for each of the 108 nations. What we shall call the Index of Ethnolinguistic Fractionalization (ELF) is derived from data reported in the authoritative *Atlas Narodov Mira* on the numbers of people in distinctive cultural, ethnic, and linguistic groups.[9] Groups were determined by their roles, descents, and relationships to others rather than by their physical characteristics. The ELF Index is constructed as follows:

$$\text{ELF} = \left[ 1 - \sum \frac{n_i\,(n_i - 1)}{N\,(N - 1)} \right] * 100$$

where   $n_i$ = number of people in the $i$th group
      $N$ = total population

Hence the larger the number of groups and the smaller the proportion of the total population in each of them, the more fractionated or differentiated is the population.

Armed with reasonably sound *aggregate* measures of mobilization and differentiation, the simplest test of Deutsch's (and Geertz's) proposition would be a multiplicative interaction model such as (5.1) or its log multiplicative counterpart, represented by (5.2).

(5.1)      $Y = \alpha + \beta_1 \ln \text{Pop.} + \beta_2\,X + \beta_3\,Z + \beta_4\,X^*Z + \varepsilon$

where      $Y$ = Mass Violence D2
      $\ln \text{Pop.}$ = ln Population 1960 (in thousands)
      $X$ = Social Mobilization 1960
      $Z$ = Ethnolinguistic Fractionalization circa 1960
      $X^*Z$ = Multiplicative Interaction Term of Social Mobilization and Ethnolinguistic Fractionalization
      $\varepsilon$ = stochastic disturbance

---

[9] The data are for circa 1960 and are generally considered to be the best available in the world. The *Atlas* is published by the N. H. Miklukho-Miklaya Institute of Ethnography of the Academy of Sciences, Department of Geodesy and Cartography of the State Geological Committee of the USSR (Moscow, 1964). The Ethnolinguistic Fractionalization Index was computed by Charles L. Taylor of the World Data Analysis Program, Yale University. It is based on the "fragmentation" index proposed by Douglas Rae and Michael Taylor in *The Analysis of Political Cleavages* (New Haven: Yale University Press, 1970), chapter 2.

(5.2) $$Y = \alpha + \beta_1 \ln \text{Pop.} + \beta_2 \ln X + \beta_3 \ln Z + \varepsilon$$

where all terms are as in (5.1).

These equations enable us to assess the direct impact of the conjunction of high mobilization *and* high differentiation on mass political violence. If the hypothesized interaction effect has systematic causal influence, then regression estimation of the models should produce a significant positive interaction coefficient in (5.1) and/or significant and positive coefficients for each term in (5.2).[10]

Tables 5.1 to 5.4 present the results for this initial test of the mobilization–differentiation thesis. None of the outcomes substantiates the hypothesized relationship. The interaction term in the multiplicative interaction formulation is positive in both the Collective Protest and Internal War regressions, and it eclipses the quite strong and positive bivariate relationship of Ethnolinguistic Fractionalization with each dimension of violence

Table 5.1  Regression of Collective Protest D2 on Social Mobilization (SM) and Ethnolinguistic Fractionalization (ELF): Multiplicative Interaction Model ($N = 108$)

| Independent Variable | Parameter Estimate[a] | $t$ Statistic |
| --- | --- | --- |
| Social Mobilization 1960 | −0.002 | −1.11 |
| Ethnolinguistic Fractionalization 1960 | −0.013 | −1.23 |
| SM*ELF | 0.00005 | 1.24 |
| ln Population 1960 | 0.606* | 4.53 |
| Constant | −1.486 | |

| $R^2$ | Regression Standard Error | $F$ | |
| --- | --- | --- | --- |
| .195 | 1.63 | 4,104 | 6.2 |

[a] Starred (*) estimate is more than twice its standard error.

[10] Recall that $Y$ is a logarithmic term and thus (5.2) reduces to $Y = \alpha^* \cdot \text{Pop.}^{\beta_1} \cdot X^{\beta_2} \cdot Z^{\beta_3} \cdot \varepsilon^*$; where $\ln \alpha^* = \alpha$, $\ln \varepsilon^* = \varepsilon$, and all the coefficients are significant and positive. The resulting expression is thus multiplicative (in $X$ and $Z$), which confirms the hypothesis of an interactive mobilization–differentiation effect on mass violence—conventionally tested by (5.1). For an evaluation of similiar (but additive) models across African nations, see Donald G. Morrison and Hugh M. Stevenson, "Integration and Instability: Patterns of African Political Development," *American Political Science Review*, Vol. 66, No. 3, September 1972, pp. 902–927.

A parallel evaluation of this proposition that relies on cruder data and different techniques of analysis has been undertaken by Ronald Inglehart and Margaret Woodward, "Language Conflicts and Political Community," *Comparative Studies in Society and History*, Vol. 10, 1967–1968, pp. 27–48.

Table 5.2   Regression of Internal War D2 on Social Mobilization (SM) and Ethnolinguistic Fractionalization (ELF): Multiplicative Interaction Model ($N = 108$)

| Independent Variable | Parameter Estimate[a] | $t$ Statistic |
|---|---|---|
| Social Mobilization 1960 | −0.010* | −3.70 |
| Ethnolinguistic Fractionalization 1960 | −0.025 | −1.50 |
| SM*ELF | 0.0001 | 1.83 |
| ln Population 1960 | 0.842* | 4.00 |
| Constant | −0.206 | |

| $R^2$ | Regression Standard Error | $F$ | |
|---|---|---|---|
| .243 | 2.57 | 4,104 | 8.3 |

[a] Starred (*) estimates are more than twice their standard error.

Table 5.3   Regression of Collective Protest D2 on Social Mobilization and Ethnolinguistic Fractionalization: ln Multiplicative Model ($N = 108$)

| Independent Variable | Parameter Estimate[a] | $t$ Statistic |
|---|---|---|
| ln Social Mobilization 1960 | 0.260 | 1.20 |
| ln Ethnolinguistic Fractionalization 1960 | 0.072 | 0.52 |
| ln Population 1960 | 0.562* | 4.32 |
| Constant | −3.402 | |

| $R^2$ | Regression Standard Error | $F$ | |
|---|---|---|---|
| .192 | 1.63 | 3,104 | 8.2 |

[a] Starred (*) estimate is more than twice its standard error.

(which is not reported here). In fact, the sign of the coefficient for ELF is now (small and insignificantly) negative in these regressions. However, the interaction coefficients are not large enough vis à vis their standard errors to permit confidence in the results. In the log multiplicative regressions, the parameter estimates are either insignificant or, as in the Internal War regression (Table 5.4), the estimate for social mobilization has the "wrong" sign.

Hence a single equation model involving the relation of mobilization and differentiation to violence is not supported by the data in the 108-

Table 5.4 Regression of Internal War D2 on Social Mobilization and Ethnolinguistic Fractionalization: ln Multiplicative Model ($N = 108$)

| Independent Variable | Parameter Estimate[a] | $t$ Statistic |
|---|---|---|
| ln Social Mobilization 1960 | −0.756* | −2.04 |
| ln Ethnolinguistic Fractionalization 1960 | 0.257 | 1.02 |
| ln Population 1960 | 0.768* | 3.56 |
| Constant | 0.746 | |

| $R^2$ | Regression Standard Error | $F$ |
|---|---|---|
| .156 | 2.70 | 3,104   6.4 |

[a] Starred (*) estimates are more than twice their standard error.

nation cross-section. Perhaps an alternative, multi-equation specification will provide a more satisfactory representation of the operative causal processes.

## Toward a Multiequation Formulation

The foregoing results do not necessarily mean that sociocultural differentiation and social mobilization are irrelevant for explaining mass violence. However, the causal processes involved are apparently more complex than the simple interaction model of (5.1) and (5.2) or the even simpler notion of a direct differentiation to violence causal relation would indicate. Indeed, Deutsch, Pye, Geertz, and others have suggested that the *immediate* consequence of differentiation, or the conjunction of mobilization *and* differentiation, is frequently political separatist activity on the part of unassimilated sociocultural groups. It may be, then, that sociocultural differentiation produces political separatism, which is what directly causes high levels of mass political violence—and, in particular, Internal War—since separatism is usually not expressed merely as protest against government, but involves attempts to fundamentally alter political arrangements.

Another possible causal path of differentiation to mass violence has been advanced by Kornhauser:

"Ethnic and racial minorities . . . rebel for corporate immunities and privileges—like special status for their languages or religions or even for self rule. . . . Unlike social classes, minorities may go so far as to seek secession—to establish a *separate state* or to join another state. Finally, like social classes, minorities may seek assimilation into the political society. Rebellions against slavery, caste, or other forms of racial or ethnic *discrimination* may facilitate the extension of full citizenship rights to members of minority groups."[11]

Thus, in addition to the causal path of differentiation → political separatism → violence (in particular, Internal War), Kornhauser notes that differentiated minority groups may also experience discrimination, which is another source of "rebellion." However, rebellions against discrimination, unlike those attendant to separatist movements, typically have the objective of redressing grievances *within* the system. In Kornhauser's words, those involved seek "assimilation into the political society." We would hypothesize, therefore, that the path from discrimination leads primarily to Collective Protest, although there may be a weaker link from discrimination to separatism and, perhaps, directly to Internal War as well.[12]

Figure 5.1 depicts this more elaborate, multiequation statement of the likely causal processes (solid and dotted lines indicate probable and possible causal relationships, respectively and the circled intersections represent hypothesized interaction effects). In addition to the cluster of relationships involving differentiation, separatism, discrimination, and mass violence, the figure includes other variables whose causal role was implied earlier. One of these is a dummy variable for Postwar Independence (1 = gained independence since World War II, 0 = did not). This is postulated to have a positive effect on ELF, since many of the most highly differentiated nations are recently independent ex-colonies which were literally carved out of Africa and Asia by European imperialists without regard for "natural" ethnolinguistic boundaries. It is also shown to have a direct and interactive (with ELF) positive impact on Political Separatism, in order to capture Geertz's thesis, discussed in the last section, that differentiated societies that have recently come under native control are especially likely to experience separatism.

Social Mobilization (SM) also appears in the model. Its negative effect on ELF simply indicates that for most nations the mobilization of differentiated underlying minorities results in their assimilation to the dominant cultural community, or at least this is the conclusion suggested by cross-

[11] William Kornhauser, "Rebellion and Political Development," in Harry Eckstein (ed.), *Internal War* (New York: The Free Press, 1964), p. 153. Emphasis added.
[12] It seems likely that those suffering from discrimination who are not able to effect change through protest would turn to separatism and the more fundamentally antisystem Internal War mode of violence. Part III deals with the general question of the escalation of violence from Collective Protest to Internal War.

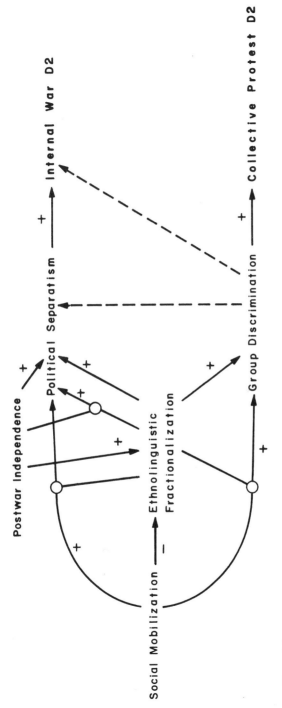

Figure 5.1.

73

sectional relationships.[13] More important is the hypothesized positive interaction effect of Social Mobilization and Ethnolinguistic Fractionalization on Political Separatism and Group Discrimination. Recall that the former effect was hypothesized by Deutsch, Geertz, and others. The latter represents the idea that the mobilized and differentiated are much more "visible" than their "underlying" counterparts and hence more readily encounter discrimination.

The operational measures of Political Separatism and Group Discrimination are estimates developed by Ted Gurr for a large number of nations, circa 1960.[14] The political separatism indicator incorporates separatist sentiment as well as overt acts. It is defined as the percentage of the population inferred to be "dissatisfied with the closeness of their political association with the polity of which they are formally members."[15] Group Discrimination is measured by the percentage of the population "which is substantially and systematically excluded from valued economic, political, or social positions because of ethnic, religious, linguistic, or regional characteristics."[16]

All the variables for the model in Figure 5.1 have now been defined. Considering Collective Protest and Internal War separately, the model subsumes two unidirectional or recursive systems. We postpone a detailed discussion of the properties of such systems and only point out here that each is certainly misspecified. They are misspecified because of the omission

---

[13] The bivariate correlation between (1n) Social Mobilization and Ethnolinguistic Fractionalization is $-.547$. No earlier argument was made for this casual relation, but it does appear that most cultural minorities have found it expedient to become assimilated into the dominant culture when mobilized into national life. There are many significant exceptions, however, and this is the rationale for the SM*ELF interaction effect on Political Separatism and Group Discrimination. That is, those who do remain differentiated when mobilized are the ones most likely to encounter discrimination and/or to engage in separatist activity. We are aware of no theory which is able to account for the resiliency of some and not other cultures in resisting or choosing to resist assimilation to a dominant culture. It obviously depends on peculiar characteristics of minority and dominant groups, the rewards and penalties attached to assimilation versus nonassimilation, and whether there is any dominant group at all (see, e.g., Deutsch, *Nationalism and Social Communication*, Chapter 7). Once we know (or can estimate from past data) the relative sizes of minority and dominant cultures and the rates of mobilization and assimilation, it is possible to make projections about future distributions and to assess the likelihood of national conflict. For example, see Deutsch, *ibid.*, Chapter 6 and Appendices 1 to 5; and the ambitious but as yet uncompleted work of Raymond Hopkins, "Mathematical Modeling of Mobilization and Assimilation Processes," International Political Science Association Paper, VIII World Congress, Munich, September 1970.

[14] These data are presented and discussed in some detail in Ted R. Gurr, *New Error-Compensated Measures for Comparing Nations; Some Correlates of Civil Violence*, Center of International Studies, Princeton University, May 1966.

[15] *Ibid.*, p. 75.

[16] *Ibid.*, p. 71.

of additional causal paths to Collective Protest and Internal War; some of these causal paths were developed in previous chapters, and others are introduced in the following chapters. The consequence of this omission is generally to *bias upward* the parameter estimates of the included variables.[17] If anything, then, we are likely to err on the "positive" side—the estimates of effects will be spuriously high. Nevertheless, the models are estimated at this point in order to secure provisional information about functional form. In particular, we are interested in determining what variables in the equations for Collective Protest and Internal War should be retained for consideration in the much larger, "final" causal model developed in Part III.

Figure 5.1 provided the basis for the equations examined. A variety of functional forms, additional two- and three-way interactions (which did not have the theoretical justification of those depicted and discussed), and direct causal paths were explored. Rather than present all these results, only the functional forms that were most compatible with the data—in the sense of maximizing linear fits—are reported here.[18] The "best" Internal War system of equations, proceeding backward in the causal chain, was as follows:

Internal War D2 $= \alpha + \beta_1 \ln$ Population 1960 $+ \beta_2 \ln$ Political Separatism 1960 $+ \beta_3$ Group Discrimination 1960 $+ \varepsilon$

ln Political
Separatism 1960 $= \alpha \pm \beta_1$ Ethnolinguistic Fractionalization 1960

---

[17] This would not be true if the omitted variables were uncorrelated with the included variables. Consider the following illustration. Assume that the "true" equation generating some $y$ is

$$E(y/x) = \beta_1 x_1 + \beta_2 x_2$$

where all variables are mean deviates.

Suppose we mistakenly omit $x_2$ and estimate

$$E(y/x) = \beta_1 x_1$$

The least-squares estimate of $\beta_1$ in the misspecified model is

$$\hat{\beta}_1 = \beta_1 + [\beta_2 \cdot b_{21}]$$

where $b_{21}$ denotes the coefficient in the (auxiliary) regression of $x_2$ on $x_1$.

The bracketed expression indicates the (usually upward) bias of $\hat{\beta}_1$ in the misspecified model. Note that if $\beta_2$ and $b_{21}$ have opposite signs, the bias will be negative. It of course will be nil when $b_{21}$ is zero, that is, when $x_2$ and $x_1$ are uncorrelated.

Similar conclusions can be derived for the more general multivariate case where there are several omitted and several included variables. See Potluri Rao and Roger L. Miller, *Applied Econometrics* (Belmont, Calif.: Wadsworth Publishing Co., Inc., 1971), Chapter 3.

[18] Recall that what is meant by "linear" is linear in the parameters. The models include nonlinear variable functional forms as well as nonadditivities.

$$- \beta_2 \text{ Social Mobilization 1960} + \beta_3 \text{ SM * ELF}$$
$$+ \beta_4 \text{ Postwar Independence} + \varepsilon$$

$$\text{Group Discrimination} = \alpha + \beta_1 \text{ Ethnolinguistic Fractionalization}$$
$$1960 + \varepsilon$$

Ethnolinguistic
$$\text{Fractionalization 1960} = \alpha - \beta_1 \text{ ln Social Mobilization 1960}$$
$$+ \beta_2 \text{ Postwar Independence} + \varepsilon$$

where all terms are as defined earlier and $\pm$ signifies an estimate less than its standard error.

The actual parameter estimates and associated statistics for each equation are shown in Tables 5.5 to 5.8 The results for the Internal War equation (Table 5.5) fully support the sequence of causes and effects outlined in Figure 5.1. As anticipated, Political Separatism is estimated to have a forceful impact on the incidence of this mode of mass political violence. Separatist movements indeed appear to challenge existing political arrangements in a sharp and fundamental way. Similarly, Group Discrimination (unlogged), which was hypothesized to have a "possible" causal influence, seems to be strongly linked to subsequent Internal War. And, as expected, the impact of Ethnolinguistic Fractionalization is entirely mediated through separatism and discrimination.

The most distinctive feature of the results for the ln Political Separatism equation (Table 5.6) is the powerful interactive impact manifested by the conjunction of Social Mobilization and Ethnolinguistic Fractionalization. It totally eclipses the positive bivariate relationship of fractionalization and separatism and provides striking evidence for theories arguing that

Table 5.5  Recursive System for Internal War D2: Internal War D2 Equation ($N = 108$)

| Independent Variable | Parameter Estimate[a] | $t$ Statistic |
|---|---|---|
| ln Political Separatism 1960 | 0.411* | 2.52 |
| Group Discrimination 1960 | 0.025* | 2.78 |
| ln Population 1960 | 0.614* | 2.90 |
| Constant | −2.150 | |

| $R^2$ | Regression Standard Error | $F$ |
|---|---|---|
| .210 | 2.61 | 3,104  9.2 |

[a] Starred (*) estimates are more than twice their standard error.

Table 5.6  Recursive System for Internal War D2: ln Political Separatism 1960 Equation ($N = 108$)

| Independent Variable | Parameter Estimate[a] | $t$ Statistic |
|---|---|---|
| Ethnolinguistic Fractionalization (ELF) 1960 | −0.002 | −0.17 |
| Social Mobilization (SM) 1960 | −0.004* | −2.31 |
| SM*ELF | 0.00009* | 2.88 |
| Postwar Independence | 0.685 | 1.90 |
| Constant | 1.310 | |

| $R^2$ | Regression Standard Error | $F$ | |
|---|---|---|---|
| .306 | 1.37 | 4,103 | 11.4 |

[a] Starred (*) estimates are at least twice their standard error.

Table 5.7  Recursive System for Internal War D2: Group Discrimination 1960 Equation ($N = 108$)

| Independent Variable | Parameter Estimate[a] | $t$ Statistic |
|---|---|---|
| Ethnolinguistic Fractionalization 1960 | 0.209* | 2.30 |
| Constant | 12.750 | |

| $R^2$ | Regression Standard Error | $F$ | |
|---|---|---|---|
| .047 | 28.5 | 1,106 | 5.3 |

[a] Starred (*) estimate is more than twice its standard error.

Table 5.8  Recursive System for Internal War D2: Ethnolinguistic Fractionalization 1960 Equation ($N = 108$)

| Independent Variable | Parameter Estimate[a] | $t$ Statistic |
|---|---|---|
| ln Social Mobilization 1960 | −12.500* | −3.60 |
| Postwar Independence | 22.800* | 3.96 |
| Constant | 98.410 | |

| $R^2$ | Regression Standard Error | $F$ | |
|---|---|---|---|
| .390 | 23.9 | 2,105 | 33.5 |

[a] Starred (*) estimates are more than twice their standard error.

a mobilized *and* differentiated population is a particularly explosive combination. The Postwar Independence estimate in this equation is not quite twice its standard error, but it is nearly so, which weakly supports the proposition that recently independent nations have greater separatism at each level of mobilization and differentiation.[19]

Unlike the case for ln Political Separatism, the Social Mobilization–Ethnolinguistic Fractionalization interaction does not have the anticipated positive effect on Group Discrimination. Apparently, minority sociocultural groups experience about the same degree of discrimination, regardless of whether they are socially mobilized in Deutsch's sense. Hence Group Discrimination is shown simply as a function of ELF (Table 5.7). Although the ELF parameter estimate is significant in Table 5.7, the Group Discrimination equation clearly leaves much to be desired in terms of goodness of fit.

Table 5.8 reports the results for the ELF equation. Both Social Mobilization and Postwar Independence have forceful effects in the hypothesized direction. Thus we have strong support for the propositions that the modal impact of mobilization is to promote cultural assimilation and that the legacy of imperialism is high sociocultural differentiation. Note that in this equation the logarithm of Social Mobilization was determined to maximize the linear relationship, whereas in the ln Political Separatism equation it is not transformed. Thus Social Mobilization appears in two linearly independent functional forms in this "partial" model.[20]

---

[19] The effect of Postwar Independence (PWI) is additive—the hypothesized interaction of PWI and ELF did not prove significant. As a dummy variable, PWI's effect thus shows up in the intercept or constant term so that the slope (or, in this *n*-dimensional case, the regression response surface) generated by the "regular" variables is the same for all nations, but recently independent states have higher separatism at each point on the slope or surface. The interpretation, then, is identical to that of the more conventional analysis of covariance with additive effects. An excellent discussion of this and related points is provided by Harold W. Watts, "An Introduction to the Theory of Binary Variables (Or All About Dummies)," Social Systems Research Institute, University of Wisconsin, April 1964. Also instructive are: William Mendenhall, *Introduction to Linear Models and the Design and Analysis of Experiments* (Belmont, Calif.: Wadsworth Publishing Co., 1968); James Fennessey, "The General Linear Model: A New Perspective on Some Familiar Topics," *American Journal of Sociology*, Vol. 72, No. 1, July 1968, pp. 1–27; Jacob Cohen, "Multiple Regression as a General Data-Analytic System," *Psychological Bulletin*, Vol. 70, No. 6, 1968, pp. 426–443; and D.B. Suits, "Use of Binary Variables in Regression Equations," *Journal of the American Statistical Association*, vol. 52, 1957, pp. 548–551.

[20] This actually serves to introduce an *additional* exogenous variable into the model. Nonlinear identities of this sort sometimes aid identification, although our purpose in using them here is to maximize linear relationships. See Franklin M. Fisher, *The Identification Problem in Econometrics* (New York: McGraw-Hill Book Company, Inc., 1966), Chapter 5. We return to the identification issue in Part III.

We now consider the system of equations that produced the best linear relationships in the Collective Protest causal chain. The equations are

Collective Protest D2 $= \alpha + \beta_1$ ln Population 1960 $+ \beta_2$ Group Discrimination 1960 $+ \varepsilon$

Group Discrimination 1960 $= \alpha + \beta_1$ Ethnolinguistic Fractionalization 1960 $+ \varepsilon$

Ethnolinguistic Fractionalization 1960 $= \alpha - \beta_1$ ln Social Mobilization 1960 $+ \beta_2$ Postwar Independence $+ \varepsilon$

The equations for Group Discrimination and Ethnolinguistic Fractionalization, of course, have the same functional form and causal interpretation in the Collective Protest causal chain as they do in that of Internal War; therefore, the regression results need not be reported again here (see Tables 5.7 and 5.8). Yet the causal sequence leading to Collective Protest is somewhat different from the analogous sequence that leads to Internal War. What differentiates the Collective Protest chain is our finding that Group Discrimination (unlogged) mediates the causal effects of all other independent variables in the model (Table 5.9). This provides a clear confirmation of the argument advanced by Kornhauser that discrimination frequently produces a reaction of mass protest.

Table 5.9  Recursive System for Collective Protest D2: Collective Protest D2 Equation $(N = 108)$

| Independent Variable | Parameter Estimate[a] | $t$ Statistic |
|---|---|---|
| Group Discrimination 1960 | 0.018* | 3.40 |
| ln Population 1960 | 0.669* | 5.56 |
| Constant | −3.103 | |

| $R^2$ | Regression Standard Error | $F$ |
|---|---|---|
| .263 | 1.55 | 2,105   18.7 |

[a] Starred (*) estimates are more than twice their standard error.

## Summary

This concludes our preliminary analysis of the impact of sociocultural differentiation on mass political violence. To recapitulate, we concluded that a single-equation, interaction specification of a direct differentiation to mass violence causal relationship was inadequate for both Internal War and Collective Protest. A richer multiequation formulation which had greater theoretical appeal proved to be more compatible with the data. This specification involved two unidirectional (recursive) causal paths, each originating in Ethnolinguistic Fractionalization and leading through Political Separatism and Group Discrimination to Internal War or Collective Protest. It was emphasized that the estimates and inferences made for the Internal War and Collective Protest equations are preliminary and intended only to sort out which of the variables and causal sequences considered in this chapter should be retained for analysis in the context of a more inclusive, final model in Part III.

CHAPTER SIX

# The Behavior of Political Elites: Government Repression and Coups

In the analyses of previous chapters, political variables entered some of the equations in interaction with the variables that were of principal concern. For example, in Chapter 4, Nondefense General Government Expenditures as a percentage of Gross Domestic Product was employed as an indicator of governmental effort to meet human needs in a ratio interaction model with the Social Mobilization Index. The single equation interaction model proved to be inadequate, however, and so an alternative multiequation causal system was specified that involved Economic Development, Social Mobilization, and Social Welfare, as well as the Government Expenditures variable. In the last chapter, single equation formulations also fared poorly; therefore, a recursive causal sequence was developed which included Political Separatism mediating the effect of Ethnolinguistic Fractionalization on Internal War.

This chapter focuses on explanations of domestic violence that involve political variables more centrally. In particular, we look at variables that pertain to the behavior of political elites and explore how these might be causally linked to mass violence. The investigation begins in the usual fashion with an examination of single equation hypotheses. These include propositions dealing with the causal influence of the coercive capability available to the governing political elite; the impact of actual acts of government repression or coercion; and, finally, the causal role of actual and attempted power seizures (coups) by elite groups, chiefly the military, that are outside of and/or disaffected from incumbent political authorities. At the same time we pursue at some length the rather complex, causal relationships among these variables, and spend a good deal of time as well in testing alternative theories that purport to explain the incidence of coups and repression. Although such theories do not concern the

causes of mass violence directly, the variables involved can have important second-order effects on Collective Protest and Internal War through
their influence on the centrally relevant coups and repression variables.
Moreover, such factors must be introduced if we are to estimate precisely
(in Part III) the causal interdependencies we tentatively conclude are
operative between mass violence, coups, and repression. Finally, the
various facets of the investigation are pulled together in the last part of
the chapter where the causal relationships provisionally established in
earlier sections are summarized and depicted diagrammatically.

Perhaps what differentiates the processes analyzed here most from
those investigated in preceding chapters is their voluntaristic or manipu-
lative character. Unlike most of the variables considered earlier, coups
and government repression are under the direct and immediate *control*
of small (elite) groups and, hence, are amenable to ready *manipulation*
if the relevant actors are so inclined. Uncovering the causal implications
of such elite behavior, then, is of more than academic interest.

## Elite Coercive Capability and Mass Violence

The capability of political authorities to exercise coercive social
control is a feature of political systems that has figured prominently
in both qualitative and quantitative research on mass political violence.
A common observation in qualitative analyses, whether of the case
study or general-theoretical variety, is that the greater the coercive or
repressive forces available to a political elite, the more successful they are
likely to be in containing or inhibiting outbreaks of mass violence.
Roberts, for example, concluded in his study of eighteenth and nineteenth
century English working class protest that "A factor of considerable
importance in the growth of mob riots was the weakness of central
authorities."[1] In an entirely different substantive context, Ake theorized
that maintaining a strong coercive capability is one way regimes in transitional societies undergoing rapid social mobilization are able to neutralize
the accompanying instabilities.[2] Similarly, Chalmers Johnson argued in
his (structural–functional) analysis of "Revolutionary Change" that if
political elites in "disequilibrated" societies are to secure the "persistence"
of the system—that is, to stave off violent, revolutionary change—then the
most important thing to be avoided is a vitiation of elite ability to apply

[1] Ben C. Roberts, "On the Origins and Resolution of English Working Class Protest," in
Hugh D. Graham and Ted R. Gurr (eds.), *Violence in America: Historical and Comparative
Perspectives*, A Report to the National Commission on the Causes and Prevention of
Violence, June 1969. (New York: Signet Books, 1969), p. 240.
[2] Claude Ake, *A Theory of Political Integration* (Homewood, Ill.: The Dorsey Press, 1969).

coercion.[3] This line of reasoning was succintly summarized by Gurr when he hypothesized that "The magnitude of systemic violence tends to vary inversely with the perceived force capability of a political regime."[4]

How might this proposition be put to the empirical test? A straight-forward specification is the model represented by (6.1).

(6.1) $$Y = \alpha + \beta_1 \ln \text{Pop.} + \beta_2 X + \varepsilon$$

where $Y$ = Mass Violence D2
$\ln \text{Pop.}$ = ln Population 1960
$X$ = Regime Coercive Capability
$\varepsilon$ = stochastic disturbance

If mass disorder is indeed inhibited in a linear and inverse way by the strength of the coercive forces available to political authorities, then estimation of (6.1) should yield a significant, negative parameter estimate for the Coercive Capability term.

The results of a number of quantitative studies stand in contrast to the inverse "deterrence" effect, which some of the qualitative and theo-retical work has attributed to regime coercive capability. These studies have reported a curvilinear relationship between the size of repressive forces available to government and mass political violence. Violence is found to be greatest not in "permissive" societies, where the forces for potential elite coercion are relatively small, nor in "repressive" nations, with relatively large coercive capabilities, but rather in those with moderate or "middle-sized" capabilities. In the latter kinds of societies, it is argued, the regime's coercive posture is sufficient to antagonize or alienate signifi-cant segments of the population, but inadequate to inhibit or effectively suppress violent expressions of discontent. Indeed, although Gurr hypothe-sized a linear inverse relationship initially, he subsequently determined that a curvilinear model best described the association between his logged measure of the "Total Magnitude of Civil Strife" and the size of regime coercive forces across 114 nations.[5] This and other evidence led Gurr to revise his initial position and conclude that ". . . curvilinearity hypotheses seem to offer the most parsimonious and convincing explanation."[6] Bwy

---

[3] Chalmers Johnson, *Revolutionary Change* (Boston: Little, Brown & Co., 1966), Chapter 5.
[4] Ted R. Gurr, "The Genesis of Violence: A Multivariate Theory of the Preconditions for Civil Strife," Ph.D. Dissertation, New York University, 1965, Table 17, M1. Note, however, that Gurr was referring to "perceptions" which we are unable to measure directly.
[5] Ted R. Gurr, "A Comparative Study of Civil Strife," in Graham and Gurr, *Violence in America*, pp. 544–605; also Ted R. Gurr and Charles Ruttenberg, *The Conditions of Civil Strife: First Tests of a Causal Model*, Research Monograph No. 28, Center of International Studies, Princeton University, April 1967.

also discerned a curvilinear relationship between a measure of "regimeforce" —Defense Expenditure as a percentage of GNP, 1959 to 1960—and "Anomic Violence" during the years 1958 to 1960 across 20 Latin American nations.[7] Similarly, a number of cross-national studies based on the Feierabend data report a curvilinear relationship between "regime coerciveness" and political violence.[8]

These investigations have typically based their conclusions on tabular arrays and scatterplots, and at best they supply the reader with summary curves of relationships. Estimates of slopes and goodness of fit for the models proposed are usually not reported or apparently even estimated.[9] Given the appropriate quantitative data, we can more rigorously evaluate the adequacy of the linear versus the curvilinear hypothesis by comparing the results of (6.1) with those generated by the curvilinear alternative represented by (6.2).

(6.2)          $$Y = \alpha + \beta_1 \ln \text{Pop.} + \beta_2 X + \beta_3 X^2 + \varepsilon$$

where                    all terms are as in (6.1).

If the curvilinear model is more compatible with the data than the linear model, then estimation of (6.2) should yield a significant and positive $\beta_2$ coefficient and a significant and negative $\beta_3$ coefficient, as well as an $R^2$ significantly larger than that produced by (6.1). Such a result would demonstrate that a one-bend curve of the appropriate form characterizes the relationship of Regime Coercive Capability $(X)$ and mass violence $(Y)$.

[6] Ted R. Gurr, *Why Men Rebel* (Princeton, N.J.: Princeton University Press, 1970), p. 251. Chapter 8 of this book reviews the literature much more extensively than we do here.

[7] "Anomic Violence" in Bwy's study closely approximates our Collective Protest dimension of violence. Bwy also found that regime force bears no relation to "Organized Violence"— a variable similar to our Internal War, but including such elite actions as coups, which are examined separately in relation to mass violence later in this chapter. See Douglas P. Bwy, "Political Instability in Latin America: The Cross-Cultural Test of a Causal Model," *Latin American Research Review*, Vol. 3, No. 2, 1968, pp. 17–66; and "Correlates of Political Instability in Latin America: Over-Time Comparisons from Brazil, Cuba, The Dominican Republic, and Panama," American Political Science Association paper, Washington, D.C., September 1968.

[8] Ivo D. Feierabend et al., "Social Change and Political Violence: Cross-National Patterns," in Graham and Gurr, *Violence in America*, pp. 606–668; and Betty A. Nesvold, Ivo D. Feierabend, and Rosalind L. Feierabend, "Regime Coerciveness and Political Instability," American Political Science Association paper, New York, September 1969. The Feierabend data consist largely of ordinal rating scores, and the *N* varies from 75 to 85.

[9] Gurr, "A Comparative Study of Civil Strife," and Gurr and Ruttenberg, *The Conditions of Civil Strife*, usually report partial correlation coefficients for the various propositions examined, but they rely on summary curves in arguing curvilinearity.

It would thereby provide the evidence necessary to soundly argue that "middle-sized" coercive postures are indeed counterproductive from the perspective of an elite anxious to maintain domestic stability, and that the "permissive" or "repressive" alternatives should therefore be considered.

A number of indicators of a regime's coercive capacity are available in order to test these competing hypotheses. Several measure the size and resources commanded by the military establishment. These include:

Defense Expenditure as a Percentage of Gross Domestic Product
Defense Expenditure as a Percentage of General Government Expenditure
Military Manpower per 10,000 Population[10]

In many nations the military has little or no external function and is correctly considered (and perceived by the population) to represent the domestic coercive capacity of political authorities. The army, in particular, is regularly employed as a coercive agent for domestic social control. In other nations, however, the military is seldom if ever used in this fashion, and by training and experience (and attitude) it is ill-suited for the task. The size and share of governmental resources of such military establishments hinge on international considerations: cold war tensions, defense of the empire, imperialist adventures of political elites, and so on. As a comparable cross-national index of regime coercive capability, then, such military variables have limited value. More useful are variables that unmistakably measure domestic coercive potential. Two variables for which data were available for the 108-nation cross-section are:

Internal Security Forces per 10,000 Population
Internal Security Forces per 1000 sq km

The Internal Security Forces variables, which include police forces at all levels of government and such paramilitary forces as gendarmeries and active national guards, overcome some of the objections raised vis à vis the military variables and tap quite independent features of an elite's repressive capability.[11] The first represents the population density of such forces; the second the spatial density.

[10] Military manpower includes the total manpower in all the armed forces of the state. It excludes civilian employees and Internal Security Forces.

[11] The correlation ($r$) between these variables is only .12. Probably more measurement error is associated with these variables than with most of the others used in the study. Internal Security Forces strength is obviously sensitive information from the point of view of many regimes, and under- (and over-) reporting in official sources is a problem. See the discussion in Charles L. Taylor and Michael C. Hudson (eds.), *World Handbook of Political and Social Indicators*, 2nd edition (New Haven: Yale University Press, 1972).

*The Behavior of Political Elites*

Both the military and the internal security variables, however, suffer from a number of additional limitations. A regime's coercive capacity clearly depends not only on the size of available forces, but also on their loyalty, training, and technological sophistication—which we are unable to assess. Moreover, the current size of these forces may in part be a *response to* the magnitude of previous mass violence, raising the problem of what causes what? However, causality here is probably not instantaneously reciprocal; it most likely involves some delayed response or lag, since it takes considerable time for political authorities to recruit and train the large numbers of personnel necessary to substantially increase Internal Security Forces. Thus the process can be captured by means of a recursive causal sequence. But even this solution is less than optimal, since three of the coercion capability indicators—Military Manpower per 10,000 Population, Internal Security Forces per 10,000 Population, and ISF per 1000 sq km—are available for the year 1965 only, and therefore in large part do not temporally precede decade 2 violence.

Despite these problems, which serve to weaken causal inferences, the linear and curvilinear models were estimated with each of the coercive capability variables for each dimension of violence.[12] Tables 6.1 to 6.8 report only the results for which the two Internal Security Forces variables are the coercive capability indicators. The only clear message that emerges from this body of statistical results (both those reported and those not) is that no strong causal relationship of any kind exists between the coercive

Table 6.1   Linear Regression of Collective Protest D2 on Internal Security Forces per 10,000 Population 1965 ($N = 108$)

| Independent Variable | Parameter Estimate[a] | $t$ Statistic |
|---|---|---|
| Internal Security Forces per 10,000 Population 1965 | −0.0002 | −0.18 |
| ln Population 1960 | 0.599* | 4.70 |
| Constant | −2.070 | |

| $R^2$ | Regression Standard Error | $F$ |
|---|---|---|
| .181 | 1.62 | 2,105   11.7 |

[a] Starred (*) estimate is more than twice its standard error.

[12] Nonlinear transformations of the capability variables were also tried in regressions and plots for the linear and curvilinear models. These produced results no better than those discussed and reported here.

capability of the political elite and mass political violence. Neither the linear nor the curvilinear hypothesis is consistently supported by the empirical data. The most we can conclude, therefore, is that the strength of coercive forces available to governing elites does not seem to bear a marked curvilinear relation to mass violence, as previous analyses have suggested, and that the strength of such forces also fails to exert a substantial linear "deterrence" effect.

Table 6.2  Linear Regression of Internal War D2 on Internal Security Forces per 10,000 Population 1965 ($N = 108$)

| Independent Variable | Parameter Estimate[a] | $t$ Statistic |
|---|---|---|
| Internal Security Forces per 10,000 Population 1965 | −0.004 | −0.28 |
| ln Population 1960 | 0.650* | 2.98 |
| Constant | −1.350 | |

| $R^2$ | Regression Standard Error | $F$ |
|---|---|---|
| .083 | 2.80 | 2,105   4.8 |

[a] Starred (*) estimate is more than twice its standard error.

Table 6.3  Curvilinear Regression of Collective Protest D2 on Internal Security Forces per 10,000 Population 1965 ($N = 108$)

| Independent Variable | Parameter Estimate[a] | $t$ Statistic |
|---|---|---|
| Internal Security Forces per 10,000 Population 1965 | 0.036 | 1.68 |
| Internal Security Forces per 10,000 Population Squared | −0.0004 | −1.90 |
| ln Population 1960 | 0.605* | 4.81 |
| Constant | −2.610 | |

| $R^2$ | Regression Standard Error | $F$ |
|---|---|---|
| .209 | 1.61 | 3,104   9.2 |

[a] Starred (*) estimate is more than twice its standard error.

Table 6.4　Curvilinear Regression of Internal War D2 on Internal Security
Forces per 10,000 Population 1965 ($N = 108$)

| Independent Variable | Parameter Estimate[a] | $t$ Statistic |
|---|---|---|
| Internal Security Forces per 10,000 Population 1965 | 0.069 | 1.90 |
| Internal Security Forces per 10,000 Population Squared | −0.0007* | −2.17 |
| ln Population 1960 | 0.662* | 3.08 |
| Constant | −2.390 | |

| $R^2$ | Regression Standard Error | $F$ |
|---|---|---|
| .123 | 2.74 | 3,104　4.9 |

[a] Starred (*) estimates are more than twice their standard error.

Table 6.5　Linear Regression of Collective Protest D2 on Internal Security
Forces per 1000 sq km 1965 ($N = 108$)

| Independent Variable | Parameter Estimate[a] | $t$ Statistic |
|---|---|---|
| Internal Security Forces per 1000 sq km 1965 | −0.0002 | −1.71 |
| ln Population 1960 | 0.592* | 4.79 |
| Constant | −1.991 | |

| $R^2$ | Regression Standard Error | $F$ |
|---|---|---|
| .203 | 1.60 | 2,105　13.4 |

[a] Starred (*) estimate is more than twice its standard error.

## Elite Repression and Mass Violence

Thus far attention has been confined to the repressive capability of
the political elite. Perhaps *actual acts of coercion and repression* have a
more direct and important influence on the incidence of domestic mass
violence. Hence we consider in this section the causal role of what are
designated as *"Acts of Negative Sanction."*

Negative sanctions are defined as actions taken by political authorities to neutralize, suppress, or eliminate a perceived threat to the security

and stability of the government, the regime, or the state itself. They include acts of censorship against mass media, political publications, and the like, as well as restrictions on the political activity and participation of the general public, or specific persons, parties, and organizations.[13] The Negative Sanction acts are aggregated into two 10-year periods that coin-

Table 6.6   Linear Regression of Internal War D2 on Internal Security Forces per 1000 sq km 1965 ($N = 108$)

| Independent Variable | Parameter Estimate[a] | $t$ Statistic |
|---|---|---|
| Internal Security Forces per 1000 sq km 1965 | −0.0003 | −1.57 |
| ln Population 1960 | 0.644* | 3.03 |
| Constant | −1.296 | |

| $R^2$ | Regression Standard Error | $F$ |
|---|---|---|
| .103 | 2.76 | 2,105   6.1 |

[a] Starred (*) estimate is more than twice its standard error.

Table 6.7   Curvilinear Regression of Collective Protest D2 on Internal Security Forces per 1000 sq km 1965 ($N = 108$)

| Independent Variable | Parameter Estimate[a] | $t$ Statistic |
|---|---|---|
| Internal Security Forces per 1000 sq km 1965 | −0.0002 | −0.21 |
| Internal Security Forces per 1000 sq km Squared | 0.000 | 0.00 |
| ln Population 1960 | 0.592* | 4.71 |
| Constant | −1.991 | |

| $R^2$ | Regression Standard Error | $F$ |
|---|---|---|
| .203 | 1.61 | 3,104   8.9 |

[a] Starred (*) estimate is more than twice its standard error.

[13] A more complete discussion of these data can be found in "Political Indicators Definitions" (mimeo., Center for Research on Conflict Resolution, University of Michigan, November 21, 1966) and in Taylor and Hudson (eds.), *World Handbook of Political and Social Indicators*.

*The Behavior of Political Elites*

Table 6.8	Curvilinear Regression of Internal War D2 on Internal Security
Forces per 1000 sq km 1965 ($N = 108$)

| Independent Variable | Parameter Estimate[a] | t Statistic |
|---|---|---|
| Internal Security Forces per 1000 sq km 1965 | −0.003 | −1.59 |
| Internal Security Forces per 1000 sq km Squared | 0.000 | 1.41 |
| ln Population 1960 | 0.690* | 3.22 |
| Constant | −1.436 | |

| $R^2$ | Regression Standard Error | F |
|---|---|---|
| .120 | 2.75 | 3,104   4.8 |

[a] Starred (*) estimate is more than twice its standard error.

cide with the aggregation periods of the mass political violence variables.
Accordingly:

Negative Sanctions D1 = total number of repressive acts during the period January 1, 1948 to December 31, 1957

Negative Sanctions D2 = total number of repressive acts during the period January 1, 1958 to December 31, 1967

In the previous section we proposed that the size of Internal Security Forces, which indexes a regime's coercive potential, may represent the response of political authorities to the magnitude of past mass violence, as well as serving to deter present and future violence. However, since the reciprocity was delayed or lagged, it was not inappropriate to regress decade 2 violence on these coercive capability variables in order to test (linear and curvilinear) single equation hypotheses.[14] But in the case of actual acts of repression or "negative sanctions," the causal relationship is likely not only to be *reciprocal*, but nearly *instantaneous* as well. It is reciprocal because although mass violence is a cause of Negative Sanctions insofar as it evokes repression from political authorities, the *immediate*

[14] Recall that the 1965 time point for these variables posed an additional problem. There are also problems associated with estimating an equation in a recursive system that includes a lagged endogenous variable further back in the causal chain. Since upward bias is the likely result, we can nevertheless safely reject hypotheses.

consequence of repression is often a response of yet greater violence by its recipients. Moreover, this reciprocity probably has a sufficiently small lag time to be best conceived (and thus estimated) as simultaneous, particularly since the aggregation periods for decade 2 Negative Sanctions and mass violence are identical. This is not to say, however, that lagged Negative Sanctions does not also play a role in such a causal scheme. Although a strong positive, simultaneous relationship is anticipated between decade 2 violence and repression, we might also hypothesize that previous repression has a strong negative or inhibitive effect. This formulation incorporates the idea that the short-term or immediate response to repression is frequently more violence on the part of its recipients, but the long-term impact of repression is to deter violent expressions of discontent.

Tables 6.9 and 6.10 provide supporting evidence for the Internal War dimension of mass violence.[15] The regression of Internal War on current and lagged Negative Sanctions (Table 6.10) yields a significant positive coefficient for the former and a significant negative coefficient for the latter. This is not true in the Collective Protest regression (Table 6.9), where only current Negative Sanctions has a significant (positive) parameter estimate. These results are compatible with the argument that events such as riots, demonstrations, and political strikes are more "spontaneous" than are the events that comprise the composite measure of Internal War.[16] In any case, Collective Protest does not appear to be

Table 6.9   Regression of Collective Protest D2 on Current and Lagged
ln Negative Sanctions ($N = 108$)

| Independent Variable | Parameter Estimate[a] | $t$ Statistic |
|---|---|---|
| ln Negative Sanctions D2 | 0.954* | 8.34 |
| ln Negative Sanctions D1 | −0.120 | −1.51 |
| ln Population 1960 | 0.240* | 2.22 |
| Constant | −2.347 | |

| $R^2$ | Regression Standard Error | $F$ |
|---|---|---|
| .544 | 1.22 | 3,104   41.4 |

[a] Starred (*) estimates are more than twice their standard error.

[15] Note that the (natural) logarithm of Negative Sanctions is used in the regressions. This specification produced the best linear fits.
[16] See the sources cited in Chapter 2, footnote 1.

Table 6.10   Regression of Internal War D2 on Current and Lagged ln Negative Sanctions

| Independent Variable | Parameter Estimate[a] | t Statistic |
|---|---|---|
| ln Negative Sanctions D2 | 1.684* | 8.29 |
| ln Negative Sanctions D1 | −0.483* | −3.43 |
| ln Population 1960 | 0.218 | 1.14 |
| Constant | −2.647 | |

| $R^2$ | Regression Standard Error | F |
|---|---|---|
| .453 | 2.17 | 3,104  28.7 |

[a] Starred (*) estimates are more than twice their standard error.

deterred by the knowledge that elites in the past have resorted to repression, whereas it does make an important difference for the subsequent incidence of Internal War.

What is of real interest, however, is a model of the sort illustrated in Figure 6.1, which captures the instantaneous reciprocity of decade 2

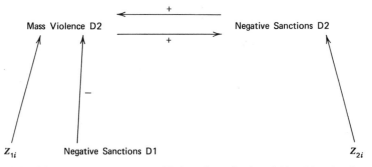

**Figure 6.1.**  Where $Z_{ni}$ represent unspecified predetermined variables. Negative Sanctions D1 appears only in the Internal War equation.

violence and repression as well as the deterrence effect of lagged repression on Internal War. Considered for the moment in isolation from the causal relations developed in previous chapters, this model would involve the estimation of a two-equation simultaneous system like that of (6.3) and (6.4):

$$(6.3) \qquad \text{Negative Sanctions D2} = \alpha + \beta \text{ Mass Violence D2} + \gamma_i Z_{2i} + \varepsilon_2$$

(6.4)          Mass Violence D2 $= \alpha + \beta$ Negative Sanctions D2
$+ \gamma_i Z_{1i} + \lambda$ Negative Sanctions D1
$+ \varepsilon_1$

where $Z_{ni}$ represent unspecified predetermined variables, $\varepsilon_n$ represent stochastic disturbances, and Negative Sanctions D1 appears only in
the equation for Internal War.

These relationships are incorporated into the larger causal system
developed in Part III, where the special problems surrounding the estimation
of simultaneous reciprocities are discussed. At this point, let us examine
how the actions of elites disaffected from the inner governing circle relate
to elite repression and mass violence.

## The Impact of Coups

A feature of political systems that is closely connected with the
government repression–domestic violence interdependency is the incidence
of (successful and unsuccessful) attempts at "irregular" government change.
These involve illegal attempts to overthrow the government by a particular
segment of the population, coalitions and factions of disaffected individuals
within the administration or ruling party, and (most commonly) the
military.[17] It closely approximates what Huntington meant by "praetorianism."[18] Since the variable consists primarily of military actions, it
is designated simply as "Coups."[19]

Coups are very likely to be causally related to domestic violence.
Actual and attempted seizures of power by the military commonly elicit
a violent response from the mass public as people spontaneously take to
the streets in protest or are mobilized by incumbent and/or opposing
political elites to defeat the attempt. Tables 6.11 and 6.12 show that the
association of Coups and each dimension of political violence is indeed
a strong one. This indicates that the response to a coup by the mass public

[17] "Irregular" and "illegal" mean outside the prevailing institutional procedures of the
political system. For a more detailed discussion of this variable, see Taylor and Hudson (eds.),
*World Handbook of Political and Social Indicators.*
[18] See Samuel P. Huntington, "Political Development and Political Decay," *World Politics,*
Vol. 17, No. 3, 1965, pp. 386–430 and *Political Order in Changing Societies* (New Haven:
Yale University Press, 1968). Huntington provides no sharp definition of "praetorianism";
but proceeds instead largely by example. The concept seems, however, to be nicely captured
by the Coups variable, although it may involve elements of what are included in Collective
Protest and Internal War. We evaluate Huntington's theoretical scheme below.
[19] Corresponding to our measures of Negative Sanctions and mass violence, Coups D1 and
D2 represent the number of such events in each of the 10-year periods.

*The Behavior of Political Elites*

may take the form of Collective Protest as well as (the more serious) Internal War. But, as in the case of elite coercion and mass violence, the causal relationship here is probably not unidirectional, as the model implied by Tables 6.11 and 6.12 suggests.[20] For example, an important stimulus of military intervention is often large-scale domestic disorder which, in the military's view, is not being dealt with effectively by incumbent political elites. The scenario of domestic disorder leading to military intervention to "handle" the situation, which provokes yet more disorder, is not uncommon. The literature on "the military and politics" provides numerous illustrations of what Huntington has called the "vicious circle of direct action" in praetorian political systems.[21] Hence a unidirectional formulation is inadequate. What is called for is a model that captures the interdependence or simultaneous causal reciprocity of Coups and mass political violence. However, Coups are not only reciprocally related to

Table 6.11   Regression of Collective Protest D2 on in Coups D2 $(N = 108)$

| Independent Variable | Parameter Estimate[a] | $t$ Statistic |
|---|---|---|
| ln Coups D2 | 0.709* | 4.57 |
| ln Population 1960 | 0.618* | 5.40 |
| Constant | −2.729 | |

| $R^2$ | Regression Standard Error | $F$ |
|---|---|---|
| .317 | 1.49 | 2,105   24.4 |

[a] Starred (*) estimates are more than twice their standard error.

[20] Note that as was true of the other event variables, the (natural) logarithm of Coups was determined to maximize linear relationships. Hence, whenever Coups appears in the equations, it has been logarithmically transformed. Recall also that the coups, mass violence, and elite repression variables are 10-year aggregates, and thus inferences must be interpreted with caution.

[21] See Huntington, *Political Order in Changing Societies*, especially Chapter 4; and *idem.*, Political Development and Political Decay." See also Martin C. Needler, *Latin American Politics in Perspective* (Princeton, N.J.: D. Van Nostrand Co., Inc., 1963), pp. 64–88; Henry Bienen, (ed.), *The Military Intervenes: Case Studies in Political Development* (New York: Russell Sage, 1968); Edwin Lieuwen, *Generals vs. Presidents: Neo-Militarism in Latin America* (New York: Praeger, 1964); and John J. Johnson (ed.), *The Role of the Military in Under-developed Countries* (Princeton, N.J.: Princeton University Press, 1962), especially the article by Edwin Lieuwen, "Militarism and Politics in Latin America," pp. 131–163. For a theoretically appealing analysis in the Latin American context which frames the relationships in terms of power "contenders" employing their available power "capabilities," see Charles W. Anderson, *Politics and Economic Change in Latin America* (Princeton, N.J.: D. Van Nostrand Co., Inc., 1967), Chapter 4.

Table 6.12  Regression of Internal War D2 on ln Coups D2
(N = 108)

| Independent Variable | Parameter Estimate[a] | T Statistic |
|---|---|---|
| ln Coups D2 | 1.717* | 7.19 |
| ln Population 1960 | 0.697* | 3.96 |
| Constant | −2.958 | |

| $R^2$ | Regression Standard Error | | F |
|---|---|---|---|
| .386 | 2.29 | 2,105 | 32.9 |

[a] Starred (*) estimates are more than twice their standard error.

violence; they are also likely to be a determinant of Negative Sanctions. This is especially probable when military intervention is spurred by mass disorder which incumbent authorities are (perceived to be) unable to properly contain. We would anticipate that in such situations the military would increase repression in order to restore stability. Yet, as was noted earlier, the immediate consequence of repression and military intervention itself is frequently to exacerbate the situation.

These relationships can be traced through Figure 6.2, which depicts the hypothesized causal linkages between mass violence, elite repression, and coups. Note that the causal system represented in Figure 6.2 is not closed. If it were, it would be hopelessly underidentified and estimation of the hypothesized causal effects would be impossible. In this sense it would be a "nonmodel." However, the model includes unspecified $Z_{ni}$, which represent additional causal influences that are *predetermined* with respect to the variables specified in the figure. Of course, the $Z_{ni}$ themselves be generated by recursive or nonrecursive causal processes in other "sectors" or "blocks"

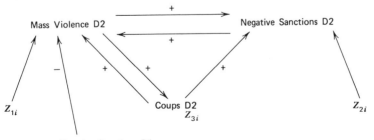

**Figure 6.2.**  Where $Z_{ni}$ are unspecified predetermined variables. Negative Sanctions D1 appears only in the Internal War equation.

of the model.[22] Included among the $Z_{1i}$, for example, are the variables that figured in causal paths to mass violence which were developed in previous chapters.

What of the other $Z_{ni}$ in Figure 6.2? That is, what factors other than Collective Protest and Internal War produce elite repression (negative sanctions) and coups? Let us pursue this question at some length, since a determination of these causal influences is necessary in order to estimate the reciprocal relationships between violence, repression, and coups in Part III. Moreover, such variables might have important second-order or indirect influences on Collective Protest and Internal War by way of their direct effects on coups and repression. Hence it is important that the causes of coups and repression be investigated carefully.

## Predetermined Causes of Coups

What other than the occurrence of mass political violence explains cross-national variation in attempts by the military and similar groups to seize power "illegally"? Huntington's analysis of the causes of "praetorian" politics provides a testable theory. He has argued that the most important causes of military intervention and praetorian politics are found not in the social and organizational features of the military establishment, as some analysts have claimed, but rather in the political and institutional structure of the larger society:

"The stability of any given polity depends upon the relationship between the level of political participation and the level of political institutionalization . . . . Political systems with low levels of institutionalization and high levels of participation are systems where social forces using their own methods act directly in the political sphere . . . . Such political systems are appropriately called praetorian polities. Conversely, political systems with a high ratio of institutionalization to participation may be termed civic polities. One society may thus have more highly developed political institutions than another and yet may also be more praetorian because of its still higher level of political participation."[23]

[22] The most notable example of a multisector, block-recursive social science model is the Brookings–SSRC econometric model of the United States economy. See J. S. Duesenberry et al., *The Brookings Quarterly Econometric Model of the United States* (Chicago: Rand McNally & Co., 1965). We present our complete model and pursue in some detail the points raised here in Part III.

[23] Huntington, *Political Order in Changing Societies*, pp. 79, 80. See also *idem.*, "Political Development and Political Decay." A similar theory is advanced by William Kornhauser, *The Politics of Mass Society* (New York: The Free Press, 1959). Also see S. N. Eisenstadt, *Modernization: Protest and Change*, (Englewood Cliffs, N.J.: Prentice-Hall, Inc., 1966), Chapter 3.

Huntington also suggests that an imbalance in the degree of social mobilization or political participation and institutionalization not only produces praetorian politics, of which the hallmark is military intervention, but general political instability and widespread domestic violence as well:

"The relationship between social mobilization and political instability seems reasonably direct. Urbanization, increases in literacy, education, and media exposure all give rise to enhanced aspirations and expectations which, if unsatisfied, galvanize individuals and groups into politics. In the absence of strong and adaptable political institutions, such increases in participation mean instability and violence."[24]

Clearly, Huntington has proposed an interaction model identical in functional form to those examined in Chapter 4. At one point in his exposition he actually specifies the equation: political participation/political institutionalization = political instability.[25] However, he supports his proposition largely by introducing typologies and citing examples. Perhaps a more rigorous test of the thesis that the conjunction of high mobilization (or participation) and low institutionalization has an impact beyond the additive effect of these variables is afforded by the ratio interaction model of (6.5):

(6.5) $$Y = \alpha + \beta_1 \ln \text{Pop.} + \beta_2 X + \beta_3 Z + \beta_4 \frac{X}{Z} + \varepsilon$$

where $Y$ = Mass Violence or Coups
$\ln$ Pop. = ln Population 1960 (appears in the equation for Mass Violence only)
$X$ = Social Mobilization, Political Participation
$Z$ = Institutionalization
$\frac{X}{Z}$ = Ratio (interaction term) of Mobilization or Participation to Institutionalization
$\varepsilon$ = stochastic disturbance

An alternative formulation, less susceptible to multicollinearity, is the log multiplicative model of (6.6a):

---

[24] Huntington, *Political Order in Changing Societies*, p. 47.

[25] *Ibid.*, p. 55. If such an imbalance affects both coups and mass violence, as Huntington suggested, then it does not, of course, constitute the kind of independent, predetermined influence on Coups that is necessary for estimation purposes, although it still should appear in the model. See the empirical results below.

For an analysis of Huntington's theory in the context of 10 highly developed nations, see P. R. Schneider and A. L. Schneider, "Social Mobilization, Political Institutions, and Political Violence, a Cross-National Analysis," *Comparative Political Studies*, Vol. 4, 1971, pp. 69–90.

(6.6a)            $Y = \alpha + \beta_1 \ln \text{Pop.} + \beta_2 \ln X + \beta_3 \ln Z + \varepsilon$

where            all terms and conditions are as in (6.5).

Recall that $Y$—Mass Violence or Coups—appears in (natural) logarithmic form. Hence (6.6a) can be rewritten:

(6.6b)

$$Y = \alpha^* \cdot \text{Pop.}^{\beta_1} \cdot X^{\beta_2} \cdot Z^{\beta_3} \cdot \varepsilon^*$$

where $\ln \alpha^* = \alpha$
$\ln \varepsilon^* = \varepsilon$

A significant negative estimate for the Institutionalization coefficient ($\beta_3$) is necessary to support the ratio interaction hypothesis, for (6.6b) then can be expressed

(6.6c)

$$Y = \alpha^* \cdot \text{Pop.}^{\beta_1} \cdot \frac{X^{\beta_2}}{Z^{\beta_3}} \cdot \varepsilon^*$$

Since Huntington attributes the same meaning to social mobilization as Deutsch, the Social Mobilization Index developed in Chapter 4 may be employed as the operational definition here. In addition to participation in national life generally implied by Huntington's use of social mobilization, he speaks specifically of "political" participation. To assess the degree of Political Participation, we use the percentage of eligible voters voting circa 1960. This indicator has a number of drawbacks, but electoral turnout is the most straightforward benchmark of politicization available for a large number of nations.[26]

A measure of sociopolitical institutionalization, which Huntington argues must be highly developed if the destabilizing consequences of high levels of social mobilization and political participation are to be effectively contained, is more difficult to devise. Huntington discusses the "criteria of institutionalization" at length, but the analysis is cast in such abstract terms that operationalization is a formidable problem. Fortunately,

---

[26] One key problem is the artificially high turnout in Communist nations and the general incomparability of this value with turnout in other nations. To control for possible distortions, the models were estimated with samples including and excluding Communist nations. Another problem, which we are unable to overcome given the available data, is that turnout is depressed in nations like the United States where it is relatively difficult to establish eligibility. This vitiates the cross-national comparability of the turnout indicator. See Stanley Kelley, et al., "Registration and Voting: Putting First Things First," *American Political Science Review*, Vol. 61, 1967, pp. 359–379.

Michael Hudson has already done a great deal of work in developing a variety of quantitative indicators to tap its key features.[27] He quite convincingly argues that although any one of the proposed indicators is in itself too crude to effectively capture the theoretical concept of institutionalization, they should prove adequate if used additively. In choosing indicators from among those suggested by Hudson, we have eliminated those which seem particularly weak or excessively redundant, as well as those measuring political stability directly. The latter exclusion is especially important if institutionalization as a structural feature of society and polity is to be differentiated from its hypothesized causal effects.

With these points in mind the following variables were selected in order to create an index of sociopolitical institutionalization: Direct Taxes as a Percentage of General Government Revenue, 1960;[28] Age in Decades of Present National Institutional Form, through 1968;[29] Union Membership as a Percentage of the Nonagricultural Work Force, 1960;[30] General Government Expenditures as a Percentage of the Gross Domestic Product, 1960;[31] Age of the Largest Political Party Divided by the Number of Parties, circa 1965;[32] and the Age of the Largest Political Party, 1965.[33]

A number of procedures were considered and experimented with in constructing a composite institutionalization index from these variables.

---

[27] Michael C. Hudson, "Some Quantitative Indicators for Explaining and Evaluating National Political Performance," American Political Science Association paper, Chicago, September 1967.

[28] Direct taxes, such as income taxes, are far more difficult to collect than indirect taxes, such as sales and customs. Hence a high proportion of government revenues coming from direct taxes indexes a sophisticated bureaucratic apparatus.

[29] The longevity of a nation's institutional form is a sign of durability and adaptability, but of course not necessarily of democratic accountability.

[30] Many studies have emphasized that unions are important institutional mechanisms for the maintenance of stability in the face of mobilization and discontent. See, for example, Ted R. Gurr, *New Error-Compensated Measures for Comparing Nations: Some Correlates of Civil Violence* (Center of International Studies, Princeton University, May 1966); and *idem.*, "A Causal Model of Civil Strife: A Comparative Analysis Using New Indices," *American Political Science Review*, Vol. 62, 1968, pp. 1104–1124, and the sources cited therein; Clark Kerr et al., *Industrialism and Industrial Man* (Cambridge, Mass.: Harvard University Press, 1960); and William Kornhauser, *The Politics of Mass Society* (New York: The Free Press, 1959).

[31] Where government resources comprise a large proportion of the total domestic product, the capabilities of political institutions are likely to be great.

[32] The fewer the parties and the older they are, the more adaptable they must be as political institutions, and the more adaptable the party system as a whole must be to changing conditions. To be included in the calculation, a party must have obtained at least 5 % of the legislative seats.

[33] Huntington emphasizes that "The principal institutional means for organizing the expansion of political participation are political parties and the party system," and so we include a second parties variable. It measures the durability and adaptability of the major party in the political system. Huntington, *Political Order in Changing Societies*, p. 398.

*The Behavior of Political Elites*

As in the case of the Social Welfare and Social Mobilization indices, a straightforward additive index was finally settled on. Hence the *Institutionalization Index* equals the mean of the sum of the six component variables.

Having operationalized all the relevant concepts, both the ratio interaction (equation 6.5) and the log multiplicative (equation 6.6) formulations of Huntington's theory were tested against the data in the 108-nation cross-section for Coups, as well as for Collective Protest and Internal War. Each equation was estimated separately with Political Participation (electoral turnout) and Social Mobilization as the "$X$" variable. Since the outcomes were not substantially different, only the Social Mobilization version of the equations is reported in Tables 6.13 to 6.18.

Table 6.13  Regression of ln Coups D2 on Social Mobilization and Institutionalization:  Ratio Interaction Model ($N = 108$)

| Independent Variable | Parameter Estimate | $t$ Statistic |
|---|---|---|
| Social Mobilization 1960 | −0.001 | −1.18 |
| Institutionalization 1960 | −0.010 | −0.69 |
| Social Mobilization/Institutionalization | 0.026 | 1.25 |
| Constant | 0.871 | |

| $R^2$ | Regression Standard Error | $F$ |
|---|---|---|
| .135 | 0.874 | 3,104   5.4 |

Table 6.14  Regression of Collective Protest D2 on Social Mobilization and Institutionalization:  Ratio Interaction Model ($N = 108$)

| Independent Variable | Parameter Estimate[a] | $t$ Statistic |
|---|---|---|
| Social Mobilization 1960 | 0.002 | 0.74 |
| Institutionalization 1960 | −0.036 | −1.38 |
| Social Mobilization/Institutionalization | −0.003 | −0.07 |
| ln Population 1960 | 0.599* | 4.69 |
| Constant | −1.669 | |

| $R^2$ | Regression Standard Error | $F$ |
|---|---|---|
| .223 | 1.60 | 4,103   7.4 |

[a] Starred (*) estimate is more than twice its standard error.

Table 6.15   Regression of Internal War D2 on Social Mobilization and Institutionalization: Ratio Interaction Model ($N = 108$)

| Independent Variable | Parameter Estimate[a] | t Statistic |
|---|---|---|
| Social Mobilization 1960 | −0.002 | −0.52 |
| Institutionalization 1960 | −0.092* | −2.26 |
| Social Mobilization/Institutionalization | −0.036 | −0.60 |
| ln Population 1960 | 0.844* | 4.26 |
| Constant | −0.131 | |

| $R^2$ | Regression Standard Error | F | |
|---|---|---|---|
| .289 | 2.49 | 4,103 | 10.5 |

[a] Starred (*) estimates are more than twice their standard error.


Table 6.16   Regression of ln Coups D2 on Social Mobilization and Institutionalization: ln Multiplicative Model ($N = 108$)

| Independent Variable | Parameter Estimate[a] | t Statistic |
|---|---|---|
| ln Social Mobilization 1960 | 0.064 | 0.55 |
| ln Institutionalization 1960 | −0.656* | −3.89 |
| Constant | 2.290 | |

| $R^2$ | Regression Standard Error | F | |
|---|---|---|---|
| .134 | 0.870 | 2,105 | 8.3 |

[a] Starred (*) estimate is more than twice its standard error.


Table 6.17   Regression of Collective Protest D2 on Social Mobilization and Institutionalization: ln Multiplicative Model ($N = 108$)

| Independent Variable | Parameter Estimate[a] | t Statistic |
|---|---|---|
| ln Social Mobilization 1960 | 0.408 | 1.88 |
| ln Institutionalization 1960 | −0.664* | −2.09 |
| ln Population 1960 | 0.570* | 4.52 |
| Constant | −2.030 | |

| $R^2$ | Regression Standard Error | F | |
|---|---|---|---|
| .224 | 1.59 | 3,104 | 10.0 |

[a] Starred (*) estimates are more than twice their standard error.

101

Table 6.18   Regression of Internal War D2 on Social Mobilization and
Institutionalization:  ln Multiplicative Model ($N = 108$)

| Independent Variable | Parameter Estimate[a] | $t$ Statistic |
|---|---|---|
| ln Social Mobilization 1960 | −0.359 | −1.05 |
| ln Institutionalization 1960 | −1.920* | −3.89 |
| ln Population 1960 | 0.796* | 3.97 |
| Constant | 5.020 | |

| $R^2$ | Regression Standard Error | $F$ |
|---|---|---|
| .256 | 2.53 | 3,104   12.0 |

[a] Starred (*) estimates are more than twice their standard error

None of the results supports Huntington's theory of the structural
conditions which produce praetorian politics and domestic violence.
In the ratio interaction equations (Tables 6.13–6.15), not one of the
interaction terms even approaches significance. Similarly, in the log
multiplicative equations [(6.16)–(6.18)], either the parameter estimates
are not consistently significant or they do not have the "correct" sign.
What is clear from these results, however, is that (ln) Institutionalization
*alone* has a negative impact on Coups, Collective Protest, and Internal
War. Weakly institutionalized societies, then, are far more likely than
those with highly developed institutions to suffer praetorian political
interventions by the military and similar groups, whatever the level of
social mobilization.

Although not as theoretically provocative as the interaction effect
proposed by Huntington, the finding that Institutionalization has an
additive, negative impact on the incidence of Coups is not unexpected.
The qualitative observations of many scholars anticipate such a result.[34]
Moreover, the significant negative impact of (ln) Institutionalization on
mass violence also lends support to the contention of Gurr and others
that "If institutions beyond the family and community level are broad in
scope, command large resources, and are stable and persisting, the

[34] See, for example, Gino Germani and Kalman Silvert, "Politics and Military Intervention
in Latin America," in J. L. Finkle and R. W. Gable (eds.), *Political Development and Social
Change* (New York: John Wiley & Sons, Inc., 1966), pp. 397–401; Dankwart A. Rustow,
"The Military in Middle Eastern Society and Politics," in *ibid.*, pp. 386–397; S. E. Finer,
*The Man on Horseback: The Role of the Military in Politics* (London: Pall Mall, 1962); and
Kalman H. Silvert, *The Conflict Society: Reaction and Revolution in Latin America* (New
Orleans: The Hauser Press, 1961), Chapter 2.

disruptive effects of [widespread domestic] discontent ought to be minimized."[35]

It is, of course, possible that the inhibitive effect of Institutionalization on mass violence is not direct but is mediated instead through its negative causal influence on Coups. Whether this is the case will be determined by the multiequation analyses in Part III. At this point, a number of other theories concerning Coups deserve attention.

One of these springs from Needler's analysis of military intervention in the domestic politics of Latin American nations.[36] Although confined to a particular region, Needler's work suggests the outlines of a generally applicable model.

Like Huntington, Needler argues that Coups are largely explainable by features of socioeconomic and political structure rather than by the internal peculiarities of the military establishment. His thesis focuses on the (potentially threatening) consequences of an imbalance between social mobilization or political participation and economic development, as opposed to disequilibrium between mobilization and institutionalization, which was the core of Huntington's argument. Social mobilization is potentially threatening because:

" . . . constitutional presidents are likely to be responsive to social classes of progressively lower status as these enter the political arena by moving to the city or otherwise become mobilized. The policies of each successive constitutional president are thus likely, on balance, to constitute a greater threat to the status quo than those of his predecessor. This may be interpreted to the military by those trying to secure their intervention as a threat to the personal economic interests of military officers, as a challenge to the military in its role of preserver of domestic order, as a threat to national unity and power, or as a long-term threat to the special

---

[35] Gurr, "A Comparative Study of Civil Strife," p. 581. This result is also anticipated by a number of qualitative analyses. Ralf Dahrendorf, in *Class and Class Conflict in Industrial Society* (Stanford, Calif.: Stanford University Press, 1959), for example, wrote "Organization is institutionalization, and whereas its manifest function is usually an increasingly articulate and outspoken defense of interests, it invariably has the latent function also of inaugurating routines of conflict which contribute to reducing violent clashes of interest" (p. 65). See also Kerr, *Industrialism and Industrial Man*; and Anthony Oberschall, "Group Violence: Some Hypotheses and Empirical Uniformities," American Sociological Society paper, San Francisco, September 1969.

[36] Needler's relevant work includes: Martin C. Needler, *Political Development in Latin America: Instability, Violence, and Evolutionary Change* (New York: Random House, 1968); "Political Development and Socioeconomic Development: The Case of Latin America," *American Political Science Review*, Vol. 62, No. 3, September 1968, pp. 889–897; "Political Development and Military Intervention in Latin America," *American Political Science Review*, Vol. 60, September 1966, pp. 616–626.

status and privileges, even to the continued existence, of the military institution."[37]

But the seriousness of the "threat" posed by social mobilization and increased mass participation in the perception of military elites (acting to secure their own interests and those of a vested economic elite) is *conditional* upon the level of economic development:

"One is thus presented with a dialectical tension: if mass participation rises faster than the level of economic development, then constitutional functioning breaks down, usually with the imposition of a military regime, as the conservative forces in the society react against the attempts of constitutional governments to gratify desires of the newly participant masses through drastic social change."[38]

What Needler means, then, is that the mobilization of mass publics into national life and political participation becomes a *serious* threat to the interests of privileged military establishments and allied economic elites *when* economic development is low. It is in such situations that the desires and demands of large numbers of mobilized low-status people are unlikely to be satisfied from a limited economic pie by responsive civilian elites. Hence the combination of high mobilization and low economic development raises the specter of "drastic" social change: for example, a fundamental *redistribution* of *existing* (though limited) economic resources. Thus, when the "dialectical tension" moves in the direction of mobilization outrunning economic development, military interventions are likely to be frequent.

Needler introduces a good deal of quantitative data on Latin American coups, levels of economic development, and so on, to support his thesis, but the evidence is presented and the discussion cast in a manner that tends to confuse rather than illuminate the issue. A proper test of his argument seems to require a ratio interaction model. The appropriate specifications, as we have noted before in conjunction with different hypotheses with the same functional form, are

$$(6.7) \quad Y = \alpha + \beta_1 X + \beta_2 Z + \beta_3 \frac{X}{Z} + \varepsilon \quad \text{Ratio Interaction Equation}$$

where  $Y = (\ln)$  Coups D2
$X = $ Social Mobilization, Political Participation

---

[37] Needler, *Political Development in Latin America*, p. 64. Note that his formulation assumes that the military usually acts conservatively and in alliance with economic elites. There are, of course, significant exceptions to such an assumption.
[38] *Ibid.*, p. 95.

$Z$ = Level of Economic Development

$\dfrac{X}{Z}$ = Ratio (interaction term) of Mobilization or Participation to Economic Development

$\varepsilon$ = stochastic disturbance

(6.8) $Y = \alpha + \beta_1 \ln X + \beta_2 \ln Z + \varepsilon \ln$ Multiplicative Equation

where     all terms are as in (6.7).

In estimating (6.7) and (6.8), GNP per capita and Energy Consumption per capita served as measures of Economic Development, and Electoral Turnout and the Social Mobilization Index were the participation variables. Since each combination of these variables furnished essentially the same answer, only the results of the Social Mobilization–GNP per capita regressions are reported here (Tables 6.19 and 6.20).

Tables 6.19 and 6.20 demonstrate that Needler's proposition is not substantiated by the data. Indeed, given the high collinearity between Social Mobilization and GNP per capita ($r = .84$), we would not expect it to be. As we noted in a different context in the last chapter, high collinearity means that there are simply too few instances, even across a very wide range of nations, of high social mobilization *and* low economic development for the interaction effect to manifest itself, *even though the interaction model may have theoretical merit*.[39] We shall have to look elsewhere for a robust explanation of coups.

Table 6.19   Regression of ln Coups D2 on Social Mobilization and Economic Development: Ratio Interaction Model ($N = 108$)

| Independent Variable | Parameter Estimate | $t$ Statistic |
|---|---|---|
| Social Mobilization 1960 | −0.0002 | −0.22 |
| GNP per capita 1960 | −0.0003 | −0.88 |
| Social Mobilization/GNP per capita | 0.141 | 0.68 |
| Constant | 0.729 | |

| $R^2$ | Regression Standard Error | $F$ |
|---|---|---|
| .070 | 0.906 | 3,104   2.62 |

[39] See the longer discussion in Chapter 4 on this issue. Collinearity was not a serious problem in the models with Social Mobilization and Institutionalization, which are only moderately highly correlated: $r = .56$.

*The Behavior of Political Elites*

Table 6.20    Regression of ln Coups D2 on Social Mobilization and
Economic Development: ln Multiplicative Model ($N = 108$)

| Independent Variable | Parameter Estimate[a] | t Statistic |
|---|---|---|
| ln Social Mobilization 1960 | 0.250 | 1.31 |
| ln GNP per capita 1960 | −0.369* | −2.43 |
| Constant | 1.390 | |

| $R^2$ | Regression Standard Error | F | |
|---|---|---|---|
| .066 | 0.904 | 2,105 | 3.7 |

[a] Starred (*) estimate is more than twice its standard error.

Recent research by Putnam on military interventions in Latin America provides further testable hypotheses that may prove to have explanatory power across a wider range of nations.[40] Drawing on the qualitative research of traditional scholars, particularly Latin American area specialists, Putnam hypothesized that "the propensity to military intervention is likely to decrease with increased social mobilization."[41] He showed that across Latin American nations the thesis is confirmed: Social Mobilization displayed a strong negative correlation with military intervention in domestic politics during the years 1956 to 1965.[42] The argument here, in contrast to the conditional specification of interaction theories, is simply that mobilization increases the political awareness and activity of mass publics and thereby supplies the political resources necessary to sustain civilian regimes and to deter arbitrary, "praetorian" power seizures by the military and other narrowly based elite groups. Conversely, a population which is largely nonpoliticized, or, in Deutsch's sense, "underlying," is far less likely to have either the political awareness or the resources that would pose an obstacle to military takeovers.

Another hypothesis for which Putnam found strong verification in his Latin American data is one proposing that "the propensity for military intervention increases with the habituation of the military to intervention."[43] Simply put, this hypothesis means that an interventionist history develops

[40] Robert D. Putnam, "Toward Explaining Military Intervention in Latin America," *World Politics*, Vol. 20, No. 1, October 1967, pp. 83–110.
[41] *Ibid.*, p. 85.
[42] *Ibid.*, p. 92ff. Putnam's social mobilization index was derived from Deutsch's work and is very similar to the index we have created. His military intervention index was based on ordinal scores assigned to each nation for each year.
[43] Putnam, "Toward Explaining Military Intervention in Latin America," pp. 87, 103ff.

and/or perpetuates a political tradition or "culture" that makes future interventions more likely than otherwise would be the case. In societies that have experienced frequent military interventions in the recent past, large segments of the general public (as well as the military establishment itself) may come to look on such interventions as a normal feature of political life.[44]

Finally, Putnam reported a strong positive correlation between Defense Expenditures as a percentage of GNP and military intervention, which supports the contention of Janowitz and others that "the size and sophistication of the military establishment are positively related to the propensity for intervention in politics."[45] However, Putnam dismissed this finding as a case of "circular" causation. Undoubtedly, there is a reciprocity to this relationship, although it is surely lagged rather than (nearly) simultaneous. A military establishment which has intervened in the past is very likely to have secured for itself a generous share of social resources, and civilian political elites anxious to avoid antagonizing the "colonels" are unlikely to diminish the share substantially. Conversely, a well-financed or privileged military has a great deal at stake in political life, and this makes future intervention more probable. Moreover, if the military's relative share of government resources is large, then its organizational capacity for domestic political involvement in relation to that of civilian actors is likely to be correspondingly great.[46] This suggests a lagged reciprocity which can be captured recursively. Hence (lagged) military expenditure should be retained as a potential causal influence on Coups D2.[47]

---

[44] On the "normalcy" of coups in Latin America, see Silvert, *The Conflict Society*, p. 20ff. "Political culture" is extensively discussed in Lucian W. Pye and Sidney Verba (eds.), *Political Culture and Political Development* (Princeton, N.J.: Princeton University Press, 1965).

[45] Putnam, "Toward Explaining Military Intervention in Latin America," pp. 87, 103ff; Morris Janowitz, *The Military in the Political Development of New Nations* (Chicago: University of Chicago Press, 1964), p. 40ff. Putnam found that such other "size" variables as military personnel as a percentage of adults and total military personnel bore little relation to coups.

[46] Janowitz (*ibid.*) provides a good discussion on this point. For Latin American evidence on the military's inclination to spend a great deal on itself, that is on defense, when it rules intermittently, see Philip Schmitter, "Military Intervention, Political Competitiveness, and Public Policy in Latin America: 1950–1967," in Morris Janowitz and Jaques Van Doorn, (eds.), *On Military Intervention* (Rotterdam, Neth.: Rotterdam University Press, 1971).

[47] If we use military expenditures as an explanatory variable for Coups as proposed, and expenditures is itself generated by a process that includes lagged Coups, then bias in parameter estimates will result if disturbances are autocorrelated. The extent of the bias will vary as a function of the magnitude of the autocorrelation; but since the data are cross-sectional, there is no way to estimate this. What can be said is that the bias in the estimated effect of military expenditures on Coups will generally be upward, and therefore hypotheses concerning this variable can safely be rejected. Estimation problems are treated in greater detail in Part III.

The hypotheses derived from the traditional literature and confirmed by Putnam's analysis suggest a straightforward model. Unlike those previously considered, it involves no complex interactions or interdependencies. Instead, the probability of military intervention is seen as additively (and linearly) inhibited by social mobilization, and increased by high military expenditure and an interventionist history. To this we add our previous conclusion that well-developed (nonmilitary) sociopolitical institutions also deter Coups. Ignoring at this point the variables hypothesized earlier (and depicted in Figure 6.2) as having an interdependent causal association with Coups D2, the following multivariate model is implied:

(6.9)      $Y = \alpha + \beta_1 X + \beta_2 Z + \beta_3 V + \beta_4 Y_{t-1} + \varepsilon$

where   $Y = \ln$ Coups D2
        $X = \ln$ Institutionalization 1960
        $Z =$ Social Mobilization 1960
        $V =$ Defense Expenditures as a $\%$ of General Government Expenditures 1960[48]
        $Y_{t-1} = \ln$ Coups D1 (interventionist history)
        $\varepsilon =$ stochastic disturbance

Equation 6.9 was estimated both with and without the term for "interventionist history"—Coups D1 $(Y_{t-1})$. Two estimations were undertaken because Coups D1 is almost surely correlated with the disturbance in the equation for Coups D2, and this upwardly biases its estimate and detracts from the potential explanatory power (downwardly biases the estimates) of the other independent variables. We say "almost surely" because there probably are some causal variables that do not appear in (6.9) but influence Coups D1. Those omitted influences appear in the disturbance for (6.9) and are correlated with Coups D1. As is well known, this biases (Ordinary Least Squares) estimates. Hence the equation is estimated both with and without Coups D1.

Table 6.21 reports the outcome of the regression of Coups D2 on (ln) Institutionalization, Social Mobilization, and Defense Expenditures. Contrary to our expectations, Social Mobilization, in the presence of the other independent variables, does not manifest a significant impact on

[48] Defense Expenditures as a percentage of General Government Expenditures rather than as a percentage of GNP (used by Putnam) appears in (6.9) because it had the best linear fit with Coups. It also squares better with our theoretical argument.

Table 6.21  Regression of ln Coups D2 on ln Institutionalization, Social Mobilization, and Defense Expenditures: Additive Model ($N = 108$)

| Independent Variable | Parameter Estimate[a] | $t$ Statistic |
|---|---|---|
| ln Institutionalization 1960 | −0.435* | −2.35 |
| Social Mobilization 1960 | −0.0002 | −0.44 |
| Defense Expenditures as a % of General Government Expenditures | 0.025* | 3.38 |
| Constant | 1.690 | |

| $R^2$ | Regression Standard Error | $F$ |
|---|---|---|
| .220 | 0.830 | 3,104   9.8 |

[a] Starred (*) estimates are more than twice their standard error.

Coups.[49] The results for Institutionalization and Defense Expenditures are as anticipated. Well-developed civilian institutions inhibit and high defense expenditures increase the frequency of "praetorian" interventions in domestic politics.

Table 6.22 provides the regression results when lagged Coups ("interventionist history") is in the equation. As expected, it strongly increases the frequency of Coups in the following decade—but recall our caution about upward bias. Social Mobilization again has no appreciable influence, but the Defense Expenditures estimate is significant and positive as before. Institutionalization, however, drops to insignificance in this equation. Although not *twice* its standard error, it *is larger than* its standard error and is undoubtedly biased downward. Therefore, (ln) Institutionalization as well as Defense Expenditures and lagged Coups should remain among the predetermined explanatory variables ($Z_{3i}$ in Figure 6.2) for Coups D2.

## Predetermined Causes of Elite Repression

The foregoing analyses disclose a number of variables which at this exploratory stage of the investigation seem to have important effects on the incidence of actual and attempted Coups. Moreover, they do so in a

---

[49] This result is not necessarily incompatible with Putnam's Latin American findings because he never evaluated the impact of social mobilization in the presence of all the other variables which he argued affect the incidence of military intervention (although some limited attempts at causal modeling were made). See Putnam, "Toward Explaining Military Intervention in Latin America," *passim.*

Table 6.22  Regression of ln Coups D2 on ln Institutionalization, Social Mobilization, Defense Expenditures, and ln Coups D1: Additive Model ($N = 108$)

| Independent Variable | Parameter Estimate[a] | $t$ Statistic |
|---|---|---|
| ln Institutionalization 1960 | −0.261 | −1.68 |
| Social Mobilization 1960 | −0.0005 | −0.96 |
| Defense Expenditures as a % of General Government Expenditures | 0.022* | 3.49 |
| ln Coups D1 | 0.528* | 6.71 |
| Constant | 0.981 | |

| $R^2$ | Regression Standard Error | $F$ |
|---|---|---|
| .457 | 0.696 | 4,103  21.7 |

[a] Starred (*) estimates are more than twice their standard error.

do so in a way that is independent of the causal reciprocities depicted in Figure 6.2. Thus they are predetermined with respect to those interdependencies. What variables might have an analogous causal impact on the extent of elite repression (negative sanctions)?

One possibility is the ratio interaction of social mobilization to institutionalization, hypothesized by Huntington to be an important cause of coups and mass violence. Although this model did not do well in explaining Coups, Collective Protest, or Internal War, it may perform better vis á vis elite repression. For when the ratio of social mobilization to institutionalization is large, the burdens generated by high mobilization may have outrun the capabilities of sociopolitical institutions and, as a consequence, elites may perceive the situation as sufficiently threatening to resort to repression as an alternative mode of social control. Deutsch predicted just such a sequence when he wrote that if political institutions are incapable of meeting the burdens imposed by a highly mobilized population, then " . . . some or many of [the regime's] subjects will cease to identify themselves with it psychologically; it will be reduced to *ruling by force* where it can no longer rule by display, example, and persuasion . . . ."[50]

Another possible predetermined influence is the degree to which elites are held accountable for their actions. We would anticipate that political authorities who are periodically held accountable to the mass public by free and competitive elections would, *ceteris paribus*, be more

[50] Deutsch, "Social Mobilization ad Political Development," p. 502. Emphasis added.

restrained in their use of repression.[51] As a measure of the democratic accountability of political authorities, we use an "Elite Electoral Accountability" score, which was created by evaluating the fairness and competitiveness of elections in each nation during the postwar period.[52]

Finally, the Internal Security Forces available to the political elite might also have an impact on the incidence of repression. Recall that in the analyses reported at the outset of the chapter, none of the coercive capability indicators appeared to have a substantial direct effect on mass political violence. However, they may influence mass violence indirectly by way of their direct effect on Negative Sanctions, since it is likely that repression would be more readily and easily applied when political authorities have sizable coercive forces at their disposal.

Considered jointly, these hypotheses imply a multivariate equation of the following form:[53]

$$(6.10) \quad Y = \alpha + \beta_1 \ln \text{Pop.} + \beta_2 X + \beta_3 Z + \beta_4 \frac{X}{Z} + \beta_5 V + \beta_6 W + \varepsilon$$

where  $Y = \ln$ Negative Sanctions D2
$\ln$ Pop. $= \ln$ Population, 1960
$X =$ Social Mobilization, 1960
$Z =$ Institutionalization, 1960

$\dfrac{X}{Z} =$ Ratio (interaction term) of Social Mobilization of Institutionalization

$V =$ Elite Electoral Accountability
$W =$ Internal Security Forces
$\varepsilon =$ stochastic disturbance

When (6.10) was estimated, each of the hypothesized predetermined causes of elite repression demonstrated a strong impact in the expected direction. An imbalance in Mobilization and Institutionalization, as well

---

[51] See, for example, Anthony Oberschall, "Group Violence: Some Hypotheses and Empirical Uniformities," American Sociological Association paper, San Francisco, September 1969.

[52] All elections during the 1945 to 1965 period were rated according to the criteria developed by W. J. M. Mackenzie in *Free Elections* (London: George Allen & Unwin, 1958). Specifically, the variable was constructed by computing the average score for elections held within the 20-year period, where: 1 = "rigged," 2 = "substantial irregularity," 3 = "competitive, reasonably free" were the ratings assigned. Nations without elections are scored zero.

[53] Population is included in the equation because a nation's size alone may have some relation to the number of "acts of negative sanction" taken by political authorities against the mass public. As in the case of Collective Protest and Internal War, we want to examine the impact of other variables after the size effect is removed. The log of population maximizes the linear fit.

as sizable Internal Security Forces, appeared to increase the inclination of political authorities to apply repression, whereas Electoral Accountability seemed to diminish it.[54] Moreover, these effects hold up, as the results in Table 6.23 verify, even when the interdependent causes of Negative Sanctions (Coups, Collective Protest, and Internal War) are in the equation— an outcome which generates a good deal of confidence in the results.

Table 6.23  Regression of ln Negative Sanctions D2 on Social Mobilization–Institutionalization Ratio Interaction, Elite Electoral Accountability, Internal Security Forces, ln Coups D2, and Mass Violence D2

| Independent Variable | Parameter Estimate[a] | t Statistic |
|---|---|---|
| Social Mobilization 1960 | −0.008 | −0.85 |
| Institutionalization 1960 | 0.018 | 1.47 |
| Social Mobilization/Institutionalization | 0.047* | 2.68 |
| Elite Electoral Accountability | −0.695* | −5.79 |
| ln Internal Security Forces per 1000 sq km | 0.122* | 2.64 |
| ln Coups D2 | 0.220* | 2.41 |
| Collective Protest D2 | 0.366* | 6.88 |
| Internal War D2 | 0.109* | 2.98 |
| ln Population 1960 | 0.202* | 3.29 |
| Constant | 0.728 | |

| $R^2$ | Regression Standard Error | F |
|---|---|---|
| .779 | 0.673 | 9,98   38.3 |

[a] Starred (*) estimates are more than twice their standard error.

This concludes our investigation of the factors that exert predetermined causal influence on elite repression and coups. Now let us briefly summarize all the results of this chapter and explore their implications for the multi-equation analyses to be undertaken in Part III.

## Summary and Implications for a Multiequation Model

In this as in previous chapters, single equation models proved to be theoretically and/or empirically inadequate to capture the complex causal processes which, we concluded, were likely to be operative among the variables considered. The analyses indicated that regime coercive capability

[54] We found ln Internal Security Forces per 1000 sq km to have a more significant impact than any of the other coercive forces variables.

is not curvilinearly related to the incidence of mass political violence across nations, as some research has suggested, nor does it have a *strong and direct* linear "deterrence" effect. However, coercive capability (in particular, Internal Security Forces) does facilitate actual acts of repression (Negative Sanctions) by incumbent political elites. Similarly, the conjunction of high social mobilization and low institutionalization seems to increase the inclination of political elites to resort to repression. Perhaps this is because in such situations the burdens created by mass mobilization have outrun the capabilities of political institutions, and elites see repression as an attractive alternative means of social control. Conversely, in nations where political elites are periodically held accountable to the mass public in free and competitive elections, the incidence of repression is much lower.

We also concluded that current Negative Sanctions have a strong positive and (nearly) simultaneous reciprocal relationship with current Collective Protest and Internal War since mass violence typically engenders repression from elites and the short-term response to such repression is often more violence by its recipients. In contrast, the exploratory evidence indicated that the lagged or long-run impact of elite repression is to deter future organized violence—Internal War—but not future Collective Protest, which is viewed by many theorists as a more spontaneous expression of discontent.

Finally, we argued that attempts at "irregular" government change, or Coups, by disaffected elite groups (chiefly the military) may also bear a reciprocal relationship to mass violence. This follows from the propensity of military establishments to intervene in situations of mass violence to restore "order," which in turn is frequently met with (violent) resistance. To the extent that Coups are in fact spurred by mass violence, they should be followed by increased repression. Hence, such a causal link was also proposed.

In addition to the interdependency with mass violence, the incidence of Coups was also shown to be influenced by a number of predetermined variables. High defense expenditures give military establishments a continuing interest in domestic political affairs and accordingly seem to increase the likelihood of "praetorian" power seizures. So does an "interventionist" history, probably because past Coups legitimate future ones, or perhaps only make them more palatable. The existence of strong and well-developed civilian sociopolitical institutions, however, diminishes the frequency of Coups—or so we inferred on the basis of the provisional estimation results.

Figure 6.3 incorporates the conclusions reached in this chapter. It illustrates the rather complex nature of the relationships implied by the numerous equations and models investigated. Yet these relationships are

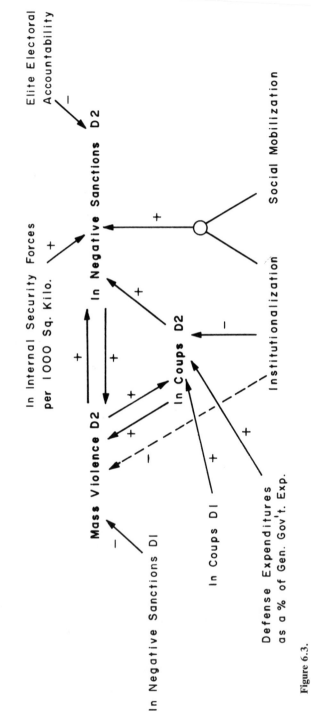

Figure 6.3.

114

provisional and must be validated in the context of a still larger causal system that includes the results of the other chapters. Before this is undertaken, however, we examine a final group of single equation hypotheses.

# CHAPTER SEVEN

# Domestic Political Structure: Political Democracy, Totalitarian Communism, and Left Party Strength

In this chapter we conclude the exploratory analysis of single equation models and partial theories of mass political violence by examining hypotheses that concern the causal influence of political democracy, Communist totalitarianism, and the strength of leftist political parties. Unlike the variables investigated in the last chapter, such as repression and coups, which are subject to more or less direct control and manipulation by elite groups, the factors examined here represent relatively fixed features of domestic political life. Hence they are not amenable to substantial change or manipulation by elites in the short term. Yet the impact these variables have on the magnitude of mass violence can illuminate the implications for domestic stability of long-run developmental patterns in some key features of political structure.

## Political Democracy and Mass Violence

Few topics have received more attention in recent years from students of comparative politics than political development—especially "democratic" political development. There is no point in reviewing the voluminous literature here. We note only that among the most important and, in the view of the majority of theorists, desirable consequences of democratic political development is the diminution of violent domestic conflict. By facilitating the "articulation" and "aggregation" of the diverse interests of the body politic, and by insuring that these are accommodated in an orderly manner, democratic political arrangements are seen as precluding the occurrence of large-scale domestic violence.

The pervasive assumption that political democracy produces social stability has not been subjected to a great deal of empirical scrutiny. Perhaps the only hard evidence that supports the assumption is provided by Flanigan and Fogelman's analysis of the relationship between democratization and political violence across 65 nations from 1800 to 1960. Relying on relatively crude ordinal rating scores to measure democracy and domestic violence, the examination of scatterplots and cross-tabulations led Flanigan and Fogelman to conclude that regardless of the level or rate of economic development, democratic nations experienced significantly less political violence than nondemocratic ones.[1]

The availability of higher quality data and the use of different analytical techniques allows us to furnish what perhaps is a more convincing test of the "democracy produces less violence" thesis here. However, it is first necessary to develop a sharper notion of the meaning of democratic political development. As conceived in virtually all the recent comparative politics literature, democratic political development is viewed as a *process* or framework that structures political activity rather than as a *condition* of socioeconomic equality, high mass social welfare, and the like. Lipset articulated well this view of the democratic political process:

"Democracy in a complex society may be defined as a political system which supplies regular constitutional opportunities for changing the governing officials, and a social mechanism which permits the largest possible part of the population to influence major decisions by choosing among contenders for political office."[2]

Therefore, fair and competitive elections and high popular participation (e.g., voting) would seem to be the key characteristics of a democratic political system. The former may be assessed with the Elite Electoral Accountability variable, which was introduced and defined in the last chapter. The most straightforward measure of mass participation that is available for a large number of nations is again electoral turnout—specifically: the percentage of eligible voters voting in national elections, circa 1960.[3]

Using Elite Electoral Accountability and mass Electoral Turnout to operationalize the process conception of democracy, the democracy–mass violence thesis was evaluated by the following model:

(7.1)     $Y = \alpha + \beta_1 \ln \text{Pop.} + \beta_2 X + \beta_3 Z + \beta_4 X^*Z + \varepsilon$

---

[1] William H. Flanigan and Edwin Fogelman, "Patterns of Political Violence in Comparative Perspective," *Comparative Politics*, Vol. 3, No. 1, October 1970, pp. 1–20.

[2] Seymour M. Lipset, *Political Man* (Garden City, N.Y.: Doubleday & Co., 1963), p. 27.

[3] See the discussion on the limitations of this variable in Chapter 6.

where        $Y$ = Mass Violence D2
    ln Pop. = ln Population 1960
        $X$ = Elite Electoral Accountability
        $Z$ = Electoral Turnout 1960
    $X*Z$ = multiplicative interaction term
        $\varepsilon$ = stochastic disturbance

The model is specified with a multiplicative interaction term. This allows for the possibility that the conjunction of fair and competitive elections *and* high mass participation may have a (negative) nonadditive impact on the incidence of domestic violence. Since voting in Communist countries (which typically is nearly 100%) has a qualitatively different meaning from voting in non-Communist nations, (7.1) was estimated for the sample of non-Communist states ($N = 99$) as well as for the full 108-nation cross-section. The results of these regressions were essentially the same, and only the latter are reported in Tables 7.1 and 7.2.

The evidence in Tables 7.1 and 7.2 suggests that neither Elite Electoral Accountability, mass Electoral Turnout, nor the conjunction of the two has any appreciable direct influence on the magnitude of political violence. Democratic nations have nearly as high levels of Collective Protest and Internal War as nondemocratic ones. It appears, then, that democracy conceived as a framework for formal political activity simply does not pacify the behavior of significant segments of the mass public, however well it serves to establish regularized rules and mechanisms (including popular ratification) through which competing political elites secure public office.[4]

An alternative explanation of these results is that democratization has not been measured with sufficient sensitivity to detect the stabilizing effect anticipated by so many theorists. Accordingly, an additional test of the proposition was undertaken, using Cutright's political development index as the democratization measure. Although designed to assess "political development" generally, the Cutright index is more properly considered an indicator of *democratic* political development as McCrone and Cnudde, and Neubauer have noted.[5] It is of course not without limitations and

---

[4] Recall, however, that elite accountability may have an indirect (negative) impact on the level of violence through its inhibitive effect on government repression, tentatively established in the last chapter.

Additive and log multiplicative versions of (7.1) were also tested but the results did not alter the inference drawn here.

[5] Donald J. McCrone and Charles F. Cnudde, "Toward a Communications Theory of Democratic Political Development: A Causal Model," *American Political Science Review*, Vol. 61, No. 1, March 1967, pp. 72–79; Deane E. Neubauer, "Some Conditions of Democracy," *American Political Science Review*, Vol. 61, No. 4, December 1967, pp. 1002–1009.

Table 7.1 Regression of Collective Protest D2 on Elite Electoral Accountability and Electoral Turnout: Multiplicative Interaction
Model ($N = 108$)

| Independent Variable | Parameter Estimate[a] | $t$ Statistic |
|---|---|---|
| Elite Electoral Accountability | −1.160 | −1.04 |
| Electoral Turnout 1960, % | −0.043 | −1.47 |
| Accountability*Turnout | 0.018 | 1.31 |
| ln Population 1960 | 0.634* | 4.84 |
| Constant | 0.358 | |
| $R^2$ | Regression Standard Error | $F$ |
| .210 | 1.61 | 4,104  6.8 |

[a] Starred (*) estimate is more than twice its standard error.

Table 7.2 Regression of Internal War D2 on Elite Electoral Accountability and Electoral Turnout: Multiplicative Interaction
Model ($N = 108$)

| Independent Variable | Parameter Estimate[a] | $t$ Statistic |
|---|---|---|
| Elite Electoral Accountability | −1.410 | −0.75 |
| Electoral Turnout 1960, % | −0.067 | −1.34 |
| Accountability*Turnout | 0.014 | 0.62 |
| ln Population 1960 | 0.807* | 3.62 |
| Constant | 2.930 | |
| $R^2$ | Regression Standard Error | $F$ |
| .135 | 2.74 | 4,103  4.0 |

[a] Starred (*) estimate is more than twice its standard error.

is available for only 67 of the 108 nations in the cross-section. Nevertheless
it is widely recognized as a reasonably good index of the development of
democratic political structures and it allows us to re-evaluate the analyses
reported in Tables 7.1 and 7.2.[6]

The model estimated was

$$(7.2) \qquad Y = \alpha + \beta_1 \ln \text{Pop.} + \beta_2 X + \varepsilon$$

[6] For a detailed explanation of the Cutright index, see Phillips Cutright, "National Political
Development: Measurement and Analysis," *American Sociological Review*, Vol. 28, April
1963, pp. 253–264.

where $X$ = the Cutright (Democratic) Political Development Index and all other terms are as in (7.1).

The regression estimates for (7.2) are provided in Tables 7.3 and 7.4. The estimates in Table 7.3 confirm our initial conclusion—that democratic political development, measured here by the Cutright index, bears no direct significant relationship to levels of Collective Protest. Contrary to our earlier inference, however, the Cutright index does exhibit a significant negative association with Internal War (Table 7.4). Yet we know from previous quantitative studies that democratic political development is highly correlated with communications development, economic development, and the like. For example, in our data the correlation of the Cutright index and ln Energy Consumption per capita (economic development) is +.609. Moreover, the analyses in Chapter 3 established that Internal War (but not Collective Protest) has a significant *linear*

Table 7.3   Regression of Collective Protest D2 on Cutright Democratic Political Development Index ($N = 67$)

| Independent Variable | Parameter Estimate[a] | $t$ Statistic |
|---|---|---|
| Cutright Political Development Index | 0.004 | 0.45 |
| ln Population 1960 | 0.516* | 3.60 |
| Constant | −1.300 | |

| $R^2$ | Regression Standard Error | $F$ |
|---|---|---|
| .169 | 1.57 | 2,64   6.5 |

[a] Starred (*) estimate is more than twice its standard error.

Table 7.4   Regression of Internal War D2 on Cutright Democratic Political Development Index ($N = 67$)

| Independent Variable | Parameter Estimate[a] | $t$ Statistic |
|---|---|---|
| Cutright Political Development Index | −0.035* | −2.31 |
| ln Population 1960 | 0.390 | 1.59 |
| Constant | 2.010 | |

| $R^2$ | Regression Standard Error | $F$ |
|---|---|---|
| .118 | 2.69 | 2,64   4.3 |

[a] Starred (*) estimate is more than twice its standard error.

negative relationship with ln Energy Consumption per capita, although we argued that the *causal* relationship was quite indirect. Therefore, in order to test for the obvious possibility of spuriousness, (7.3) was estimated.

(7.3)     Internal War D2 $= \alpha + \beta_1$ ln Pop. $+ \beta_2 X + \beta_3 Z + \varepsilon$

where ln Pop.    $=$ ln Population 1960
     $X$        $=$ Cutright (Democratic) Political Development Index
     $Z$       $=$ ln Energy Consumption per capita 1960
     $\varepsilon$       $=$ stochastic disturbance

The results for this equation reported in Table 7.5 clearly demonstrate that the significant negative association of the Cutright index and Internal War (Table 7.4) does not hold up in the presence of ln Energy Consumption per capita. Hence the original relationship was most likely a spurious artifact of the joint linear association of Internal War and democratization with economic development. Our initial conclusion, then, is substantiated. Political democracy, defined in terms of process and structure, has little or no *direct* causal impact on the incidence of *either* dimension of mass violence.

Table 7.5   Regression of Internal War D2 on Cutright Democratic Political Development Index and Economic Development ($N = 67$)

| Independent Variable | Parameter Estimate[a] | $t$ Statistic |
|---|---|---|
| Cutright Political Development Index | 0.010 | 0.56 |
| ln Energy Consumption per capita 1960 | −1.030* | −3.97 |
| ln Population 1960 | 0.664* | 2.87 |
| Constant | 4.510 | |
| $R^2$ | Regression Standard Error | $F$ |
| .295 | 2.43 | 3,63  8.7 |

[a] Starred (*) estimates are more than twice their standard error.

## Totalitarian Communism and Mass Violence

Having concluded that democratization as conventionally conceived does not have a substantial direct effect on the magnitude of mass political violence, we now consider the impact of a particularly salient kind of nondemocratic political structure: totalitarian Communism.

A good deal has been writen about the "total" control exercised over the citizenry of Communist nations. Rather than review this literature in detail, we simply note that despite occasional outbursts of violent rebellion and protest that have occurred in a number of European Communist nations during the last few decades, the police-state atmosphere characteristic of Communist regimes would lead us to expect much less domestic violence, especially organized violence, in these countries. If the simple classification of nations as Communist and non-Communist in fact has any relevance for explaining differing levels of mass political violence, then (7.4) should yield a significantly negative parameter estimate for the Communist Regime "dummy" variable.

(7.4)        $Y = \alpha + \beta_1 \ln \text{Pop.} + \beta_2 X + \varepsilon$

where        $Y$ = Mass Violence D2
         $\ln$ Pop. = ln Population 1960
         $X$ = Communist Regime Dummy: $1 = CR, 0 = $ non-CR
         $\varepsilon$ = stochastic disturbance

Furthermore, this effect of Regime type should be relatively larger in the Internal War equation than in the Collective Protest equation, since the more "spontaneous" Collective Protest mode of discontent is probably less readily deterred by a pervasive state apparatus for social control than is the more "organized" Internal War dimension of violence. Accordingly, the *standardized* regression estimate for the Communist Regime Dummy in the equation for Collective Protest should be smaller than its Internal War counterpart.

Tables 7.6 and 7.7 reveal that the Communist Regime dummy variable is indeed significantly negative in the regression for each dimension of political violence. Moreover, the *standardized* coefficient in the Internal War equation, $-.331$, is larger than the corresponding coefficient in the Collective Protest equation, $-.283$, thus confirming the proposition that Internal War is more easily deterred by "totalitarianism" than is Collective Protest.[7] As is true of all the single equation findings, however, this con-

---

[7] We did not find Regime type significantly related to acts of Negative Sanction (government repression). Hence our interpretation that the (direct) Regime effect reflects the police-state *atmosphere* and constant *potential* for repression in Communist nations rather than a high level of specific acts of repression which are catalogued by the Negative Sanctions variable.

   An alternative explanation for the Regime effect is that bias in the collection of the data is responsible for the lower levels of violence in Communist nations. Two facts suggest that this is not a dominant explanation. First, the widely respected "Pica" index of press freedom developed by the University of Missouri School of Journalism (available for 87 of the 108 nations) does not correlate highly with the mass violence measures: its $r$ with Internal War D2 is $-.11$; with Collective Protest D2, $r = +.17$. Second, the Regime effect is greater on Internal War, yet deaths, guerrilla attacks, and assassinations are in general more difficult to conceal than are riots, demonstrations, and strikes.

Table 7.6    Regression of Collective Protest D2 on Communist Regime
             Dummy ($N = 108$)

| Independent Variable | Parameter Estimate[a] | $t$ Statistic |
|---|---|---|
| Communist Regime Dummy | −1.816* | −3.32 |
| ln Population 1960 | 0.672* | 5.56 |
| Constant | −2.604 | |
| $R^2$ | Regression Standard Error | $F$ |
| .259 | 1.55 | 2,105   18.4 |

[a] Starred (*) estimates are more than twice their standard error.

Table 7.7    Regression of Internal War D2 on Communist Regime
             Dummy ($N = 108$)

| Independent Variable | Parameter Estimate[a] | $t$ Statistic |
|---|---|---|
| Communist Regime Dummy | −3.447* | −3.71 |
| ln Population 1960 | 0.792* | 3.86 |
| Constant | −2.412 | |
| $R^2$ | Regression Standard Error | $F$ |
| .189 | 2.63 | 2,105   12.3 |

[a] Starred (*) estimates are more than twice their standard error.

clusion is only provisional. It may be that the relationship observed here
is simply a function of variables such as the level of mass social welfare
or the extent of government efforts to meet human needs, which are likely
to be jointly related to Regime type and levels of political violence. If
this is the case, the association between Regime type and violence reported
in Tables 7.6 and 7.7 might be spurious, and the causal inference concerning
"totalitarianism" should be revised accordingly. Or the correct conclusion
may lie somewhere between these interpretations. In any case, these issues
are best resolved in the context of the larger, integrative causal system
examined in Part III.

*Communist Parties and Mass Violence*

The influence of Communist parties on the incidence of mass violence
in non-Communist nations would seem to be even more problematic than

that of Communist Regimes, although social scientists have typically attributed to such parties a disruptive and destabilizing role. Lipset, for example, has written of the "challenge" to democratic order and political stability posed by Communist parties in nations where they appear on the political scene before the working class had become "integrated" into the body politic—that is, in nations that currently have large Communist parties:

"Communist workers, their parties and trade-unions, cannot possibly be accorded the right of access to actual political power by a democratic society. The Communists' self-image, and more particularly their ties to the Soviet Union, lead them to accept the self-fulfilling prophecy that they cannot secure their ends by democratic means. This belief prevents them from being allowed access, which in turn reinforces the Communist workers' sense of alienation from the government. The more conservative strata in turn are strengthened in their belief that giving increased rights to workers or their representatives threatens all that is good in life. Thus the presence of Communists precludes the easy prediction that economic development will stabilize democracy in these European countries."[8]

Gurr also expressed the common belief that large Communist parties make for unstable and violent politics when he asserted that the size and status of Communist parties form a "facilitating" factor in the cross-national magnitude of civil strife. Yet he presented no evidence to support this supposition, since his measure of the status and characteristics of Communist parties cross-nationally is aggregated with other variables in a composite "Facilitation" index.[9] Kornhauser made an analogous argument in his well-known study, *The Politics of Mass Society*, when he wrote of the "widespread use of violence on the part of . . . the Communists in all countries in which they have developed organizations."[10] But nowhere does Kornhauser offer hard evidence to justify such a generalization.

Observations like the foregoing concerning the role of Communist parties in promoting domestic violence and instability may derive from ideological bias rather than from an impartial review of the evidence. It is asserted, largely without supporting data, that Communist parties

[8] Lipset, *Political Man*, p. 83.
[9] See Ted R. Gurr, "A Causal Model of Civil Strife: A Comparative Analysis Using New Indices," *American Political Science Review*, Vol. 62, No. 4, December 1968, pp. 1104–1124. Since this was first written I have been informed by Gurr in private communication that unpublished bivariate correlation analyses justified his procedure.
[10] William Kornhauser, *The Politics of Mass Society* (New York: The Free Press, 1959), p. 46.

inevitably instigate political violence. Or it is assumed that existing socio-economic and political arrangements are legitimate, and hence attempts to mobilize mass publics for fundamental socioeconomic and political change (as opposed to the incremental reformism that is characteristic of "moderate" parties) are by definition illegitimate, as well as disruptive of political stability.[11]

Clearly, Communist parties are often in the forefront in pressing militantly the demands of working people. Frequently, these efforts take the form of what we have denoted as Collective Protest: antigovernment demonstrations, political strikes, and even riots. On the other hand, large domestic Communist parties can in many ways be viewed as performing an integrating, if not moderating, role. At times they have even acted in a *counter*revolutionary fashion. Che Guevara's experience with the largely urban-oriented Bolivian Communist Party while trying to build a peasant insurgency in the Bolivian countryside is instructive here, as is the parliamentary mentality of Latin American and European Communist parties generally—a mentality that is especially characteristic of the dominant pro-Soviet factions of these parties.[12] Further illustrations include the moderating or "counterrevolutionary" efforts of the French Communist Party, especially the leadership, during the May 1968 rebellion of workers and students, and the important "integrating" role played by the Communist Party in the industrial triangle of northern Italy through its efforts to settle into the new urban–industrial environment recently mobilized and potentially "anomic" migrants from the rural South.[13] What we are arguing, then, is that although it is reasonable to expect Communist parties in non-Communist nations to promote Collective Protest, their impact on the magnitude of Internal War, if any, may be just the opposite.

The most appropriate measure of the potential influence of Communist parties on domestic social stability is simply the size of the party

[11] See Gabriel Almond and Sidney Verba, *The Civic Culture* (Boston: Little, Brown and Co., 1965), p. 106 ff., Chapter 13, and *passim*.

[12] On Che's problems with the antirevolutionary Bolivian Communist Party, see Robert Scheer (ed.), *The Diary of Che Guevara* (New York: Bantam Books, 1968). Maoist (and Fidelista) factions within the larger Communist parties in Europe and Latin America are generally small and isolated.

[13] On the Italian Communist Party see Sidney G. Tarrow, "Economic Development and the Transformation of the Italian Party System," *Comparative Politics*, Vol. 1, No. 2, January 1969, especially p. 181 ff. Also Tarrow, "Political Dualism and Italian Communism," *American Political Science Review*, Vol. 61, No. 1, March 1967, pp. 39–53.

The behavior of the French Communist leadership during the May revolt has been analyzed by Daniel Singer in *Prelude to Revolution, France in May 1968* (New York: Hill and Wang, 1970).

membership.[14] In order to rigorously evaluate the Communism–political violence hypotheses, the following model was estimated against the data in the 108 nation cross-section:

(7.5)      $Y = \alpha + \beta_1 \ln \text{Pop.} + \beta_2 X + \beta_3 Z + \varepsilon$

where      $Y$ = Mass Violence D2
   $\ln \text{Pop.}$ = ln Population 1960
   $X$ = Communist Regime Dummy: $1 = CR$, $0 = $ non-CR
   $Z$ = ln Communist Party Membership 1960
   $\varepsilon$ = stochastic disturbance

The (natural) logarithm of Communist Party Membership appears in (7.5) because the untransformed variable has a very skewed distribution across the 108 nations in the sample, and, more important, the ln transformation maximized linear fits. Note also that the Communist Regime dummy variable is included in the equation. Since Communist Regimes obviously have large Communist Parties, the dummy variable is entered in the model to differentiate the potential party membership effect from the negative impact of Regime type which was established previously.

Tables 7.8 and 7.9 report the least-squares estimates for (7.5). As anticipated, the size of Communist parties appears to influence the magnitude of Collective Protest (Table 7.8)—large parties are associated with

Table 7.8   Regression of Collective Protest D2 on Communist Party Membership and Communist Regime Dummy ($N = 108$)

| Independent Variable | Parameter Estimate[a] | $t$ Statistic |
|---|---|---|
| ln Communist Membership 1960 | 0.088* | 2.18 |
| Communist Regime Dummy | −2.427* | −4.00 |
| ln Population 1960 | 0.519* | 3.76 |
| Constant | −1.701 | |

| $R^2$ | Regression Standard Error | $F$ |
|---|---|---|
| .291 | 1.52 | 3,104   14.3 |

[a] Starred (*) estimates are more than twice their standard error.

[14] The data on Communist Party memberships cross-nationally were obtained from United States Department of State, Bureau of Intelligence and Research, *World Strength of the Communist Party Organizations*, January 1961 Intelligence Report No. 4489 R-13. Although there undoubtedly are errors in these data, they are compiled with great care and are considered to be the best available.

The Non-Communist Left and Mass Violence 127

comparatively high levels of this type of violence. However, Table 7.9 demonstrates that the impact of Communist Party Membership on the incidence of Internal War is negligible, although the parameter estimate is negative. Equation 7.5 was re-estimated (without the Regime dummy term) for the $\neq$ 99 non-Communist nations, and almost exactly the same parameter values were obtained. Thus it may be inferred with considerable confidence that Communist party size has no consistent influence on levels of Internal War cross-nationally, but that it should be retained as a potentially important explanatory variable in the multiequation analysis of Collective Protest.[15]

Table 7.9  Regression of Internal War D2 on Communist Party Membership and Communist Regime Dummy ($N = 108$)

| Independent Variable | Parameter Estimate[a] | $t$ Statistic |
|---|---|---|
| ln Communist Membership 1960 | −0.062 | −0.89 |
| Communist Regime Dummy | −3.013* | −2.87 |
| ln Population 1960 | 0.901* | 3.78 |
| Constant | −3.052 | |

| $R^2$ | Regression Standard Error | $F$ | |
|---|---|---|---|
| .195 | 2.63 | 3,104 | 8.4 |

[a] Starred (*) estimates are more than twice their standard error.

## The Non-Communist Left and Mass Violence

We conclude this chapter with an attempt to assess the impact of parties of the *non*-Communist left on the incidence of political violence.

[15] We also tested, but do not report here, models that examined the main and interaction effects of the "radicalism" of Communist parties on levels of political violence. Communist party radicalism was measured on a four-point ordinal scale derived from information in the U.S. Department of State, Bureau of Intelligence and Research source cited in footnote 17. The scale was as follows: 1 = pro-Soviet CP (moderate, least radical); 2 = independent or factionalized CP; 3 = CP openly split, Soviet and Maoist wings; 4 = pro-Chinese CP (least moderate, most radical). The expectation was that the effect of large and moderate (pro-Soviet) Communist parties on the magnitude of political violence in non-Communist nations would differ greatly (nonadditively) from the effect of large and radical (Maoist) Communist parties. However, the regression results indicated that no additive or interactive effects could be attributed to Communist Party "radicalism" and thus the conclusions and results reported in the text were not altered. It should be noted, however, that most Communist parties of significant size are quite moderate (pro-Soviet), and hence there is very little opportunity for the manifestation of interaction effects or even additive effects involving Communist Party radicalism.

Socialist and Labor parties are typically a good deal more moderate in rhetoric as well as in activity than are their Communist counterparts—at least this has been the case in recent decades. At the same time they have a mass social base and represent, or are perceived to represent, popular interests. This combination of moderate political style and mass social base leads us to anticipate that where Socialist and Labor parties are large and influential, the level of mass violence will be relatively low.

To index the political importance and influence of Communist parties on mass publics we used the size of membership. This was appropriate for parties that seek to cultivate a mass *membership* and are often frozen out of positions of formal political authority, harassed, or actively suppressed by incumbent political elites. No doubt there is a reciprocal or reinforcing relationship between the immoderation of Communist parties and their isolation from formal political influence, as Lipset has suggested. What is relevant here, however, is that size of membership is not a particularly good measure of the strength of parties on the non-Communist left, since they usually seek what primarily is an electoral rather than a membership constituency.[16] Hence, to measure the potential importance of Socialist and Labor parties for domestic political stability, the following variable seems more appropriate: Percentage of Legislative Seats Held by Parties of the Non-Communist Left, circa 1960.

In order to determine the influence of the strength of the moderate left on the incidence of mass violence, variables that were inferred earlier in this chapter to have a significant impact are retained in the following equations. This allows us to observe the contrasting effects of "radical" versus "moderate" left parties as well as Communist versus non-Communist regime types. Accordingly, the equation estimated for the Collective Protest dimension of violence was

(7.6)   Collective Protest D2 $= \alpha + \beta_1$ ln Pop. $+ \beta_2$ Regime Type $+ \beta_3$ ln Communist Membership $+ \beta_4 \%$ Legislative Seats Held by Non-Communist Left $+ \varepsilon$

The model for Internal War was

(7.7)   Internal War D2 $= \alpha + \beta_1$ ln Pop. $+ \beta_2$ Regime Type $+ \beta_3 \%$ Legislative Seats Held by non-Communist Left $+ \varepsilon$

---

[16] This of course is not true of all non-Communist left parties at all times and places, but it does seem to be increasingly the case in recent years. See Leon D. Epstein, *Political Parties in Western Democracies* (New York: Frederick A. Praeger, 1967), Chapters 5, 6, and 8.

The regression results for (7.6) and (7.7) are displayed in Tables 7.10 and 7.11. As before, Communist Regime type appears to inhibit outbreaks of Collective Protest, whereas the consequence of large Communist parties is just the opposite (Table 7.10). In contrast, the strength of parties of the non-Communist left, or more precisely, the extent of their parliamentary representation, exhibits a significant (although modest) negative impact on the level of mass protest. These results bring into focus the moderate

Table 7.10 Regression of Collective Protest D2 on Communist Regime Dummy, Communist Party Membership, and Legislative Representation of the Non-Communist Left ($N = 108$)

| Independent Variable | Parameter Estimate[a] | $t$ Statistic |
|---|---|---|
| Communist Regime Dummy | $-2.691*$ | $-4.41$ |
| ln Communist Membership 1960 | $0.092*$ | $2.33$ |
| % Legislative Seats Held by Non-Communist Left 1960 | $-0.010*$ | $-2.09$ |
| ln Population 1960 | $0.491*$ | $3.60$ |
| Constant | $-1.211$ | |

| $R^2$ | Regression Standard Error | $F$ |
|---|---|---|
| .320 | 1.50 | 4,103  12.1 |

[a] Starred (*) estimates are more than twice their standard error.

Table 7.11 Regression of Internal War D2 on Communist Regime Dummy, and Legislative Representation of the Non-Communist Left ($N = 108$)

| Independent Variable | Parameter Estimate[a] | $t$ Statistic |
|---|---|---|
| Communist Regime Dummy | $-3.797*$ | $-4.04$ |
| % Legislative Seats Held by Non-Communist Left 1960 | $-0.015$ | $-1.84$ |
| ln Population 1960 | $0.763*$ | $3.75$ |
| Constant | $-1.741$ | |

| $R^2$ | Regression Standard Error | $F$ |
|---|---|---|
| .215 | 2.60 | 3,104  9.4 |

[a] Starred (*) estimates are more than twice their standard error.

character of Socialist and Labor parties, at least in nations where they have achieved political representation. The results do not mean that such parties are inherently moderate but only that left *representation* seems to diminish Protest. Moreover, this effect is perhaps best modeled sequentially—since it might well reflect the influence of Socialist and Labor representation on increasing government efforts to improve social welfare, or decreasing elite readiness to meet protest with repression rather than with accommodation. If this is the case, then it is the latter factors that have a *direct* (negative) impact on the magnitude of Collective Protest. These possibilities, however, are best sorted out when we examine multi-equation formulations in Part III.

What is appropriate to pursue here is the possibility that a similar result also accompanies Communist political representation. We investigated this by incorporating a term for the percentage of legislative seats held by Communists in (7.6) and (7.7). But the estimation results did not yield anything significant, undoubtedly because so few nations outside the Communist world have much Communist representation: the cross-national mean (for non-Communist nations) of Percentage Legislative Seats Held by Communists is 2.0% versus 26.5% mean representation for the non-Communist left. If there is a "moderation" effect that is produced by political representation, it has had little opportunity to manifest itself in the case of Communist parties.

Table 7.11 reports the regression estimates for the Internal War equation [(7.7)]. Communist Regime type again demonstrates a strong deterrence effect on this dimension of civil strife. However, the extent of political representation of the non-Communist left appears to have little relevance for explaining Internal War.

*Summary*

We established in this chapter that democratic political structures and processes apparently bear no direct relation to the cross-national incidence of mass political violence. Democratic nations experience about as much violent mass conflict as do nondemocratic nations. Hence a democratized world would not necessarily be a nonviolent one. We also concluded (tentatively) that Communist societies have considerably less violence than non-Communist ones and that this deterrence effect of "totalitarianism" is more effective vis à vis organized Internal War than it is for spontaneous Collective Protest. Furthermore, we saw in the latter sections of the chapter that sizable Communist parties in non-Communist nations serve to promote mass protest but have no systematic impact on the incidence of Internal War. Large-scale Communist movements are typically "destabilizing", but only up to a point. Finally, the legislative representation of the non-Communist left was inferred to diminish the level of Protest, but it appeared to have no influence on outbreaks of Internal War.

This concludes our survey of single equation hypotheses and partial theories. We explore now the implications all the findings in Part II have for the development of a more completely specified multiequation model of mass political violence.

PART THREE

# Multiequation Formulations and Final Causal Inferences

# CHAPTER EIGHT

# A Multiequation Model of Mass Political Violence

At the outset of this study we argued that multiequation models in general provide a more realistic mathematical representation of socioeconomic and political phenomena than single equation formulations, and that this is especially true for relationships as complex as those which underlie cross-national variation in levels of mass political violence. However, in the absence of any single theory that specified a comprehensive and convincing multiequation model of mass violence, we proceeded by examining single equation hypotheses and partial theories derived from the pertinent literature. The decision rule in evaluating the results of these analyses was that the variables under investigation had to manifest estimated coefficients at least twice their respective standard errors, unless there were sound theoretical reasons to believe that respecification of the initial hypothesis was in order. In this manner numerous hypotheses have been rejected as empirically unsound, some have been retained, and others have been reformulated as recursive and nonrecursive partial causal systems.

In what follows, the provisional conclusions and formulations of previous chapters, which were developed largely in isolation from one another, are summarized, integrated, and elaborated on by the specification of our "final" multiequation causal model. Of course the model is not all-inclusive, but it does represent the best theoretical structure we have been able to incrementally develop from available theory, data, and techniques of non-experimental causal inference. As the presentation should make clear, the model has what is known as a "block recursive" structure. Hence equations are arrayed in functional sectors or "blocks" that can be isolated for estimation purposes—all cross-sector causal influences are unidirectional (recursive) and all simultaneous (nonrecursive) relationships and feedback loops operate within blocks.

Since many of the sectors or blocks of the model are identical for Collective Protest and Internal War, we specify (and estimate) one combined system that includes both dimensions of violence. However, we do *not* specify causal relations *directly* between Collective Protest and Internal War, although, as would be expected, they are moderately strongly correlated: $r$ Internal War D2, Collective Protest D2 $= +.63$. The question of when Collective Protest leads to Internal War or conversely is of course a very important one. Yet theory provides no clear message about the dynamics of this relationship, and nothing is to be gained from positing a causal link a priori. All that can now be said about the interrelationship of Collective Protest and Internal War is summarized in the converging and diverging causal paths from other variables to each dimension of violence.

In the model below, the $Y_m$ with coefficients $\alpha_m$ denote endogenous variables that are simultaneously determined in the block of equations that includes Collective Protest and Internal War. These are the equations of primary interest. They also pose the most difficult estimation problems. The $Y_m^*$ with coefficients $\alpha_m^*$ denote *lagged* endogenous $Y_m$ variables that appear in the model. Endogenous variables that are generated in "prior" blocks or sectors of the model and are predetermined vis à vis the simultaneously determined $Y_m$ are denoted $X_k$ and have coefficients $\beta_k$. Variables that are purely exogenous, that is, independently determined vis à vis the *entire* system, are denoted $Z_i$ with coefficients $\gamma_i$.[1] Finally, the $X_k^*$ and $Z_i^*$ with coefficients $\beta_k^*$ and $\gamma_i^*$ refer to predetermined and exogenous variables that are nonlinear functions of the corresponding $X_k$ and $Z_i$.[2] Appendix 2 lists all the variables in the model, along with their denotations; this appendix also reports the chapter in which each variable was first introduced.

---

[1] Appendix 3 provides a detailed discussion of what properties lagged endogenous, predetermined endogenous, and exogenous variables must have in order to obtain consistent estimates of their parameters.

[2] For example, note that in Appendix 2, which lists all the variables in the final model, $X_8$ and $X_8^*$ refer to Social Welfare 1960 and ln Social Welfare 1960, respectively. The asterisk (*) notation is used only to remind the reader that the variables involved appear in the model in two linearly independent functional forms. They are, however, considered *distinct* variables for identification and estimation purposes, although we write equations for only one of the functional forms. We take up the identification-estimation issue in Appendix 3. On this particular point, see Franklin M. Fisher, *The Identification Problem in Econometrics* (New York: McGraw-Hill Book Company, Inc., 1966), Chapter 5. Interactions between the $X_k$, $Z_i$ are also linearly independent of the component variables and hence are considered to be additional variables which we always denote as $Z_i$.

## The Simultaneously Determined $Y_m$ Block: Mass Violence, Elite Repression, Coups, and Economic Change

The core of the multiequation model of Collective Protest and Internal War is a block of equations that expresses mathematically the causal interdependencies inferred in Part II to be operative among mass violence, elite repression, coups, and the rate of economic change. It consists of six structural equations for these simultaneously determined endogenous variables. The equations are as follows:[3]

(8.1)    COLLECTIVE PROTEST D2 $= +\alpha_3$ ln Negative Sanctions D2

$$Y_1 \qquad\qquad\qquad\qquad Y_3$$

$+ \alpha_4$ ln Coups D2

$$Y_4$$

$- \alpha_5$ Av. Annual % Change in Energy Consumption pc 1955–1965

$$Y_5$$

$+ \alpha^*{}_1$ Collective Protest D1 $+ \beta_1$ Group Discrimination 1960

$$Y_1^* \qquad\qquad\qquad X_1$$

$+ \beta_4$ ln Communist Party Membership 1960

$$X_4$$

$- \beta_5$ % Legislative Seats Held by Non-Communist Left 1960

$$X_5$$

$- \beta_7$ ln Nondefense General Govt. Expenditures as a % of GDP 1960

$$X_7$$

$- \beta_9^*$ ln Institutionalization 1960

$$X_9^*$$

$+ \beta_{10}$ Av. Annual % Change in Population 1955–1965

$$X_{10}$$

$\pm \beta_8$ Social Welfare 1960 $\pm \gamma_2$ Social Mobilization 1960

$$X_8 \qquad\qquad\qquad Z_2$$

$+ \gamma_{12}$ (Soc. Mob./Soc. Welfare) $+ \gamma_1$ ln Population 1960

$$Z_{12} \qquad\qquad\qquad Z_1$$

$- \gamma_3$ Communist Regime Dummy $+ \varepsilon_1$

$$Z_3$$

[3] Assume that all equations are normalized so that each endogenous variable appears on the left-hand side of its equation with an implicit coefficient of unity. Constant terms are omitted from all equations. Note also that the equations are numbered opposite to the conventional manner. Hence, when proceeding from Equations 8.1–8.6 to 8.7–8.16 we are moving "backward" in the causal ordering.

(8.2)　INTERNAL WAR D2 $= +\alpha_3$ ln Negative Sanctions D2 $+ \alpha_4$ ln Coups D2
$\quad\quad\quad\quad\underset{Y_2}{} \quad\quad\quad\quad\quad\quad\quad\underset{Y_3}{} \quad\quad\quad\quad\quad\quad\underset{Y_4}{}$

$- \alpha_6$ Av. Annual % Change in GNP pc 1955–1965 $+ \alpha_2^*$ Internal War D1
$\quad\quad\underset{Y_6}{} \quad\quad\quad\quad\quad\quad\quad\quad\quad\quad\quad\quad\quad\quad\underset{Y_2^*}{}$

$- \alpha_3^*$ ln Negative Sanctions D1 $+ \beta_1$ Group Discrimination 1960
$\quad\quad\underset{Y_3^*}{} \quad\quad\quad\quad\quad\quad\quad\quad\quad\underset{X_1}{}$

$+ \beta_2$ ln Political Separatism 1960
$\quad\quad\underset{X_2}{}$

$- \beta_7$ ln Nondefense General Govt. Expenditures as a % of GDP 1960
$\quad\quad\underset{X_7}{}$

$- \beta_8^*$ ln Social Welfare 1960 $- \beta_9^*$ ln Institutionalization 1960
$\quad\underset{X_8^*}{} \quad\quad\quad\quad\quad\quad\quad\quad\underset{X_9^*}{}$

$+ \beta_{10}$ Av. Annual % Change in Population 1955–1965
$\quad\quad\underset{X_{10}}{}$

$+ \gamma_1$ ln Population 1960 $- \gamma_3$ Communist Regime Dummy $+ \varepsilon_2$
$\quad\underset{Z_1}{} \quad\quad\quad\quad\quad\quad\quad\underset{Z_3}{}$

(8.3)　LN NEGATIVE SANCTIONS D2 $= +\alpha_1$ Collective Protest D2
$\quad\quad\quad\quad\quad\quad\underset{Y_3}{} \quad\quad\quad\quad\quad\quad\quad\quad\quad\quad\underset{Y_1}{}$

$+ \alpha_2$ Internal War D2 $+ \alpha_4$ ln Coups D2
$\quad\underset{Y_2}{} \quad\quad\quad\quad\quad\quad\underset{Y_4}{}$

$- \beta_5$ % Legislative Seats Held by Non-Communist Left 1960
$\quad\quad\quad\quad\quad\quad\underset{X_5}{}$

$- \beta_6$ Elite Electoral Accountability $\pm \beta_9$ Institutionalization 1960
$\quad\quad\underset{X_6}{} \quad\quad\quad\quad\quad\quad\quad\quad\quad\underset{X_9}{}$

$\pm \gamma_2$ Social Mobilization 1960 $+ \gamma_{11}$ (Soc. Mob./Institutionalization)
$\quad\quad\underset{Z_2}{} \quad\quad\quad\quad\quad\quad\quad\quad\quad\underset{Z_{11}}{}$

$+ \gamma_1$ ln Population 1960
$\quad\underset{Z_1}{}$

$+ \gamma_9$ ln Internal Security Forces per 1000 sq km 1965 $+ \varepsilon_3$
$\quad\quad\underset{Z_9}{}$

(8.4)　LN COUPS D2 $= +\alpha_1$ Collective Protest D2 $+ \alpha_2$ Internal War D2
$\quad\quad\quad\underset{Y_4}{} \quad\quad\quad\quad\quad\underset{Y_1}{} \quad\quad\quad\quad\quad\quad\quad\underset{Y_2}{}$

$+ \alpha_4^*$ ln Coups D1 $- \beta_9^*$ ln Institutionalization 1960
$\quad\underset{Y_4^*}{} \quad\quad\quad\quad\quad\quad\underset{X_9^*}{}$

$+ \gamma_{10}$ Defense Expenditures as a % of General Govt. Expenditures 1960 $+ \varepsilon_4$
$\quad\quad\quad\quad\underset{Z_{10}}{}$

(8.5)   AV. ANNUAL % CHANGE IN ENERGY CONSUMPTION
$$Y_5$$

PER CAPITA 1955–1965 $= -\alpha_1$ Collective Protest D2
$$Y_1$$

$- \alpha_1^*$ Collective Protest D1
$$Y_1^*$$

$- \beta_{10}$ Av. Annual % Change in Population 1955–1965
$$X_{10}$$

$+ \gamma_6$ ln Energy Consumption pc 1960
$$Z_6$$

$+ \gamma_8$ Gross Fixed Domestic Capital Formation as % of GNP 1960 $+ \varepsilon_5$
$$Z_8$$

(8.6)   AV. ANNUAL % CHANGE IN GNP PER CAPITA 1955–1965 $=$
$$Y_6$$

$-\alpha_2$ Internal War D2 $- \alpha_2^*$ Internal War D1
$$Y_2 \qquad\qquad Y_2^*$$

$- \beta_{10}$ Av. Annual % Change in Population 1955–1965 $+ \gamma_7$ ln GNP pc 1960
$$X_{10} \qquad\qquad\qquad\qquad\qquad Z_7$$

$+ \gamma_8$ Gross Fixed Domestic Capital Formation as % of GNP 1960 $+ \varepsilon_6$
$$Z_8$$

Figure 8.1 delineates the relationships in this sector of the model. It depicts the hypothesized simultaneous causal reciprocities between the $Y_m$, notes where lagged endogenous variables are expected to exert causal effects, and represents predetermined and purely exogenous influences by generalized $X_k$, $Z_i$ terms.

Consider first the relationships between the simultaneously determined $Y_m$ in (8.1) through (8.6). As we pointed out in previous chapters, the simultaneous specification does not deny that causality is inherently a phenomenon that involves lags, however finite, between reciprocally related variables. Indeed, Herman Wold and others have objected on philosophical grounds to simultaneous specification and estimation of economic relations for just this reason.[4] But this objection is really beside the point. It is *not* maintained that the reciprocal relationships among the $Y_m$ are

---

[4] See, for example: Herman Wold, in association with L. Jureen, *Demand Analysis: A Study in Econometrics* (New York: John Wiley & Sons, Inc., 1953); *idem.*, "A Generalization of Causal Chain Models," *Econometrica*, Vol. 28, No. 2, April 1960, pp. 443–463; and Robert H. Strotz and Herman Wold, "Recursive vs. Nonrecursive Systems: An Attempt at Synthesis," *Econometrica*, Vol. 28, No. 2 (April 1960), pp. 417–427.

140

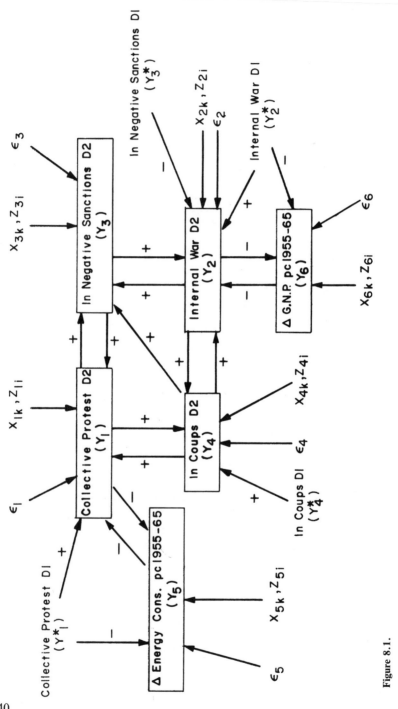

Figure 8.1.

actually *instantaneous*, but only that the causal interdependencies have a *sufficiently small lag time* in relation to the observed data periods that they are best *approximated mathematically* by simultaneous specification and estimation. Hence, simultaneous formulations are simply limiting approximations to underlying nonsimultaneous relationships with relatively short stimulus–response, lag–reaction times.[5]

With this in mind, the simultaneous reciprocities hypothesized in this first and most important block of equations may be reviewed. In Figure 8.1 ln Negative Sanctions D2 ($Y_3$), or government repression, is depicted as bearing a simultaneous, positive relationship to each dimension of violence. Thus elite repression ($Y_3$) appears with a positive coefficient in the equations for Collective Protest and Internal War [(8.1) and (8.2)], and the mass violence variables ($Y_1$ and $Y_2$) have positive parameters in the equation for ln Negative Sanctions (8.3). These specifications are based on the discussion in Chapter 6, where we argued that mass violence typically engenders negative sanctions from political authorities, and this is followed (nearly instantaneously) by a response of more violence from its recipients.

A similar logic underlies the causal reciprocity of ln Coups D2 ($Y_4$) with Collective Protest and Internal War which is depicted in Figure 8.1 and expressed mathematically in (8.1), (8.2), and (8.4). It conforms with the conclusion of Chapter 6 that Coups are (in part) the consequence of mass violence as the military reacts to the (perceived) inability of incumbent authorities to effectively maintain social stability. Yet in the short-term Coups often exacerbate the level of violence as people spontaneously take to the streets in protest or are mobilized by counterelites to defeat the attempted seizure of power. Hence a positive reciprocity is proposed. Coups are also linked (unidirectionally) to repression, and thus $Y_4$ appears in the structural equation for $Y_3$. As we argued in Chapter 6, it is expected that Coups lead to increased government repression, especially when they are spurred by the occurrence of mass violence.

The last simultaneous relationship hypothesized among the $Y_m$ is the interdependence of Collective Protest D2 and Internal War D2 with the average rate of economic growth 1955 to 1965. It is designed to incorporate

---

[5] Therefore, even if observations have been aggregated monthly and the causal reciprocity involves lags of, say, a few days, then the best specification and estimation strategy is clearly to treat the relationship as simultaneous. This line of argument is more fully developed in Franklin M. Fisher, "Causation and Specification in Economic Theory and Econometrics," *Synthése*, Vol. 20, 1969, pp. 489–500 and *idem.*, "Simultaneous Equations Estimation: The State of the Art," Working Paper, Department of Economics, M.I.T., Cambridge, Mass., July 1970. Fisher treats the issue at a more technical level in "A Correspondence Principle for Simultaneous Equation Models," *Econometrica*, Vol. 38, January 1970, pp. 73–92.

the view of economists such as Kuznets, who contend that mass disorder inhibits economic growth, as well as the findings of political scientists who report that economic growth seems to produce lower levels of violence.[6] Accordingly, the economic growth variables appear with negative coefficients in the political violence equations [(8.1) and (8.2)], and the violence variables are specified with negative coefficients in the economic growth equations [(8.5) and (8.6)]. Two measures of economic growth are involved here because the provisional analyses in Chapter 3 indicated that change in Energy Consumption per capita had the strongest linear association with Collective Protest and that change in Gross National Product per capita had the stronger association with Internal War.

Equations 8.1 through 8.6 also contain a number of lagged endogenous variables—$Y_m^*$. The equations for Collective Protest and Internal War [(8.1) and (8.2)] are specified with lagged levels of violence terms ($Y_1^*$ and $Y_2^*$) in order to test the "culture of violence" proposition that previous violence makes current violence more likely. As Gurr put it

". . . the greater strife has been in a country's past, the more likely some of its citizens are to regard it as justifiable, and the more likely some of them would have found it partially successful in the past, and hence regard it as potentially useful in the future. A history of civil strife should thus facilitate future strife . . . ."[7]

The Internal War equation includes a second lagged endogenous variable: ln Negative Sanctions D1 ($Y_3^*$). This corresponds to the tentative conclusion in Chapter 6 which indicated that although a reciprocal and *positive* causal interdependency describes the linkage between current mass violence and elite repression, the impact of past repression is to *deter* current outbreaks of Internal War. Hence, $Y_3^*$ appears in (8.2) with a negative coefficient. Similarly, lagged Coups ($Y_4^*$) is in the equation for current Coups. It derives from the provisional finding in Chapter 6 that an "interventionist history" makes current "praetorian" attempts to seize power more probable (and perhaps more acceptable) than otherwise would be the case. Finally, lagged political violence variables ($Y_1^*$, $Y_2^*$) are specified with negative coefficients in the rate of economic growth equations [(8.5) and (8.6)]. This represents the hypothesis that current violence is not only negatively and reciprocally related to current economic growth but that

---

[6] See the discussion in Chapter 3.

[7] Ted R. Gurr, in Hugh D. Graham and Ted R. Gurr (eds.), *Violence in America: Historical and Comparative Perspectives*, A Report to the National Commission on the Causes and Prevention of Violence (New York: Signet Books, 1969), p. 576. Also see Chapters 6 and 7 of Gurr, *Why Men Rebel* (Princeton, N. J.: Princeton University Press, 1970) for a detailed discussion and review of the literature on this and related propositions.

large-scale violence in the recent past has an *additional* detrimental effect on the pace of current growth.

The predetermined endogenous variables $X_k$ and the purely exogenous variables $Z_i$ that appear in (8.1) through (8.6) are best introduced equation by equation. The first equation, Collective Protest D2, includes seven $X_k$ and four $Z_i$. Group Discrimination $(X_1)$ is specified in this equation with a positive coefficient in conformity with the results of Chapter 5, which established that discrimination mediates the impact of cultural differentiation and has a direct positive impact on the incidence of Protest. In Chapter 7 the (ln transformed) size of Communist Party Memberships was inferred to promote Protest, whereas the legislative representation of the non-Communist left was inferred to diminish it. Accordingly, $X_4$ appears in (8.1) with a positive parameter and $X_5$ has a negative parameter. The results (8.1) with a positive parameter and $X_5$ has a negative parameter. The results of Chapter 7 also indicated that totalitarian Communism deters outbreaks of violence, and thus (8.1) is specified with a negative or "deterrence effect" coefficient for the Communist Regime dummy variable $(Z_3)$.

In the analysis of Huntington's theory concerning the consequences of imbalances in social mobilization and institutionalization on the cross-national incidence of Coups and mass violence in Chapter 6, (ln) institutionalization manifested a singular negative impact on the level of Protest. Hence $X_9^*$ is entered in (8.1) with a negative parameter. Similar evaluations of the effect of imbalances between social mobilization and government performance or social welfare in Chapter 4 suggested that the conjunction of high mobilization and low social welfare produces increased Collective Protest. But these exploratory analyses also revealed that high (ln) civilian government expenditures relative to Gross Domestic Product ("government performance") singularly diminishes the level of Protest. Therefore, (8.1) is specified with a negative coefficient for $X_7$, a positive coefficient for $Z_{12}$, and indeterminate coefficients for the (probably insignificant) main effects terms $X_8$ and $Z_2$.

The average rate of population growth between 1955 and 1965 appears in the Collective Protest equation with a positive coefficient. This corresponds to the result in Chapter 3—namely, that the pressure of rapidly increasing population has a strong impact on the magnitude of Protest. Finally, (8.1) includes an ln Population term $(Z_1)$. This takes account of the theoretically uninteresting (but necessary) linear effect of a nation's size alone; $\varepsilon_1$ is the stochastic error term for the equation.

The second equation in the simultaneously determined $Y_m$ block is for Internal War D2. It shares quite a number of $X_k$ and $Z_i$ with the Collective Protest equation—which is not surprising, given the moderately high correlation between the two dimensions of mass violence. The single equation results in Part II indicated that Group Discrimination $(X_1)$ and the pressure of rapid population growth $(X_{10})$ increase the level of Internal War as well as Collective Protest, and so these variables appear with positive coefficients in (8.2). The investigation in previous chapters also established that ln Institutionalization $(X_9^*)$, ln Civilian Government Expenditures as a Percentage of GDP $(X_7)$, and Communist Regime type $(Z_3)$ serve to diminish the magnitude of Internal War; therefore these terms are specified with negative coefficients.

In contrast to the results for Protest, Chapter 5 demonstrated that (ln) Political Separatism, in addition to Group Discrimination, mediates the effect of cultural differentiation in a causal sequence leading to Internal War. Thus the latter $(X_1)$ as well as the former $(X_2)$ are included in (8.2) with positive coefficients. Although we did not find a Social Mobilization–Social Welfare interaction operative for the Internal War dimension of violence, we did tentatively conclude in Chapter 4 that (ln) Social Welfare has a significantly negative additive impact. Accordingly, $X_8^*$ appears with a negative parameter. Finally, ln Population is incorporated into the equation to account for the linear effect of size, and $\varepsilon_2$ represents the disturbance term.

Equation 8.3 articulates the causal processes that are hypothesized to underlie ln Negative Sanctions (elite repression). Since the regression outcomes in Chapter 6 indicated that political authorities with large coercive forces at their disposal—in particular, ln Internal Security Forces per 1000 sq km—more readily resort to repression, $Z_9$ is specified in this equation with a positive coefficient. We determined in the same chapter that there is less repression in nations where political elites are democratically held accountable for their actions, and suggested in the following chapter that where the non-Communist left is politically influential, elites might similarly be less inclined to resort to "acts of Negative Sanction." Hence $X_6$ and $X_5$ are hypothesized to have an inhibitive or negative impact on the extent of repression.

The ratio of Social Mobilization to Institutionalization $(Z_{11})$ appears in (8.3) with a positive coefficient. This stems from the analyses in Chapter 6, which revealed that in societies where social mobilization has outrun institutional development, elites apparently resort to repression as a means of social control. Corresponding to the earlier single equation findings, the main effects terms for this ratio interaction $(X_9, Z_2)$ are shown with indeterminate parameters. Finally, (8.3) also includes a term for (ln) Population, since it is reasonable to expect (other things being equal) that the larger the population, the greater will be the number of repressive acts. $\varepsilon_3$ is the disturbance term.

The causal structure for ln Coups D2 is expressed in (8.4). It is specified with only two predetermined endogenous and exogenous variables in addition to the endogenous and lagged endogenous variables discussed previously. These variables are ln Institutionalization $(X_9^*)$ and Defense Expenditures as a % of General Government Expenditures $(Z_{10})$. The inclusion of ln Institutionalization with a negative coefficient derives from the analysis in Chapter 6, which established that nations with well-developed sociopolitical institutions were much less likely to suffer "praetorian" seizures of power by the military and other organized groups. The appearance of Defense Expenditures as a % of General Government Expenditures with a positive parameter is also based on results developed in Chapter 6. It represents our inference that where the military's share of governmental resources is large, their "stake" in domestic politics as well as their organizational capacity relative to civilian sectors of government is correspondingly high. Consequently, the probability of political intervention is increased. The stochastic error in (8.4) is represented by $\varepsilon_4$.

Equations 8.5 and 8.6 pertain to the rate of change in Energy Consumption per capita and GNP per capita, respectively. One predetermined endogenous variable and two exogenous variables appear in these equations. In accordance with the discussion in Chapter 3, where we argued that the rates of population and economic growth are inversely related, the average rate of population change from 1955 to 1965 $(X_{10})$ is specified with a negative coefficient in these equations. This formally articulates the common notion that a key prerequisite to economic growth is a diminution of the birthrate. Gross Fixed Capital Formation as a % of GNP $(Z_8)$ appears in the equations with a positive coefficient for the obvious reason: The larger the proportion of the Gross National Product allocated to reinvestment and capitalization, the greater should be the rate of economic growth. Finally, the rate of economic growth expressions include terms for the *level* of economic development: ln Energy Consumption per capita $(Z_6)$ in (8.5) and ln GNP per capita $(Z_7)$ in (8.6). They are hypothesized to have positive parameters because the more highly developed nations seem to sustain the highest per capita economic growth rates.[8] $\varepsilon_5$ and $\varepsilon_6$ are the disturbance terms.

This concludes the introduction of the block of equations for the simultaneously determined $Y_m$ variables. Although these equations comprise the core of the model and are of central importance, we also need to specify equations for the $X_k$ which are predetermined with respect to the $Y_m$ but endogenous to the entire causal system. Specification of structural

---

[8] We shall experiment with alternatives to the linear, ln transformed economic development terms in (8.5) and (8.6). For example, as we initially suggested in Chapter 3 (see Figure 3.3), an exponential specification may be more appropriate.

equations for the $X_k$ is particularly important if we are to detect *indirect* influences on the $Y_m$ (especially Collective Protest and Internal War) which work through the $X_k$ variables that appear explicitly in (8.1) through (8.6). Some of these indirect causal paths have been developed in earlier chapters, and others are introduced here. The equations for the $X_k$ include lagged endogenous variables $Y_m^*$ as well as other endogenous $X_k$ and exogenous $Z_i$ variables. These equations are introduced and discussed by groups or "blocks" that index distinguishable sectors of the model.

## *The Cultural Differentiation Block*

The first block of equations for the $X_k$ variables centers on cultural differentiation, or what we denoted as Ethnolinguistic Fractionalization in Chapter 5. This sector has three equations. They are as follows:

(8.7)  GROUP DISCRIMINATION 1960 =
$$X_1$$

$+\beta_3$ Ethnolinguistic Fractionalization 1960 $+ \varepsilon_7$
$$X_3$$

(8.8)  LN POLITICAL SEPARATISM 1960 =
$$X_2$$

$+\beta_3$ Ethnolinguistic Fractionalization 1960 $- \gamma_2$ Social Mobilization 1960
$$X_3 \hspace{5cm} Z_2$$

$+ \gamma_{13}$ (Ethnolinguistic Fractionalization*Social Mobilization)
$$Z_{13}$$

$+ \gamma_5$ Postwar Independence $+ \varepsilon_8$
$$Z_5$$

(8.9)  ETHNOLINGUISTIC FRACTIONALIZATION 1960 =
$$X_3$$

$-\gamma_2^*$ ln Social Mobilization 1960 $+ \gamma_5$ Postwar Independence $+ \varepsilon_9$
$$Z_2^* \hspace{5cm} Z_5$$

Equation 8.7 expresses Group Discrimination simply as a function of the extent of Ethnolinguistic Fractionalization and a stochastic disturbance. In Chapter 5 more complex, multivariate interaction formulations were evaluated, but the specification given here was determined to be the most satisfactory.

The most notable feature of the ln Political Separatism equation (8.8) is the positive Social Mobilization–Ethnolinghistic Fractionalization interaction term. It derives from the analyses in Chapter 5, which disclosed that the conjunction of high mobilization and differentiation produces, as Deutsch theorized, political separatism and thus indirectly Internal War.[9] Equation 8.8 also includes a dummy Postwar Independence term which articulates the hypothesis of Geertz and others that "new" nations are especially (but not exclusively) susceptible to separatist movements and sentiment.

The last equation in this block pertains to sociocultural differentiation itself. Chapter 5 established that the modal pattern was for social mobilization to promote assimilation and hence $Z_2^*$ appears in (8.9) with a negative coefficient.[10] The Postwar Independence term is also specified in the differentiation function with a negative parameter. It reflects our previous inference that many of the most differentiated nations are recently independent ex-colonies whose boundaries were created without regard for ethnolinguistic composition.

The relationships in (8.7) through (8.9) are delineated in Figure 8.2 within the Cultural Differentiation Block.

## The Domestic Politics Block

The next block of equations to index a distinct sector of the multi-equation model involves variables denoting Regime type, Democratization, and the political influence of the Communist and non-Communist Left. These variables were first introduced in Chapter 7. This sector also has three equations:

(8.10) ELITE ELECTORAL ACCOUNTABILITY =
$$X_6$$

$+\gamma$ Economic Development 1960 $+ \varepsilon_{10}$

(8.11) LN COMMUNIST PARTY MEMBERSHIP 1960 =
$$X_4$$

$+\gamma$ Economic Development 1960 $- \gamma$ (Economic Development 1960)$^2$

$+ \beta_6$ Elite Electoral Accountability $+ \gamma_1$ ln Population 1960
$\qquad\qquad X_6 \qquad\qquad\qquad\qquad\qquad\qquad Z_1$

$+ \gamma_2^*$ ln Social Mobilization 1960 $+ \gamma_3$ Communist Regime dummy
$\qquad\quad Z_2^* \qquad\qquad\qquad\qquad\qquad\qquad Z_3$

$+ \gamma_4$ Communist Party Legal Status Dummy $+ \varepsilon_{11}$
$\qquad\quad Z_4$

---

[9] Recall that ln Political Separatism was found to have a strong positive effect on the incidence of Internal War in Chapter 5 and therefore appears in (8.2) with a positive coefficient.

[10] However, where mobilization does not produce assimilation—that is, where mobilization *and* differentiation are high—separatism and Internal War are the likely consequences. Compare the previous discussion and the interaction term in (8.8).

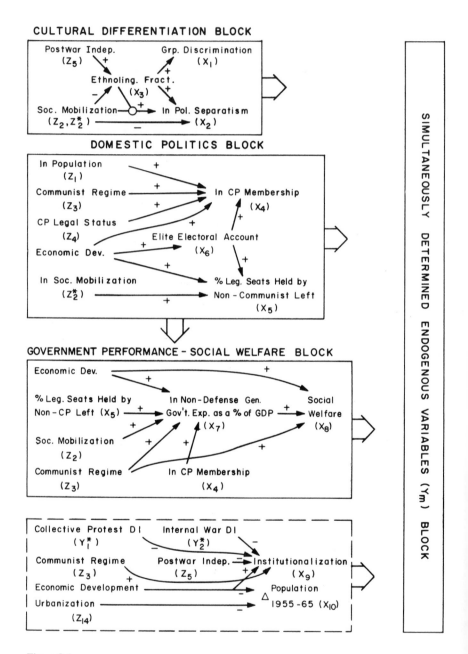

**Figure 8.2.**

(8.12) % LEGISLATIVE SEATS HELD BY THE NON-COMMUNIST LEFT 1960 =

$+ \beta_6$ Elite Electoral Accountability $+ \gamma_2^*$ ln Social Mobilization 1960
$\qquad X_6 \qquad\qquad\qquad\qquad\qquad\qquad\qquad\qquad Z_2^*$

$+ \gamma$ Economic Development 1960 $+ \varepsilon_{12}$

The Elite Electoral Accountability variable, or what has been called "democratization," is expressed in (8.10) as a function only of the level of economic development.[11] We might have specified a more elaborate equation or multiequation causal sequence for this variable on the order of Cutright's analysis of Lipset's theory or McCrone and Cnudde's formalization of the Lerner model, but the crudeness of the democratization measure does not merit more than the simple expression of (8.10).[12]

The equation for ln Communist Party Membership (8.11) is more complex. It is specified with linear and quadratic level of economic development terms to test the thesis of Benjamin and Kautsky that large Communist parties represent a mass response to the discontinuities of early and middle stages of economic development, and hence Communist membership typically grows with economic development but tends to drop off at the higher levels.[13] However, the size of Communist parties cross-nationally is unlikely to be explained well by the elementary model of Benjamin and Kautsky. For example, we would anticipate that where the Party is not suppressed its membership would be larger than otherwise. Thus we specify a positive coefficient for a Communist Legal Status dummy variable $Z_4$ (1 = legal, tolerated; 0 = illegal, suppressed).[14] Similarly, we might expect democratic nations, which have relatively pluralistic political systems, to

---

[11] In equations where "economic development" appears without specification of a particular indicator, we establish later what measure maximizes linear fits.

[12] See Phillips Cutright, "National Political Development: Measurement and Analysis," *American Sociological Review*, Vol. 28, April 1963, pp. 253–264; and Donald J. McCrone and Charles F. Cnudde, "Toward a Communications Theory of Democratic Political Development: A Causal Model," *American Political Science Review*, Vol. 61, No. 1, March 1967, pp. 72–79.

[13] Roger W. Benjamin and John H. Kautsky, "Communism and Economic Development," *American Political Science Review*, Vol. 62, March 1968, pp. 110–123.

[14] This variable was coded from information provided in the same source used to obtain Communist Party membership data: United States Department of State, Bureau of Intelligence and Research, *World Strength of the Communist Party Organizations*, January 1961, Intelligence Report No. 4489 R-13.

have larger Communist parties than nondemocratic ones. Hence the democratization variable $(X_6)$ appears with a positive parameter in (8.11). Communist membership is also hypothesized to be larger where the population is highly mobilized and thus more easily politicized and recruited. Therefore, social mobilization is specified with a positive parameter in the equation. Finally, (8.11) appears with a positive coefficient for ln Population (since Communist Party Membership has not been per capitized) as well as a positive coefficient for the Communist Regime dummy variable.[15]

The function for the Legislative Representation of the Non-Communist Left (8.12) hypothesizes that the left will be more influential in democratized nations allowing open political activity, in economically advanced nations where the industrial work force is large, and in nations where the population is mobilized and therefore more readily politicized by mass-oriented parties. Accordingly, $X_6$, $Z_2^*$, and an unspecified economic development term are entered in this equation with positive parameters.

The causal relationships modeled by (8.10) through (8.12) are depicted within the Domestic Politics Block in Figure 8.2.

## The Government Performance—Social Welfare Block

The final group of equations to comprise a distinguishable block consists of variables for government expenditures to meet human needs and the actual state of mass social welfare. The two equations in this sector are:

(8.13)  LN NONDEFENSE GENERAL GOVERNMENT EXPENDITURES AS
$$X_7$$

A % OF GDP $= +\beta_4$ ln Communist Party Membership 1960
$$X_4$$

$+ \beta_5$ % Legislative Seats Held by Non-Communist Left 1960
$$X_5$$

$+ \gamma_2$ Social Mobilization 1960 $+ \gamma$ Economic Development 1960
$$Z_2$$

$+ \gamma_3$ Communist Regime Dummy $+ \varepsilon_{13}$
$$Z_3$$

---

[15] We of course expect Communist nations to have large Communist parties. The Communist Regime dummy variable takes out the additive effect of Regime type. Interaction effects (non-parallel slopes) are also possible here.

(8.14)  SOCIAL  WELFARE  1960 =
$$X_8$$

$+ \beta_7$ ln Nondefense General Govt. Expenditures as a $\%$ of GDP 1960
$$X_7$$

$+ \gamma_3$ Communist Regime Dummy $+ \gamma$ Economic Development 1960 $+ \varepsilon_{14}$
$$Z_3$$

Note that this pair of equations, designated as the Government Performance–Social Welfare Block in Figure 8.2, includes causal influences from the preceding Domestic Politics group of equations. Specifically, Legislative Representation of the Non-Communist Left $(X_5)$ and the (ln) Communist Party Membership $(X_4)$ appear in (8.13) with positive coefficients. This represents the proposition that where the left is politically influential, government efforts to meet human needs will be correspondingly high. Civilian government expenditure is expressed as a function of the pressures generated by social mobilization, as Deutsch argued, as well as of the level of ecκnomic development, since economically advanced societies are typically better able to devote a large proportion of their resources to government services. Mobilization and Economic Development, therefore, are entered in (8.13) with positive parameters. The Communist Regime dummy variable is also specified with a positive coefficient to reflect the comparatively high government expenditures of Communist systems.

As suggested in Chapter 4, Social Welfare [(8.14)] is likely to be increased by high civilian government spending and also by the level of economic development, for it seems that independent of government efforts to improve social welfare, the lower strata in rich nations fare better than their counterparts in poor nations. Hence these variables have positive coefficients in (8.14). Finally, the Communist Regime dummy variable is incorporated in the equation to evaluate the thesis that Communist nations do better in promoting Social Welfare than non-Communist ones, regardless of levels of economic development and government spending.

## Additional Predetermined Endogenous Influences

Equations for the two remaining $X_k$ variables, Institutionalization and the Rate of Population Growth, do not fall within any particular topical sector or block. The equations are:

(8.15)  INSTITUTIONALIZATION 1960 $= -\alpha_1^*$ Collective Protest D1
$$X_9 \qquad\qquad\qquad\qquad Y_1^*$$

$- \alpha_2^*$ Internal War D1 $+ \gamma_3$ Communist Regime Dummy
$$Y_2^* \qquad\qquad\qquad Z_3$$

$$- \gamma_5 \text{ Postwar Independence} + \gamma \text{ Economic Development 1960}$$
$$Z_5$$

$$+ \varepsilon_{15}$$

(8.16)   AV. ANNUAL % CHANGE IN POPULATION 1955–1965 =
$$X_{10}$$

$$-\gamma \text{ Economic Development 1960}$$

$$- \gamma_{14} \text{ Population in Cities of 100,000 or More Residents per 1000 Pop. 1965}$$
$$Z_{14}$$

$$+ \varepsilon_{16}$$

In the Institutionalization equation, lagged violence terms are specified with negative coefficients. This formalizes the proposition that nations experiencing severe mass political violence in the recent past, especially Internal War, are unlikely to be able to establish or sustain well-developed sociopolitical institutions. Since Institutionalization itself appears in the mass violence equations [(8.1) and (8.2)], we are hypothesizing a lagged reciprocity between these variables. Institutionalization is also viewed as depending on high economic development, and so this variable is entered in (8.15) with a positive parameter. The highly developed political apparatus of Communist nations is allowed for by a positive coefficient for the Communist Regime dummy variable in the equation. Finally, the negative coefficient for the Postwar Independence dummy variable reflects the especially low institutional development that typifies recently independent, ex-colonial nations.[16]

The last equation in the model expresses the rate of population growth as a negative linear function of urbanization and the level of economic development.[17] It reflects our knowledge that population growth is highest in rural and underdeveloped nations and lowest in urban and industrialized ones. The linear formulation is tentative, however, since the rate of population growth may in fact increase from low to middle ranges of economic development where societies frequently experience dramatic improvements in food production and public health without a corresponding drop in the

[16] Occasionally the legacy of imperialism is high, rather than low, institutionalization. For example, an anti-imperialist independence movement may spur the development of well-articulated political parties, or the imperialist power may have developed an extensive native bureaucracy to handle much of the colonial administration. India experienced both possibilities. In general, however, we expect especially low institutionalization in recently independent ex-colonies.

[17] Unfortunately, urbanization data are available for a large number of nations only for the year 1965. However, 1965 urbanization is probably a good surrogate for an earlier time point.

birthrate. Hence the equation will also be estimated with an additional quadratic term in economic development.

## Conclusion

The multiequation model of mass political violence is now fully specified. It should be apparent from the discussion that the model has a block recursive structure; that is, variables endogenous to the entire system, the $X_k$, are considered predetermined in relation to the simultaneously determined mass violence, coups, elite repression, and economic change variables $(Y_m)$.[18] Our formulation of the model has specified only recursive (unidirectional) causal relationships within blocks involving the $X_k$, although had theory so indicated we might have hypothesized simultaneities here as well as between the $Y_m$. Figure 8.2 provides an overview of the complete model which delineates the constituent equations in distinguishable blocks or sectors. The relationships within the $Y_m$ block were depicted in Figure 8.1 and so are not outlined in Figure 8.2. Note that only two of the $X_k$ blocks are functionally related, although they all share exogenous variables $(Z_i)$ and of course all exert causal influence on the simultaneously determined $Y_m$ variables.

The methodological issues involved in identifying and estimating block recursive models are rather complex. They are treated in some detail in Appendix 3, where we establish the identifiability of the model and discuss the appropriate estimation methods. Readers who are unfamiliar with these issues or wish to carefully evaluate identification conditions and estimation strategies should consult Appendix 3 at this point.

We turn now to an analysis of the estimation results of the model and ascertain what "final" inferences about the causal processes underlying mass political violence may be drawn.

---

[18] Strictly speaking, a block recursive model should have not only unidirectional relationships between blocks but also a block-diagonal disturbance covariance matrix. Similar considerations hold for simple recursive models. Appendix 3 develops these points more fully.

# CHAPTER NINE

# Estimation Results and Causal Inferences

The last chapter and Appendix 3 furnish the background necessary to present and evaluate the estimation results for the multiequation model of mass political violence. Chapter 8 specified the form of the model which, for the most part, was derived from the results and conclusions developed in Part II. Appendix 3 outlines the methods and assumptions necessary for structural estimation generally, and establishes the identifiability of this particular causal model. The model includes a block of equations for the simultaneously determined, endogenous $Y_m$ variables which comprise the core of the model, as well as a number of blocks of equations for the predetermined but endogenous $X_k$. Since we are primarily concerned with the causal processes generating the $Y_m$—especially those underlying cross-national differences in Collective Protest and Internal War—the $Y_m$ block is estimated first. We then need estimate equations for *only* the $X_k$ that are inferred to exert nontrivial causal effects on the $Y_m$.

## The Simultaneously Determined $Y_m$ Block: Initial Estimation Results

Recall that the six structural equations for the $Y_m$, specified in Chapter 8, are as follows:

(9.1)   COLLECTIVE PROTEST D2 $= +\alpha_3$ ln Negative Sanctions D2
$\qquad\quad Y_1 \qquad\qquad\qquad\qquad\qquad\qquad Y_3$

$+ \alpha_4$ ln Coups D2
$\quad\; Y_4$

$- \alpha_5$ Av. Annual % Change in Energy Consumption pc 1955–1965
$\qquad\qquad\qquad\qquad Y_5$

$+ \alpha_1^*$ Collective Protest D1 $+ \beta_1$ Group Discrimination 1960
$\quad\; Y_1^* \qquad\qquad\qquad\qquad\qquad X_1$

$+ \beta_4 \underset{X_4}{\ln \text{Communist Party Membership 1960}}$

$- \beta_5 \underset{X_5}{\% \text{Legislative Seats Held by Non-Communist Left 1960}}$

$- \beta_7 \underset{X_7}{\ln \text{Nondefense General Govt. Expenditures as a }\% \text{ of GDP 1960}}$

$- \beta_9^* \underset{X_9^*}{\ln \text{Institutionalization 1960}}$

$+ \beta_{10} \underset{X_{10}}{\text{Av. Annual }\% \text{ Change in Population 1955-1965}}$

$\pm \beta_8 \underset{X_8}{\text{Social Welfare 1960}} \pm \gamma_2 \underset{Z_2}{\text{Social Mobilization 1960}}$

$+ \gamma_{12} \underset{Z_{12}}{\text{(Soc. Mob./Soc. Welfare)}} + \gamma_1 \underset{Z_1}{\ln \text{Population 1960}}$

$- \gamma_3 \underset{Z_3}{\text{Communist Regime Dummy}} + \varepsilon_1$

(9.2)    INTERNAL WAR D2 $= +\alpha_3 \underset{Y_3}{\ln \text{Negative Sanctions D2}} + \alpha_4 \underset{Y_4}{\ln \text{Coups D2}}$
        $\underset{Y_2}{}$

$- \alpha_6 \underset{Y_6}{\text{Av. Annual }\% \text{ Change in GNP pc 1955-1965}} + \alpha_2^* \underset{Y_2^*}{\text{Internal War D1}}$

$- \alpha_3^* \underset{Y_3^*}{\ln \text{Negative Sanctions D1}} + \beta_1 \underset{X_1}{\text{Group Discrimination 1960}}$

$+ \beta_2 \underset{X_2}{\ln \text{Political Separatism 1960}}$

$- \beta_7 \underset{X_7}{\ln \text{Nondefense General Govt. Expenditures as a }\% \text{ of GDP 1960}}$

$- \beta_8^* \underset{X_8^*}{\ln \text{Social Welfare 1960}} - \beta_9^* \underset{X_9^*}{\ln \text{Institutionalization 1960}}$

$+ \beta_{10} \underset{X_{10}}{\text{Av. Annual }\% \text{ Change in Population 1955-1965}}$

$+ \gamma_1 \underset{Z_1}{\ln \text{Population 1960}} - \gamma_3 \underset{Z_3}{\text{Communist Regime Dummy}} + \varepsilon_2$

(9.3)    LN NEGATIVE SANCTIONS D2 $= +\alpha_1 \underset{Y_1}{\text{Collective Protest D2}}$
        $\underset{Y_3}{}$

$+ \alpha_2 \underset{Y_2}{\text{Internal War D2}} + \alpha_4 \underset{Y_4}{\ln \text{Coups D2}}$

$- \beta_5 \ \% $ Legislative Seats Held by Non-Communist Left 1960
$$X_5$$

$- \beta_6$ Elite Electoral Accountability $\pm \ \beta_9$ Institutionalization 1960
$$X_6 \hspace{6cm} X_9$$

$\pm \ \gamma_2$ Social Mobilization 1960 $+ \ \gamma_{11}$ (Soc. Mob./Institutionalization)
$$Z_2 \hspace{5cm} Z_{11}$$

$+ \ \gamma_1 \ln$ Population 1960
$$Z_1$$

$+ \ \gamma_9 \ln$ Internal Security Forces per 1000 sq km 1965 $+ \ \varepsilon_3$
$$Z_9$$

(9.4) LN COUPS D2 $= \ +\alpha_1$ Collective Protest D2 $+ \ \alpha_2$ Internal War D2
$$Y_4 \hspace{3.5cm} Y_1 \hspace{3.5cm} Y_2$$

$+ \ \alpha_4^* \ln$ Coups D1 $- \ \beta_9^* \ln$ Institutionalization 1960
$$Y_4^* \hspace{4cm} X_9^*$$

$+ \ \gamma_{10}$ Defense Expenditures as a $\%$ of General Govt. Expenditures 1960 $+ \ \varepsilon_4$
$$Z_{10}$$

(9.5) AV. ANNUAL $\%$ CHANGE IN ENERGY CONSUMPTION
$$Y_5$$

PER CAPITA 1955–1965 $= \ -\alpha_1$ Collective Protest D2
$$Y_1$$

$- \ \alpha_1^*$ Collective Protest D1
$$Y_1^*$$

$- \ \beta_{10}$ Av. Annual $\%$ Change in Population 1955–1965
$$X_{10}$$

$+ \ \gamma_6 \ln$ Energy Consumption pc 1960
$$Z_6$$

$+ \ \gamma_8$ Gross Fixed Domestic Capital Formation as a $\%$ of GNP 1960 $+ \ \varepsilon_5$
$$Z_8$$

(9.6) AV. ANNUAL $\%$ CHANGE IN GNP PER CAPITA 1955–1965 $=$

$-\alpha_2$ Internal War D2 $- \ \alpha_2^*$ Internal War D1
$$Y_2 \hspace{4cm} Y_2^*$$

$- \ \beta_{10}$ Av. Annual $\%$ Change in Population 1955–1965 $+ \ \gamma_7 \ln$ GNP pc 1960
$$X_{10} \hspace{6cm} Z_7$$

$+ \ \gamma_8$ Gross Fixed Domestic Capital Formation as a $\%$ of GNP 1960 $+ \ \varepsilon_6$
$$Z_8$$

Appendix 3 points out that Ordinary Least Squares is not an appropriate technique for estimating blocks of structural equations that incorporate simultaneous interdependencies, since least-squares regression assumes that disturbances are uncorrelated with independent variables. It is demonstrated in the appendix that this fundamental assumption is always violated in simultaneous specifications—the jointly determined endogenous variables ($Y_m$) are by definition of the model correlated with the disturbance terms. Hence, to proceed with Ordinary Least Squares regression would yield incorrect (inconsistent) estimates of the true causal parameters.

An alternative estimation procedure, Instrumental Variables-Two Stage Least Squares (IV-2SLS), resolves this problem in the following way. In the "first stage" the simultaneously determined, endogenous $Y_m$ variables are regressed on all the predetermined endogenous $X_k$ and exogenous $Z_i$ which are known or assumed to be uncorrelated with the disturbances. The fitted values or "systematic parts" of the $Y_m$ generated by these first-stage regressions are thus linear functions of ("instrumental") variables that are uncorrelated with the disturbance terms and, therefore, are themselves uncorrelated with the disturbances. Hence the fitted values are used as surrogates for the original $Y_m$ variables in a "second-stage" regression estimation of the model. If the theoretical specification of the system incorporates the required a priori information concerning the equations to be estimated (the identification problem), then these second-stage regressions are solvable and yield correct (consistent) estimates of the causal parameters.

For reasons developed in Appendix 3, we employed two versions of the IV-2SLS procedure to estimate equations for the jointly determined $Y_m$ variables. The *primary* estimation method treats lagged endogenous variables ($Y_m^*$) as predetermined, and thus they are used as instrumental variables in the first-stage regressions. Parameter estimates produced by this method appear in the main text. The *supplementary* estimation strategy treats the $Y_m^*$ as endogenous, that is, in exactly the same way as their simultaneously determined $Y_m$ counterparts. Estimates from this method are reported in Appendix 4.

Tables 9.1 through 9.6 report the IV-2SLS estimates of the structural parameters in (9.1) through (9.6) that are produced by the primary estimation strategy.[1] How may these results be used to evaluate the hypothesized causal model? At this initial estimation stage we confine our attention to "theory trimming"; that is, we concentrate on revising the original model

---

[1] The Instrumental Variables–Two Stage Least Squares results were generated by the *Econometric Software Package*, a batch process statistical package developed by the Department of Economics, Massachusetts Institute of Technology, and by *TROLL/1*, an interactive econometric system also developed at M.I.T.

in order to resolve the most obvious conflicts between the postulated structure and the empirically derived parameter estimates.[2]

An essential prerequisite for retaining an *equation* in the causal system is that its $R^2$ be nontrivial. Our principal objective is of course not to maximize goodness of fit but to secure sharp and consistent parameter estimates. If multiple correlations were the overriding consideration then Ordinary Least Squares regression would be the optimum estimation technique because it best minimizes error sums of squares. Yet a nontrivial $R^2$ is clearly a necessary, although by no means sufficient, first condition. On this condition alone, (9.5) and (9.6) are failures as the $R^2$'s for each of the economic change equations reported in Tables 9.5 and 9.6 and Tables

Table 9.1    Equation for Collective Protest D2 ($Y_1$)

| Independent Variable | Parameter Estimate | *t* Statistic |
|---|---|---|
| ln Negative Sanctions D2 | 0.896 | 2.81 |
| ln Coups D2 | −0.471 | −1.13 |
| Average Annual % Change in Energy Consumption per capita 1955–1965 | −0.134 | −1.99 |
| Collective Protest D1 | 0.056 | 0.46 |
| Group Discrimination 1960 | 0.012 | 2.24 |
| ln Communist Party Membership 1960 | 0.065 | 1.20 |
| ln Nondefense General Government Expenditures as a % of GDP 1960 | 0.026 | 0.09 |
| ln Institutionalization 1960 | 0.200 | 0.56 |
| % Legislative Seats Held by Non-CP Left 1960 | −0.005 | −1.20 |
| Average Annual % Change in Population 1955–1965 | −0.010 | −0.07 |
| Social Welfare 1960 | 0.0004 | −0.15 |
| Social Mobilization 1960 | 0.0005 | 0.10 |
| Social Mobilization/Social Welfare | −1.200 | −0.38 |
| ln Population 1960 | 0.084 | 0.48 |
| Communist Regime Dummy | −3.000 | −4.33 |
| Constant | −0.881 | −0.35 |

| $R^2$ | Regression Standard Error | $F$ | |
|---|---|---|---|
| .595 | 1.22 | 15,92 | 9.0 |

[2] For a discussion of "theory trimming" in the context of recursive path models see David R. Heise, "Problems in Path Analysis and Causal Inference," in Edgar F. Borgatta and George W. Bohrnstedt (eds.), *Sociological Methodology 1969* (San Francisco: Jossey-Bass, Inc., 1969), p. 55 ff.

### Table 9.2  Equation for Internal War D2 ($Y_2$)

| Independent Variable | Parameter Estimate | $t$ Statistic |
|---|---|---|
| ln Negative Sanctions D2 | 1.570 | 3.43 |
| ln Coups D2 | 0.433 | 0.89 |
| Average Annual % Change in GNP per capita 1955–1965 | 0.100 | 0.54 |
| Internal War D1 | 0.488 | 4.76 |
| ln Negative Sanctions D1 | −0.764 | −3.04 |
| Group Discrimination 1960 | 0.005 | 0.80 |
| ln Political Separatism 1960 | 0.308 | 2.22 |
| ln Nondefense General Government Expenditures as a % of GDP 1960 | −0.337 | −0.66 |
| ln Social Welfare 1960 | 0.011 | 0.01 |
| ln Institutionalization 1960 | 0.462 | 0.90 |
| Average Annual % Change in Population 1955–1965 | −0.203 | −1.11 |
| ln Population 1960 | 0.060 | 0.28 |
| Communist Regime Dummy | −2.820 | −3.57 |
| Constant | −2.470 | −0.49 |

| $R^2$ | Regression Standard Error | $F$ |
|---|---|---|
| .705 | 1.68 | 13,94  17.2 |

### Table 9.3  Equation for ln Negative Sanctions D2 ($Y_3$)

| Independent Variable | Parameter Estimate | $t$ Statistic |
|---|---|---|
| Collective Protest D2 | 0.372 | 3.65 |
| Internal War D2 | 0.087 | 1.33 |
| ln Coups D2 | 0.458 | 2.94 |
| % Legislative Seats Held by Non-CP Left 1960 | 0.0009 | 0.37 |
| Elite Electoral Accountability | −0.622 | −4.70 |
| Institutionalization 1960 | 0.021 | 1.61 |
| Social Mobilization 1960 | −0.0008 | −0.82 |
| Social Mobilization/Institutionalization | 0.041 | 2.19 |
| ln Population 1960 | 0.209 | 2.96 |
| ln Internal Security Forces per 1000 sq km 1965 | 0.140 | 2.70 |
| Constant | 0.332 | 0.45 |

| $R^2$ | Regression Standard Error | $F$ |
|---|---|---|
| .762 | 0.70 | 10,97  31.0 |

*Estimation Results and Causal Inferences*

### Table 9.4 Equation for ln Coups D2 ($Y_4$)

| Independent Variable | Parameter Estimate | $t$ Statistic |
|---|---|---|
| Collective Protest D2 | 0.017 | 0.21 |
| Internal War D2 | 0.035 | 0.62 |
| ln Coups D1 | 0.495 | 6.30 |
| ln Institutionalization 1960 | −0.298 | −2.08 |
| Defense Expenditures as a % of General Government Expenditures 1960 | 0.018 | 2.70 |
| Constant | 0.822 | 1.68 |

| $R^2$ | Regression Standard Error | $F$ | |
|---|---|---|---|
| .502 | 0.67 | 5,102 | 20.6 |

### Table 9.5 Equation for Average Annual Percentage Change in Energy Consumption per capita 1955–1965 ($Y_5$)

| Independent Variable | Parameter Estimate | $t$ Statistic |
|---|---|---|
| Collective Protest D2 | −0.432 | −1.21 |
| Collective Protest D1 | 0.158 | 0.59 |
| Average Annual % Change in Population 1955–1965 | −0.093 | −0.29 |
| ln Energy Consumption per capita 1960 | −0.537 | −1.96 |
| Gross Fixed Domestic Capital Formation as a % of GNP 1960 | 0.069 | 0.68 |
| Constant | 6.086 | 2.62 |

| $R^2$ | Regression Standard Error | $F$ | |
|---|---|---|---|
| .069 | 3.74 | 5,102 | 1.5 |

A4.5 and A4.6 (in Appendix 4) plainly evidence. We can therefore conclude immediately that *mass political violence has no systematic relation to the rate of economic growth*, and neither do any of the other variables that appear in the Energy Consumption and GNP growth rate equations.[3]

---

[3] The small $R^2$'s (and insignificant $t$ statistics) for these equations signify that the causes of economic growth have not been adequately specified. However, this does not vitiate the inference concerning the impact of mass violence. The growth equations were also estimated with a term for ln population to residualize the mass violence variables by size, but this did not alter the results appreciably.

Table 9.6    Equation for Average Annual Percentage Change in Gross National
Product per capita 1955–1965 ($Y_6$)

| Independent Variable | Parameter Estimate | $t$ Statistic |
|---|---|---|
| Internal War D2 | −0.056 | −0.38 |
| Internal War D1 | −0.128 | −1.15 |
| Average Annual % Change in Population 1955–1965 | 0.344 | 1.60 |
| ln GNP per capita 1960 (in thousands of 1965 U.S. dollars) | 0.067 | 0.23 |
| Gross Fixed Domestic Capital Formation as a % of GNP 1960 | 0.109 | 1.54 |
| Constant | −0.847 | −0.41 |

| $R^2$ | Regression Standard Error | $F$ |
|---|---|---|
| .087 | 2.50 | 5,102    1.9 |

We of course do not claim from these results that particularly severe and protracted violence in specific places and times does not hinder economic growth or indeed fundamentally disrupt economics. We do maintain, however, that *the level of violence has no consistent and continuous impact on such growth.*

Equations 9.1 through 9.4 easily satisfy the first criterion. So much for accepting or rejecting whole equations in the $Y_m$ block. What of individual variables? Clearly, a minimum condition for a *variable* to be retained in the model is that its parameter have the "correct" or theoretically postulated sign. A number of variables in (9.1) through (9.4) fail to meet this minimum condition. In the first equation (Collective Protest D2) both estimation methods yield a negative (and insignificant) coefficient estimate for ln Coups D2. Moreover, Collective Protest D2 has an insignificantly positive estimate in the Coups equation in the primary estimation results reported in Table 9.4, and an insignificantly negative estimate in the supplementary estimation results reported in Appendix A4.4. The directional instability and insignificance of these estimates suggests that *the hypothesized direct causal reciprocity of Coups and Collective Protest should be rejected as empirically unsound. Coups apparently do not directly elicit Collective Protest and Protest does not directly spur Coups.*

The coefficient estimate for ln Institutionalization also has the "wrong" sign in the estimation results for the Collective Protest and Internal War equations (Tables 9.1 and 9.2). The positive (but insignificant) coefficients for ln Institutionalization in these tables indicate that *our provisional specification that sociopolitical institutionalization has a direct negative impact of levels of Collective Protest and Internal War was erroneous.*

The rate of population growth also fails to meet the minimum condition for a variable to be retained in the revised model. We had hypothesized on the basis of tentative results reported in Chapter 3 that the pressure of rapidly growing population produces increases in Collective Protest and Internal War. However, both estimation methods produce negative (and insignificant) parameter estimates for this variable. Hence it appears that, *other factors held constant, the rate of population growth does not influence magnitudes of mass political violence within nations.* It is possible, however, that rapid population growth does have a disruptive impact which is lagged and therefore not captured by the specification here.

The remaining variables whose estimated coefficients have "incorrect" signs in these initial estimation results are ln Nondefense General Government Expenditures as a % of GDP and the Social Mobilization–Social Welfare interaction in the equation for Collective Protest; ln Social Welfare in the equation for Internal War; and the Legislative Representation of the Non-Communist Left in the equation for Elite Repression (ln Negative Sanctions D2). The positive and insignificant parameter estimate for ln Nondefense Expenditures indicates that high civilian government spending, or what was denoted earlier as "government performance," does not have the anticipated negative impact on levels of Protest. *High nondefense government spending apparently does not buy domestic stability.*

Similarly, the insignificant and negative estimate for the Social Mobilization-Social Welfare interaction does not support our expectation, based on the single equation results in Part II, that Protest would be relatively high in societies where social mobilization is substantially greater than the level of actual social welfare. The same is true of the initial finding that high Social Welfare singularly diminishes the incidence of Internal War—the insignificantly positive coefficient for the welfare variable shown in Table 9.2 indicates that this is not the case. Thus Social Welfare does not exert any appreciable causal influence, additively or interactively, on the magnitude of political violence. Like civilian government spending, *a high level of mass social welfare simply does not seem to contribute in an important way to the diminution of mass political violence.*[4]

Finally, the proposition that *executive* elites are less likely to resort to Repression in nations where the Non-Communist Left has substantial

---

[4] Although the variables used to construct the Social Welfare measure were chosen because they indexed *mass* levels of well-being, we should emphasize that this is an *aggregate* result. It does not necessarily mean that individuals within a society who enjoy high standards of living are just as likely to engage in violent expressions of discontent as are more deprived groups. We pursue this point further in Chapter 10.

*parliamentary* representation is belied by the parameter estimate for this variable reported in Table 9.3. The insignificantly positive coefficient requires that this initial specification be rejected. *In comparable situations, political authorities are not less inclined to apply "Negative Sanctions" just because the Left has significant legislative political representation.*

Two observations should be made about the findings just cited which have led to the elimination of variables because they do not meet the minimum requirement of having the hypothesized coefficient sign. First, in every case but one [ln Nondefense Government Expenditures in (9.1)] both the *primary* and *supplementary* estimation strategies produced the same incorrect sign for the parameter in question. This convergence of results is persuasive evidence that we are making the correct causal inference by excluding these variables from the model. Second, and equally important, in every instance the *t* statistic associated with each estimate is very insignificant. Thus, not only did the parameters have the wrong signs, but they also had small magnitudes relative to their standard errors.

The reference to *t* statistics and significance levels brings us to the next requirement for retaining a variable in the model. In addition to the proper coefficient sign, a variable should have a "significant" causal parameter. Recall that our criterion for evaluating single equation results was that a particular coefficient estimate must have been at least *twice* its estimated standard error. Since we are now evaluating more complex systems of equations, which suffer from more severe problems of multicollinearity, let us adopt a more relaxed significance condition. At this point only those variables whose coefficients are not at least three-quarters as large as their standard errors will be eliminated. This is indeed a liberal (radical?) significance condition. It insures that a variable which truly exerts important causal effects will not be too hastily excluded from the model[5].

What variables do not satisfy the three-quarters rule? In the Collective Protest D2 equation (Table 9.1) the estimate for lagged Protest not only is very small but also is less than half its standard error. This indicates that the *"culture of violence" hypothesis is inadequate vis à vis the Collective Protest dimension of violence. High Protest in the recent past does not increase the likelihood of high Protest in the current period.* But this is not the case in the Internal War equation, where lagged Internal War is estimated by both the primary and supplementary methods (Tables 9.2 and A4.2) to have a substantial impact. However, the rate of economic growth and ln Nondefense General Government Expenditures as a % of GDP both fail the three-quarters rule in the Internal War equation.

[5] Throughout we exempt ln Population from significance conditions. Even where not statistically or causally important, we want to residualize some dependent variables by size. See the discussion in Chapter 3 and the sources cited in footnote 11 of that chapter.

Thus, unlike the case for Collective Protest, *a high rate of economic growth does not diminish outbreaks of Internal War*. Moreover, by rejecting the initial hypothesis that high civilian government expenditure has a negative impact on the incidence of Internal War, we have excluded all the equations in the Government Performance–Social Welfare Block from the revised model. This means that *neither high government spending for civilian needs nor high levels of mass social welfare exert any discernible causal influence on either dimension of mass political violence.*

Since all the variables that have not already been eliminated from the Negative Sanctions equation (Table 9.3) satisfy the minimum significance condition, only the equation for ln Coups D2 remains to be examined. In the primary estimation results for the Coups equation reported in Table 9.4, both Internal War and Collective Protest have parameter estimates less than three-quarters the size of their standard errors. But in the supplementary estimation results shown in Table A4.4 the coefficient of Collective Protest has the wrong sign, as we noted earlier, and that of Internal War is positive and nearly *twice* its standard error.

What this suggests is that *although Coups are not directly influenced by Collective Protest, they are spurred in part by Internal War*. Since Internal War clearly is a more threatening type of political violence than Collective Protest, we would expect it to more readily produce Coups by military establishments committed to the preservation of stability and/or the maintenance of their own vested interests as well as those of other privileged groups. The implication of these results is that Internal War but not Collective Protest should be retained in the revised equation for ln Coups D2.

All the equations and variables that did not meet the minimal criteria for retention in a revised model have now been noted. Let us recapitulate the findings thus far. Perhaps the most fundamental revision of the core $Y_m$ sector of the model derives from the conclusion that no important and consistent causal reciprocity exists between the rate of economic change and the incidence of mass violence. At most, the rate of economic growth has a modest negative impact on the magnitude of Collective Protest. Hence the revised $Y_m$ block consists of four rather than six interdependent equations. Equally important for the original structure of the model are the results indicating that government expenditure for civilian purposes as well as the actual state of mass social welfare—alone and in interaction with the level of social mobilization—has no appreciable effect on levels of political violence. Therefore equations for the endogenous $X_k$ variables in the Government Performance–Social Welfare Block (depicted in Figure 8.2) are not relevant for a revised multiequation model of mass political violence.

The remaining inferences that have been drawn from these initial IV-2SLS estimation results do not alter the fundamental structure of the model; nevertheless, they are important for the development of a properly specified causal system. To summarize, we established that neither the degree of sociopolitical institutionalization nor the rate of population growth appear to have a substantial impact on either dimension of violence. Furthermore, Internal War in the recent past makes current Internal War more likely, but this does not hold for Collective Protest. Finally, the evidence demonstrated that leftist parliamentary representation has no discernible influence on the extent to which executive political elites resort to repression and moreover, that Internal War rather than Collective Protest provides a significant stimulus for praetorian seizures of power by the military and other groups.

Let us pursue the implications of these results for a revised block of equations for the simultaneously determined $Y_m$ variables.

*The Simultaneously Determined $Y_m$ Block: Revised Estimation Results*

Eliminating equations and variables that failed to meet the minimum significance criteria produces the following revised system of four equations for the $Y_m$ sector of the model:

(9.7) COLLECTIVE PROTEST D2 = $+\alpha_3$ ln Negative Sanctions D2
             $Y_1$                                 $Y_3$

    $- \alpha_5$ Av. Annual % Change in Energy Consumption pc 1955–1965
                   $Y_5$

    $+ \beta_1$ Group Discrimination 1960 $+ \beta_4$ ln Communist Party Membership 1960
              $X_1$                                $X_4$

    $- \beta_5$ % Legislative Seats Held by Non-Communist Left 1960
                   $X_5$

    $+ \gamma_1$ ln Population 1960 $- \gamma_3$ Communist Regime Dummy $+ \varepsilon_1$
           $Z_1$                          $Z_3$

(9.8) INTERNAL WAR D2 = $+\alpha_3$ ln Negative Sanctions D2 $+ \alpha_4$ ln Coups D2
        $Y_2$                          $Y_3$                 $Y_4$

    $+ \alpha_2^*$ Internal War D1 $- \alpha_3^*$ ln Negative Sanctions D1
         $Y_2^*$                       $Y_3^*$

    $+ \beta_1$ Group Discrimination 1960 $+ \beta_2$ ln Political Separatism 1960
            $X_1$                        $X_2$

    $+ \gamma_1$ ln Population 1960 $- \gamma_3$ Communist Regime Dummy $+ \varepsilon_2$
          $Z_1$                         $Z_3$

(9.9)  LN NEGATIVE SANCTIONS D2 $= +\alpha_1$ Collective Protest D2
$$\quad\quad\quad\quad\quad Y_3 \quad\quad\quad\quad\quad\quad\quad\quad\quad Y_1$$

$\quad + \alpha_2$ Internal War D2 $+ \alpha_4$ ln Coups D2 $- \beta_6$ Elite Electoral Accountability
$$\quad\quad\quad Y_2 \quad\quad\quad\quad\quad Y_4 \quad\quad\quad\quad\quad\quad\quad\quad X_6$$

$\quad \pm \beta_9$ Institutionalization 1960 $\pm \gamma_2$ Social Mobilization 1960
$$\quad\quad\quad\quad X_9 \quad\quad\quad\quad\quad\quad\quad Z_2$$

$\quad + \gamma_{11}$ (Soc. Mob./Institutionalization) $+ \gamma_1$ ln Population 1960
$$\quad\quad\quad\quad Z_{11} \quad\quad\quad\quad\quad\quad\quad\quad\quad Z_1$$

$\quad + \gamma_9$ ln Internal Security Forces per 1000 sq km 1965 $+ \varepsilon_3$
$$\quad\quad\quad\quad Z_9$$

(9.10)  LN COUPS D2 $= +\alpha_2$ Internal War D2 $+ \alpha_4^*$ ln Coups D1
$$\quad\quad\quad Y_4 \quad\quad\quad\quad\quad\quad\quad Y_2 \quad\quad\quad\quad\quad\quad Y_4^*$$

$\quad - \beta_9^*$ ln Institutionalization 1960
$$\quad\quad\quad\quad X_9^*$$

$\quad + \gamma_{10}$ Defense Expenditures as a % of General Govt. Expenditures 1960 $+ \varepsilon_4$
$$\quad\quad\quad\quad Z_{10}$$

Figure 9.1 illustrates the causal relations in the revised $Y_m$ sector. Instrumental Variables–Two StageLeastSquares estimation results for the revised four-equation system appear in Tables 9.7 to 9.10 and A4.7 to A 4.10.[6] Since each equation in the simultaneously determined $Y_m$ block now has fewer variables, multicollinearity is a less serious problem and we can expect commensurately sharper estimates of causal effects. Hence it is appropriate to impose a stricter "significance" condition which variables must satisfy in order to be retained in the model. A not overly demanding criterion is that a coefficient be at least 1.5 times its standard error. Naturally, we anticipate most variables to have considerably sharper parameter estimates.

The estimation results for the first equation, Collective Protest D2, are reported in Tables 9.7 and A4.7. In neither set of results does the parameter of the Legislative Representation of the Non-Communist Left meet the significance condition for the revised equations. Hence we may safely *reject the hypothesis that the legislative representation of the left has a*

---

[6] We do not show formally that each equation in the revised four-equation $Y_m$ block is identified—the reader may verify this for himself by inspection. In estimating the revised equations, we used the same list of instrumental variables as before (although it has been inferred that some of these variables do not exert causal effects). This aids estimation efficiency but of course not identification. (cf. the discussion of the rank condition for identification in Appendix 3.)

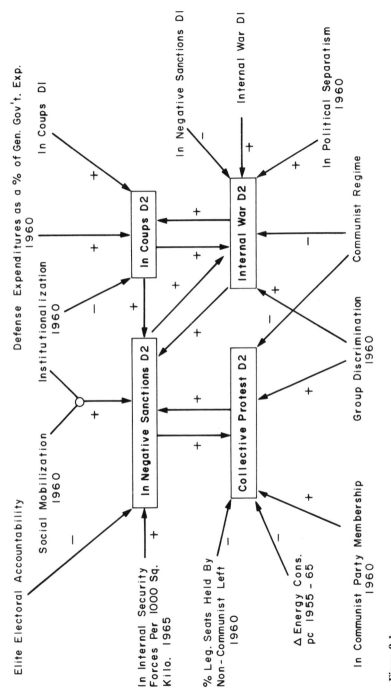

**Figure 9.1.**

167

*Estimation Results and Causal Inferences*

consistent impact on the incidence of *Collective Protest.* "Socialist" political influence simply does not diminish the frequency with which mass publics resort to Collective Protest.

Two variables fail to satisfy the significance condition in the revised equation for Internal War D2 (Tables 9.8 and A4.8). These variables are ln Coups D2 and Group Discrimination. Coupled with our previous

Table 9.7   First Revised Equation for Collective Protest D2 ($Y_1$)

| Independent<br>Variable | Parameter<br>Estimate | $t$<br>Statistic |
|---|---|---|
| ln Negative Sanctions D2 | 0.654 | 5.22 |
| Average Annual % Change in<br>Energy Consumption per capita<br>1955–1965 | −0.062 | −2.16 |
| Group Discrimination 1960 | 0.011 | 2.68 |
| ln Communist Party<br>Membership 1960 | 0.063 | 2.10 |
| % Legislative Seats Held by<br>Non-Communist Left 1960 | −0.003 | −0.83 |
| ln Population 1960 | 0.261 | 2.39 |
| Communist Regime Dummy | −2.501 | −5.68 |
| Constant | −1.894 | −2.18 |

| $R^2$ | Regression Standard Error | $F$ |
|---|---|---|
| .660 | 1.07 | 9,98   27.8 |

Table 9.8   First Revised Equation for Internal War D2 ($Y_2$)

| Independent<br>Variable | Parameter<br>Estimate | $t$<br>Statistic |
|---|---|---|
| ln Negative Sanctions D2 | 1.553 | 3.81 |
| ln Coups D2 | 0.192 | 0.47 |
| Internal War D1 | 0.429 | 5.44 |
| ln Negative Sanctions D1 | −0.669 | −3.89 |
| Group Discrimination 1960 | 0.003 | 0.48 |
| ln Political Separatism 1960 | 0.299 | 2.64 |
| ln Population 1960 | 0.069 | 0.37 |
| Communist Regime Dummy | −2.800 | −4.10 |
| Constant | −2.223 | −1.75 |

| $R^2$ | Regression Standard Error | $F$ |
|---|---|---|
| .706 | 1.64 | 8,99   29.5 |

Table 9.9   First Revised Equation for ln Negative Sanctions D2 ($Y_3$)

| Independent Variable | Parameter Estimate | $t$ Statistic |
|---|---|---|
| Collective Protest D2 | 0.371 | 3.70 |
| Internal War D2 | 0.103 | 1.61 |
| ln Coups D2 | 0.449 | 2.93 |
| Elite Electoral Accountability | −0.621 | −4.75 |
| Institutionalization 1960 | 0.021 | 1.60 |
| Social Mobilization 1960 | −0.0008 | −0.80 |
| Social Mobilization/Institutionalization | 0.040 | 2.19 |
| ln Population 1960 | 0.208 | 2.98 |
| ln Internal Security Forces per 1000 sq km 1965 | 0.132 | 2.80 |
| Constant | 0.437 | 0.61 |

| $R^2$ | Regression Standard Error | $F$ |
|---|---|---|
| .764 | 0.69 | 9,98   35.3 |

Table 9.10   First Revised Equation for ln Coups D2 ($Y_4$)

| Independent Variable | Parameter Estimate | $t$ Statistic |
|---|---|---|
| Internal War D2 | 0.056 | 1.65 |
| ln Coups D1 | 0.496 | 6.35 |
| ln Institutionalization 1960 | −0.272 | −2.18 |
| Defense Expenditures as a % of General Government Expenditures 1960 | 0.018 | 2.77 |
| Constant | 0.749 | 1.65 |

| $R^2$ | Regression Standard Error | $F$ |
|---|---|---|
| .502 | 0.66 | 4,103   25.9 |

inference that Coups and Protest are not directly related, this result means that *the empirical observations do not support the proposition that Coups have a direct causal reciprocity with either dimension of political violence,* although a simultaneous causal loop between Coups and Internal War remains in the model.[7] The insignificant coefficient of Group Discrimination indicates that *Political Separatism mediates entirely the impact of Cultural Differentiation in the causal path that leads from differentiation to Internal War.* This finding is of course quite consistent with the theoretical

---

[7] The implications of this are pursued later in the chapter.

discussion of sociocultural differentiation and national integration in Chapter 5.

The parameters of all variables in the equations for Elite Repression (ln Negative Sanctions D2) and ln Coups D2 (Tables 9.9 and 9.10) are sharply estimated, and further revision is unnecessary. Hence we need only undertake a "second revised" IV-2SLS estimation of the equations for Collective Protest and Internal War. These revised equations are as follows:

(9.11)　$\underset{Y_1}{\text{COLLECTIVE PROTEST D2}} = \underset{Y_3}{+\alpha_3 \text{ Negative Sanctions D2}}$

$\qquad - \underset{Y_5}{\alpha_5 \text{ Av. Annual \% Change in Energy Consumption pc 1955–1965}}$

$\qquad + \underset{X_1}{\beta_1 \text{ Group Discrimination 1960}}$

$\qquad + \underset{X_4}{\beta_4 \text{ ln Communist Party Membership 1960}} + \underset{Z_1}{\gamma_1 \text{ ln Population 1960}}$

$\qquad - \underset{Z_3}{\gamma_3 \text{ Communist Regime Dummy}} + \varepsilon_1$

(9.12)　$\underset{Y_2}{\text{INTERNAL WAR D2}} = \underset{Y_3}{+\alpha_3 \text{ ln Negative Sanctions D2}}$

$\qquad + \underset{Y_2^*}{\alpha_2^* \text{ Internal War D1}} - \underset{Y_3^*}{\alpha_3^* \text{ ln Negative Sanctions D1}}$

$\qquad + \underset{X_2}{\beta_2 \text{ ln Political Separatism 1960}} + \underset{Z_1}{\gamma_1 \text{ ln Population 1960}}$

$\qquad - \underset{Z_3}{\gamma_3 \text{ Communist Regime Dummy}} + \varepsilon_2$

The *primary* regression estimates for these equations are reported in Tables 9.11 and 9.12; the *supplementary* results appear in Tables A4.11 and A4.12. Each term in the expressions for Collective Protest and Internal War now easily satisfies the significance condition that parameters have a *t* statistic of at least 1.5. Indeed, almost all the coefficients are far more precisely estimated than the 1.5 rule requires. Therefore the $Y_m$ block of interdependently related endogenous variables has now been estimated in its final functional form. The "final form" results for Collective Protest, Internal War, ln Negative Sanctions and ln Coups D2, appear in Tables 9.11, 9.12, 9.9, and 9.10, respectively.

Table 9.11    Second Revised Equation for Collective Protest D2 ($Y_1$)

| Independent Variable | Parameter Estimate | $t$ Statistic |
|---|---|---|
| ln Negative Sanctions D2 | 0.672 | 5.49 |
| Average Annual % Change in Energy Consumption per capita 1955–1965 | −0.060 | −2.10 |
| Group Discrimination 1960 | 0.012 | 2.86 |
| ln Communist Party Membership 1960 | 0.062 | 2.07 |
| ln Population 1960 | 0.264 | 2.44 |
| Communist Regime Dummy | −2.431 | −5.65 |
| Constant | −2.087 | −2.50 |
| $R^2$ | Regression Standard Error | $F$ |
| .661 | 1.07 | 6,101   32.8 |

Table 9.12    Second Revised Equation for Internal War D2 ($Y_2$)

| Independent Variable | Parameter Estimate | $t$ Statistic |
|---|---|---|
| ln Negative Sanctions D2 | 1.736 | 6.61 |
| Internal War D1 | 0.431 | 5.34 |
| ln Negative Sanctions D1 | −0.711 | −4.39 |
| ln Political Separatism 1960 | 0.292 | 2.55 |
| ln Population 1960 | 0.002 | 0.01 |
| Communist Regime Dummy | −2.911 | −4.42 |
| Constant | −2.026 | −1.61 |
| $R^2$ | Regression Standard Error | $F$ |
| .681 | 1.68 | 6,101   36.0 |

Figure 9.2 depicts the final form relationships in the revised $Y_m$ sector and indicates which $X_k$ and $Z_i$ exert direct causal effects. This final causal structure represents the best model we have been able to final causal structure represents the best model we have been able to devise from an extensive search of the literature and rather involved applications of nonexperimental estimation and inference techniques. So far we have only highlighted the hypothesized influences in the simultaneously deter-mined $Y_m$ block that have *not* stood up to empirical scrutiny. Little has been said about the implications for mass political violence of the causal relations we *have* found to be operative, and nothing has been said about

172

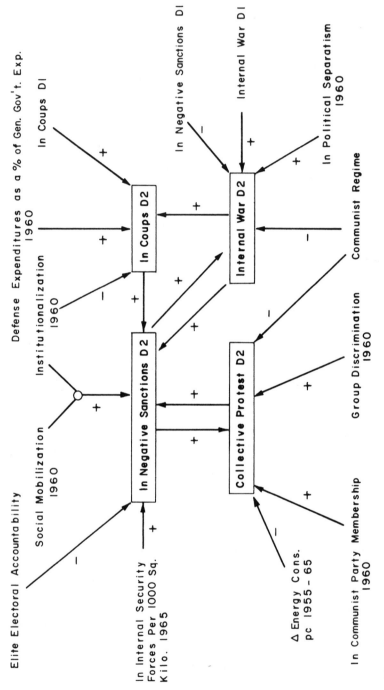

**Figure 9.2.**

the implications of the relative sizes of the parameters. Let us postpone this important discussion for the moment, since it should include not only direct influences to and among the $Y_m$, but also indirect influences from causal variables that appear in equations for the predetermined $X_k$.

*Predetermined Causal Influences: Estimation Results*

Many of the predetermined and endogenous $X_k$ that appeared in the initial specification of the multiequation model in Chapter 8 were shown to have inconsequential causal effects on the $Y_m$. Hence it is necessary to estimate equations only for those $X_k$ that remain in the revised model. These variables are:

1. Group Discrimination 1960 $(X_1)$, which appears in the equation for Collective Protest D2.
2. In Political Separatism 1960 $(X_2)$, which appears in the equation for Internal War D2.
3. Ethnolinguistic Fractionalization 1960 $(X_3)$, which appears in the equations for Group Discrimination and ln Political Separatism.
4. ln Communist Party Membership 1960 $(X_4)$, which appears in the Collective Protest D2 equation.
5. Elite Electoral Accountability $(X_6)$, which appears in the ln Negative Sanctions (Elite Repression) equation.
6. Institutionalization 1960 $(X_9)$, which appears interactively in the ln Negative Sanctions equation and additively (but ln transformed, $X_9^*$) in the ln Coups D2 equation.

The equations for these remaining $X_k$, as they were first specified in Chapter 8, are as follows:

(9.13)　GROUP DISCRIMINATION 1960
$$X_1$$

$$= + \beta_3 \text{ Ethnolinguistic Fractionalization 1960} + \varepsilon_5$$
$$X_3$$

(9.14)　LN POLITICAL SEPARATISM 1960
$$X_2$$

$$= \pm\beta_3 \text{ Ethnolinguistic Fractionalization 1960} - \gamma_2 \text{ Social Mobilization 1960}$$
$$X_3 \qquad\qquad\qquad\qquad\qquad\qquad Z_2$$

$$+ \gamma_{13} \text{ (Ethnolinguistic Fractionalization * Social Mobilization)}$$
$$Z_{13}$$

$$+ \gamma_5 \text{ Postwar Independence Dummy} + \varepsilon_6$$

(9.15)  ETHNOLINGUISTIC FRACTIONALIZATION 1960
$$X_3$$

$= -\gamma_2^* \ln \text{Social Mobilization 1960} + \gamma_5 \text{ Postwar Independence} + \varepsilon_7$

$\phantom{= -\gamma_2^*}Z_2^* \phantom{\ln \text{Social Mobilization 1960} + \gamma_5 \text{ Postwar}}Z_5$


(9.16)  LN COMMUNIST PARTY MEMBERSHIP 1960
$$X_4$$

$= +\beta_6 \text{ Elite Electoral Accountability} + \gamma \text{ Economic Development 1960}$

$\phantom{= +\beta_6 \text{ Elite Electoral}}X_6$

$- \gamma \text{ (Economic Development 1960)}^2 + \gamma_1 \ln \text{Population 1960}$

$\phantom{- \gamma \text{ (Economic Development 1960)}^2 + \gamma_1 \ln}Z_1$

$+ \gamma_2^* \ln \text{Social Mobilization 1960} + \gamma_3 \text{ Communist Regime Dummy}$

$\phantom{+ \gamma_2^*}Z_2^* \phantom{\ln \text{Social Mobilization 1960} + \gamma_3 \text{ Communist}}Z_3$

$+ \gamma_4 \text{ Communist Party Legal Status Dummy} + \varepsilon_8$

$\phantom{+ \gamma_4 \text{ Comm}}Z_4$


(9.17)  ELITE ELECTORAL ACCOUNTABILITY

$= + \gamma \text{ Economic Development 1960} + \varepsilon_9$


(9.18)  INSTITUTIONALIZATION 1960 $= -\alpha_1^* \text{ Collective Protest D1}$

$\phantom{(9.18)  INSTITUTIONALIZATION 1960 }X_9 \phantom{= -\alpha_1^* \text{ Collective}}Y_1^*$

$- \alpha_2^* \text{ Internal War D1} + \gamma_3 \text{ Communist Regime Dummy}$

$\phantom{- \alpha_2^*}Y_2^* \phantom{\text{ Internal War D1} + \gamma_3 \text{ Communist}}Z_3$

$- \gamma_5 \text{ Postwar Independence Dummy}$

$\phantom{- \gamma_5 \text{ Postwar}}Z_5$

$+ \gamma \text{ Economic Development 1960} + \varepsilon_{10}$


The first three equations—Group Discrimination (9.13), ln Political Separatism (9.14), and Ethnolinguistic Fractionalization (9.15)—comprise what was designated as the "Cultural Differentiation Block" when the complete model was introduced in Chapter 8. They were initially developed in Chapter 5 where more complex interaction formulations were examined, but the specifications here were determined to be the most satisfactory. Hence the (OLS) results reported in Tables 9.13 to 9.15 represent the final estimates of the parameters in these equations. Without repeating the earlier discussion of these findings, we note at this point only that the equation for Group Discrimination yields a particularly poor fit to the observed data. Although Ethnolinguistic Fractionalization manifests an important causal influence on the extent of discrimination cross-nationally, most of the variance in this variable remains to be explained. The development of a powerful explanation of group discrimination clearly requires extensive study.

Table 9.13  Equation for Group Discrimination 1960 ($X_1$)

| Independent Variable | Parameter Estimate | $t$ Statistic |
|---|---|---|
| Ethnolinguistic Fractionalization 1960 | 0.209 | 2.30 |
| Constant | 12.750 | 2.81 |
| $R^2$ | Regression Standard Error | $F$ |
| .047 | 28.5 | 1,106   5.3 |

Table 9.14  Equation for ln Political Separatism 1960 ($X_2$)

| Independent Variable | Parameter Estimate | $t$ Statistic |
|---|---|---|
| Ethnolinguistic Fractionalization 1960 | $-0.002$ | $-0.17$ |
| Social Mobilization 1960 | $-0.004$ | $-2.31$ |
| Social Mobilization*ELF | 0.00009 | 2.88 |
| Postwar Independence Dummy | 0.685 | 1.90 |
| Constant | 1.310 | 2.36 |
| $R^2$ | Regression Standard Error | $F$ |
| .306 | 1.3 | 4,103   11.4 |

Table 9.15  Equation for Ethnolinguistic Fractionalization 1960 ($X_3$)

| Independent Variable | Parameter Estimate | $t$ Statistic |
|---|---|---|
| ln Social Mobilization 1960 | $-12.500$ | $-3.60$ |
| Postwar Independence Dummy | 22.800 | 3.96 |
| Constant | 98.400 | 4.89 |
| $R^2$ | Regression Standard Error | $F$ |
| .390 | 23.9 | 2,105   33.5 |

Before analyzing the implications of these parameter estimates for the overall model of mass political violence, the other $X_k$ equations should be estimated.

Equations 9.16 and 9.17 are what is left in the model of the Domestic Politics Block. The equation for the (ln transformed) size of Communist Party Membership (9.16) includes linear and quadratic terms in economic development in order to test the hypothesis of Benjamin and Kautsky that Communist Party membership grows with economic development but tends to decline at the higher development levels. We also hypothesized that Communist parties should be larger where populations are mobilized for potential politicization, as well as in nations where democratic political processes prevail and the Party is not actively suppressed. Of course, Communist parties are also large in nations with Communist Regimes, and since the membership data are not standardized for population, size alone is expected to have some effect.

Equation 9.16 was estimated with a number of economic development measures and various combinations of independent variables. Table 9.16 reports the final form of this equation. In all estimations, *economic development evidenced a significant curvilinear relationship of the type predicted by Benjamin and Kautsky.* The most pronounced version of this curvilinearity involved GNP per capita, and that variable appears in the reported results. *In none of the estimations did democratization or the Communist Legal Status Dummy display a nontrivial effect* and so these variables are excluded from the final results. As hypothesized, *Communist parties are larger where (ln) Social Mobilization is high.* This is clearly demonstrated by the large and significant positive coefficient for Social Mobilization in Table 9.16. Less central, but no less necessary for the proper specification of the equation, are the anticipated *positive and significant effects of ln Population and the Communist Regime Dummy on membership size.*

Equation 9.17 expresses Elite Electoral Accountability—the measure of democratization—simply as a function of the level of economic develop-

Table 9.16    Equation for ln Communist Party Membership 1960 ($X_4$)

| Independent Variable | Parameter Estimate | $t$ Statistic |
|---|---|---|
| GNP per capita 1960 (in thousands of 1965 U.S. dollars) | 4.970 | 2.60 |
| GNP per capita 1960 Squared | −1.990 | −2.63 |
| ln Social Mobilization 1960 | 2.260 | 4.27 |
| ln Population 1960 | 1.490 | 6.53 |
| Communist Regime Dummy | 5.010 | 4.86 |
| Constant | −21.080 | −7.37 |

| $R^2$ | Regression Standard Error | $F$ |
|---|---|---|
| .688 | 2.79 | 5,102    44.9 |

Table 9.17   Equation for Elite Electoral Accountability ($X_6$)

| Independent Variable | Parameter Estimate | $t$ Statistic |
|---|---|---|
| GNP per capita 1960 (in thousands of 1965 U.S. dollars) | 0.480 | 4.54 |
| Constant | 1.977 | 24.98 |

| $R^2$ | Regression Standard Error | $F$ |
|---|---|---|
| .163 | 0.62 | 1,106   20.6 |

ment. As we noted earlier, a number of studies provide convincing evidence that more complex formulations are in order, but the crudeness of the democratization variable does not warrant anything beyond the simple specification of (9.17). The economic development indicator that maximized a linear fit with Elite Electoral Accountability was GNP per capita. The results reported in Table 9.17 show that *although GNP per capita displays a substantial impact on democratization, the equation provides a relatively poor fit to the data.* A more sensitive measure of democratization which would allow more realistic causal formulations and better fits to the data remains to be developed for cross-national samples as large as ours. However, the Elite Electoral Accountability variable is sufficiently discriminating for the limited purposes of this study.

The last predetermined and endogenous $X_k$ for which an equation must be estimated is Institutionalization (9.18).[8] In Chapter 8 we hypothesized that lagged violence, especially Internal War, would have an adverse impact on the current development of sociopolitical institutions. It was also anticipated that recently independent ex-colonies would on the whole have lower institutional development than similar nations that did not experience imperial rule. Finally, (9.18) specifies a positive coefficient for economic development, which is an important foundation of sociopolitical organizational capability, as well as a positive coefficient for the Communist Regime Dummy variable, since a highly developed political apparatus is characteristic of Communist nations.

The estimation results for the final functional form of this equation appear in Table 9.18. In analyzing the regression outcomes, it became apparent that *Internal War in the recent past has a strong adverse effect on subsequent Institutionalization, whereas Collective Protest does not.* This

[8] Although Institutionalization also appears in the model in ln transformed functional form, we only estimate an equation for the untransformed version.

of course is not at all inconsistent with our initial expectation that institutional development would be especially impaired by the more disruptive Internal War mode of violence. Moreover, *no particularly strong relationship between recent independence and sociopolitical institutionalization was discernible when other variables were controlled. This suggests that imperialism had no direct and consistent impact one way or the other on institutional development in the "new" states.* Perhaps this accounts for the conflicting observations on this issue.

In any case, to sort the matter out further requires the development of one or more variables that precisely measure differences in colonial experience. A simple dummy variable is clearly inadequate. Finally, the

Table 9.18   Equation for Institutionalization 1960 ($X_9$)

| Independent Variable | Parameter Estimate | $t$ Statistic |
|---|---|---|
| Internal War D1 | − 0.930 | − 3.16 |
| ln GNP per capita 1960 (in hundreds of 1965 U.S. dollars) | 6.648 | 7.91 |
| Communist Regime Dummy | 17.710 | 5.69 |
| Constant | − 12.275 | − 2.45 |

| $R^2$ | Regression Standard Error | $F$ | |
|---|---|---|---|
| .540 | 8.77 | 3,104 | 40.8 |

estimation results in Table 9.18 reveal that *Communist Regimes manifest considerably higher institutionalization than non-Communist ones as we anticipated, and that the expected facilitation effect of economic development is borne out and most sharply displayed by ln GNP per capita.*

Equations for all the predetermined and endogenous $X_k$, and simultaneously determined, endogenous $Y_m$ have now been estimated in their final functional forms. It is appropriate therefore to determine what "final" causal inferences and dynamic implications may be derived from these results.

## Causal Inferences and Dynamic Implications

How is the final structure of the multiequation model of mass political violence best evaluated? That is, what is the most effective way to pursue its implications in order to further our understanding of the causal processes underlying cross-national differences in levels of political violence? What need not be undertaken at this stage is any additional theory "trimming", since we have already validated the model in the sense of eliminating variables with incorrect signs and trivial causal effects. One way to evaluate the system is to analyze the causal structure in terms of *exact* coefficient magnitudes. This approach requires that the model be well specified, that variables have interpretable metrics and be measured without great error, and that coefficients be sharply estimated. It is not entirely out of order because we utilized the best available data, were careful to preserve interpretable metrics when creating composite variables, tried to avoid major specification errors by carefully examining numerous single and multiequation models suggested by existing theory, and employed rather sophisticated estimation techniques in order to secure sharp and consistent parameter estimates. However, for very large cross-national samples even the best available data are not likely to be free of significant measurement errors. Moreover, the complete absence of data on some variables, as well as the underdeveloped state of existing theory, undoubtedly has led to some specification error in the structural equations.[9] The wisest strategy, therefore, is not to put too much confidence in exact parameter values but to focus instead on their *relative* magnitudes. *Path coefficients* provide a useful measure of relative causal effects.[10]

Path coefficients are generated by the regression of standardized, "Z-scored" variables or, alternatively, by multiplying the structural regression coefficients produced by OLS and IV-2SLS by $\sigma_x/\sigma_y$—the ratio of the standard deviation of the right-hand side "independent" variable to the standard deviation of the left-hand side "dependent" variable. Thus they represent the change in dependent variables that can be attributed to (unit) changes in independent variables in terms of standard deviation units.

The magnitudes of path coefficients, unlike those of unstandardized regression coefficients, are not influenced by the metrics or units of measurement that variables happen to be expressed in. If we think of typical or "equally likely" changes in variables as $\sigma_i$, path coefficients assess the typical changes in dependent variables produced by typical changes in independent variables. However, they may be "sample specific" in the sense that their magnitudes are dependent on variances and standard deviations that may not obtain in another body of data. Thus path coefficients are best suited for assessing relative parameter values in a particular sample, especially when the metrics of independent variables are markedly different

---

[9] We take this up again in the following chapter.

[10] Recent expositions of path analysis include: Otis D. Duncan, "Path Analysis: Sociological Examples," *American Journal of Sociology*, Vol. 72, July 1966, pp. 1–16, and David Heise, "Problems in Path Analysis and Causal Inference," in Edgar Borgatta and George Bohrnstedt (eds.), *Sociological Methodology* 1969 (San Francisco: Jossey-Bass, Inc., 1969), pp. 38–73. Note that path coefficients are the same as standardized $\beta$ coefficients.

(as is the case here), whereas structural regression coefficients may be more appropriate for generalizing across bodies of data[11]. Hence the following analysis is framed in terms of path coefficients, although none of the inferences drawn would be vitiated by reference to the unstandardized structural parameters reported in the tables.

Figure 9.3 depicts the complete, revised causal model and exhibits the path coefficients for each causal link.[12] Consider first the relationships between the jointly determined $Y_m$. Two *direct* simultaneous reciprocities remain between these variables and they are among the strongest relationships in the entire model. These are the reciprocal linkages between Elite Repression (ln Negative Sanctions D2) and each dimension of mass political violence. Figure 9.4 excerpts these causal reciprocities from the larger arrow diagram in Figure 9.3.

It is clear from these results that *each type of mass violence typically evokes repression from political elites, although the relative coefficient magnitudes ( + .483 versus + .182) suggest that this is more uniformly true of Collective Protest than of Internal War.* Hence elites appear to be more inclined to deal in a repressive fashion with Protest than with Internal War. This may be because Internal War is in general more threatening to the status of incumbent elites than is Protest, and thus elites more often feel compelled to meet such situations with accommodation and compromise than they do when Protest alone is involved. Of course we would expect this to depend on the (perceived) strength of the insurgents in particular instances—a condition that cannot be investigated rigorously without hard data. Alternatively, these results may simply reflect the tendency of elites to respond directly to Internal War with military action which is not indexed by the Negative Sanctions variable. In any case, each of the path coefficients is positive, which means that repression is the most likely

---

[11] On the standardized versus nonstandardized coefficient issue, see H. M. Blalock, "Causal Inferences, Closed Populations, and Measures of Association," *American Political Science Review*, Vol. 61, March 1967, pp. 130–136; Otis D. Duncan, "Partials, Partitions, and Paths," in Edgar Borgatta and George Bohrnstedt (eds.), *Sociological Methodology* 1970 (San Francisco: Jossey-Bass Inc., 1970), pp. 38–47; John W. Tukey, "Causation, Regression, and Path Analysis," in Oscar Kempthorne et al. (eds.), *Statistics and Mathematics in Biology* (Ames, Iowa: Iowa State College Press, 1954), Chapter 3; and Sewall Wright, "Path Coefficients and Path Regressions: Alternative or Complimentary Concepts?" *Biometrics*, 1960, Vol. 16, pp. 189–202.

The argument that path coefficients index the relative importance of variables in terms of "equally likely" changes is based on Arthur S. Goldberger, *Econometric Theory* (New York: John Wiley & Sons, Inc., 1964) pp. 197–198.

[12] As in Figures 9.1 and 9.2, we omit ln Population from Figure 9.3. Circled intersections represent interactions in the model. Unless significant, arrows and coefficients for the "main effects" of variables appearing in interactions are not shown.

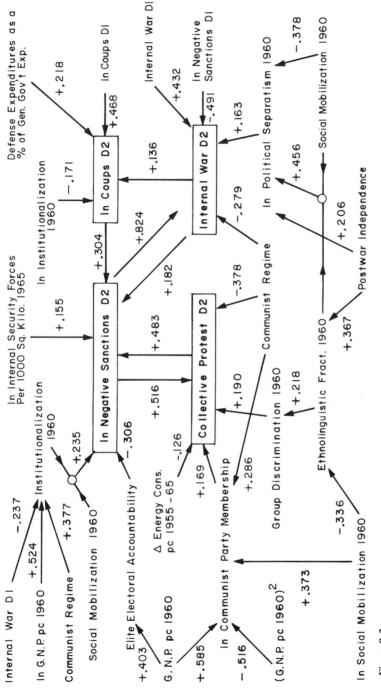

**Figure 9.3.**

181

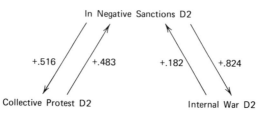

**Figure 9.4.**

response of elites to *both* kinds of domestic violence. The reciprocal nature of these causal relations also demonstrates that Collective Protest and Internal War not only engender repression from elites, but that *the nearly instantaneous response to repression is most often more mass violence.* This is not at all surprising, for it is a common observation that meeting mass protest or rebellion with repression frequently only exacerbates the situation, at least in the *short term.*

Another important feature of the elite repression–mass political violence reciprocity should be noted. It concerns the indirect causal relationship of Collective Protest and Internal War which may be traced through this part of the model. The relative parameter estimates indicate that *the dominant causal sequence that indirectly relates the dimensions of violence is one in which Protest is met with repression by elites, which produces in turn an escalated response of Internal War from its recipients.*

What we are arguing, then, is that the indirect relationship of Collective Protest and Internal War is dominated by the causal sequence schematized in Figure 9.5. Comparing the product of the coefficients along this path

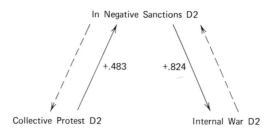

**Figure 9.5.**

(.483*.824 = .397) with the product of the coefficients along the alternative Internal War to Collective Protest path represented by dotted lines in Figure 9.5 (.182*.516 = .094) shows clearly which is predominant: The

Collective Protest to Internal War path is more than four times as strong.[13] Moreover, this finding squares with our intuitive expectations. Many examples come to mind of situations when nonviolent or only marginally violent Protests were met with rigidity and repression by elites and as a result escalated to Internal War. Tilly, for example, found that this was most often the scenario for the cases examined in his historical survey of European mass disorders:

"The authorities also have some choice of whether, and with how much muscle, to answer political challenges and illegal actions that are not intrinsically violent: banned assemblies, threats of vengeance, wildcat strikes. [Note how closely this corresponds to our Collective Protest variable.] A large proportion of the European disturbances we have been surveying turned violent at exactly that moment when the authorities intervened to stop an illegal but nonviolent action. This is typical of violent strikes and demonstrations. Furthermore the great bulk of the killing and wounding in those same disturbances was done by troops or police rather than by insurgents or demonstrators."[14]

Another set of relationships among the $Y_m$, which is as important theoretically as those discussed so far, is implied by the simultaneous causal loop between Internal War, Coups, and Negative Sanctions. This causal sequence is abstracted from the arrow diagram of the complete model and depicted in Figure 9.6.

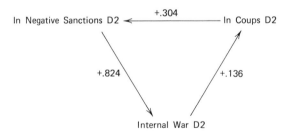

**Figure 9.6.**

---

[13] We multiply along paths only to illustrate the predominant linkages. The formal theorems of path analysis whereby variance in dependent variables can be partitioned among direct and indirect effects of independent variables breaks down in models that have simultaneous reciprocities or feedback loops.

[14] Charles Tilly, "Collective Violence in European Perspective," in Hugh D. Graham and Ted R. Gurr (eds.), *Violence in America: Historical and Comparative Perspectives*, A Report to the National Commission on the Causes and Prevention of Violence (New York: Signet Books, 1969), p. 39.

*Estimation Results and Causal Influences*

This segment of the model provides a striking illustration of what Huntington has called the "vicious circle of direct action" that characterizes "praetorian" societies. It reveals that *the occurrence of Internal War, Coups, or Repression may initiate a sequence of relationships resulting in positive feedback.* For example, an outbreak of Internal War (for whatever reason) often provides the stimulus for a "praetorian" political takeover by the military, which perceives the situation as ineffectively handled by incumbent authorities as well as threatening to its own vested interests. The result of successful takeovers is more often than not increased repression which is designed to defeat or contain the insurgency. In the short run, however, repression is likely to increase rather than diminish the severity of Internal War. This in turn may produce additional attempted seizures of power by military factions which want to implement an even "harder line." And so the "vicious circle" may continue in an escalatory fashion.[15] Therefore, Internal War not only has a direct feedback reciprocity with Repression (In Negative Sanctions) which we have already discussed, but an indirect one as well that operates through Coups.

This process may also be catalyzed by Collective Protest. It was established earlier (Figure 9.5) that Collective Protest is causally linked to Internal War by way of Elite Repression. *Hence a causal sequence may originate with Protest which evokes Repression and then escalates to Internal War. Internal War may then initiate the causal loop that leads to Coups, increased Repression, more internal war, and so on.* Figure 9.7 excerpts this series of relationships from the larger causal system in Figure 9.3.

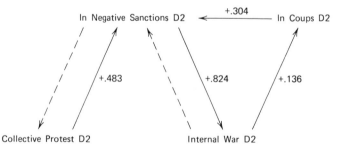

**Figure 9.7.**

[15] Whether it does is partly contingent on the circumstances of particular cases, which we are unable to assess. The model only captures the broad outlines of such a scenario. Even if it is unsuccessful, an attempted Coup by "hard-line" military factions in response to a situation of Internal War may encourage incumbent political authorities to increase Repression.

Also note that the above does not imply that the "vicious circle" or any of the other positive feedback linkages are explosive. The product of the (unstandardized) structural coefficients as well as the path coefficients for all feedback relationships is less than 1.0. Mitigating influences from other sectors of the model are discussed below.

If we had great confidence in the exact values of the parameter estimates, it would be meaningful to pursue the implications of these relationships more formally. What is worthwhile exploring, however, is the impact of predetermined and exogenous influences on these variables. Since all the direct and indirect feedback relationships between the simultaneously determined $Y_m$ are positive, let us first consider those predetermined $X_k$ and exogenous $Z_i$ that tend to mitigate these reinforcing feedback effects. Thus we are interested in those causal influences that either directly diminish the incidence of mass political violence or mitigate violence indirectly by deactivating the positive relations from other $Y_m$ to Collective Protest and Internal War.

The strongest negative causal influence on any of the $Y_m$ is that of lagged Repression (ln Negative Sanctions D1) on current Internal War. Its path coefficient of $-.491$ is considerably larger than any of the other negative coefficients in the model (see Figure 9.3). As we pointed out when a preliminary version of this result was encountered in Chapter 6, it indicates that *although the short-term consequence of repression is even more violence, the long-term impact is to deter outbreaks of Internal War.* Hence, from the perspective of elites who seek to suppress popular expressions of discontent and to maintain domestic stability, repression appears to be an efficacious long-term strategy vis à vis the more threatening Internal War dimension of mass violence.[16] *However, this is not the case for Collective Protest—the knowledge that political authorities have in the recent past responded to Protest with repression does not appear to inhibit the current incidence of this type of political violence.* These findings firmly support the proposition that "organized" and purposeful kinds of mass violence are more easily discouraged by sustained repression than are "spontaneous" and nonpurposeful expressions of discontent. Moreover, since organized violence (Internal War) is far more threatening to the tenure of elites than is unorganized violence (Collective Protest), perhaps this partially explains why the most repressive ruling classes are typically more secure in their *long-run* position than are elite classes who waver between "soft" and "hard" lines. Although, as we have noted, the *short-term*

---

[16] Even though repression appears to be an effective *long-term* strategy against Internal War, elites are less inclined to rely on repression in such situations than they are in cases of Protest, as was demonstrated earlier. We remarked then that this may be because insurgencies are inherently more threatening to elites—especially if they have wide popular support. An additional reason is implied in Figure 9.6 and the subsequent discussion. The immediate consequence of repression is typically more severe Internal War, which tends to produce "praetorian" power seizures and attempted seizures by what usually are "hard-line" military factions. Hence, a strategy of repression rather than accommodation threatens the tenure of *incumbent* elites in this manner as well. This line of reasoning is of course in large part speculative. The crudeness of the model does not support precise interpretations firmly.

consequence of repression often is to exacerbate the situation.[17]

A powerful inhibitive factor that affects both dimensions of mass political violence is regime type. Figure 9.3 illustrates that the Communist Regime Dummy variable has relatively large negative coefficients in paths to both Collective Protest and Internal War ($-.378$ and $-.279$, respectively).[18] Such results might well reflect the influence of any number of variables that systematically differentiate Communist from non-Communist regimes. Since we tried to examine most of the relevant possibilities—for example, levels of Civilian Government Expenditure and mass Social Welfare—*the negative association of Communist Regime type with each dimension of violence probably reflects the deterrence effect produced by the police-state atmosphere and constant potential for actual repression characteristic of totalitarian, Communist systems.*

The last predetermined or exogenous variable to directly diminish mass violence is the rate of economic growth. Previous results demonstrated that neither Collective Protest nor Internal War consistently inhibits the pace of economic development. Moreover, high rates of growth did not manifest the anticipated negative influence on the magnitude of Internal War. However, economic growth, or more precisely the Average Annual Percentage Change in Energy Consumption per capita 1955–1965, does exert a significantly negative (although modest) effect on Collective Protest. Hence *growing affluence does avert outbreaks of Protest but does not seem to have any systematic impact on the incidence of Internal War.*

A number of variables determined outside the $Y_m$ sector of the model serve to reduce the magnitude of mass violence indirectly. For example, Elite Electoral Accountability, a crude index of democratization, has a strong negative effect on ln Negative Sanctions D2 (Repression). The path coefficient is $-.306$. It substantiates our previous conclusion that *in otherwise comparable situations, elites are less inclined to resort to repression in nations where political authorities are held accountable for their actions by free and competitive elections.* Therefore, even though democratization does not

---

[17] Thus repression has contrasting short- and long-term consequences, which may be why incumbent political elites often waver in their application of "negative sanctions," even though sustained repression might better secure the long-run position of the ruling class as a whole. Our findings here square well with the qualitative observations of Eckstein and others. See Harry Eckstein, "On the Causes of Internal Wars," in Eric Nordlinger (ed.), *Politics and Society* (Englewood Cliffs, N.J.: Prentice Hall, Inc., 1970), pp. 287–309, and the sources cited therein.

[18] Path coefficients for dummy variables like the Communist Regime Dummy and the Post-war Independence Dummy are of course much less meaningful than they are for conventional variates. More appropriate for such variables are the unstandardized structural coefficients reported in the tables. Path coefficients for these variables are shown here only to give a very rough idea of relative effects.

have a significant direct impact on the level of violence it clearly does have a causally important indirect influence by diminishing the extent of government repression. The dominant form of this indirect causal influence is delineated in Figure 9.8.

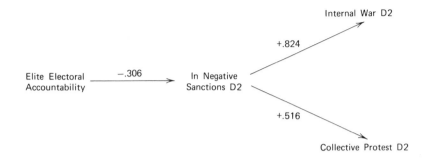

**Figure 9.8.**

In a similar fashion, Institutionalization exerts an indirect negative influence on the magnitude of violence. It does so in two ways. First, ln Institutionalization has a negative parameter in a path to ln Coups D2 ( − .171). This confirms the inference, initially made in Chapter 6, *that societies with well-developed civilian sociopolitical institutions are less susceptible to "praetorian" seizures of power by the military and other organized elite factions.* Since those who "illegally" seize power usually increase repression, which in turn produces (in the short run) additional mass violence, institutionalization contributes to the diminution of domestic violence, albeit in an indirect way. The second way institutionalization decreases violence is through its appearance in a ratio interaction term with Social Mobilization. Figure 9.3 shows that the ratio interaction term of Social Mobilization to Institutionalization has a substantial positive impact on Repression ( + .235). This suggests that *in nations where the burdens generated by social mobilization outrun the capabilities of sociopolitical institutions, political elites tend to resort to repression as an alternative means of social control.* Hence high institutionalization, relative to the level of social mobilization, reduces the size of the mobilization–institutionalization ratio, and thereby contributes directly to the diminution of repression and indirectly to the reduction of mass violence. Conversely, high social mobilization relative to institutionalization increases this ratio, which tends to increase repression directly and violence indirectly. Ignoring simultaneous reciprocities and feedback loops, Figure 9.9 isolates the indirect influence of Institutionalization on Collective Protest and Internal War.

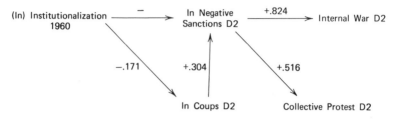

**Figure 9.9.**

Thus far we have shown how Elite Electoral Accountability and Institutionalization indirectly mitigate violence through their negative causal influence on $Y_m$ variables that have direct effects on Collective Protest and Internal War. But each of these variables is endogenous to the entire model, although predetermined vis à vis the $Y_m$ sector. Therefore, variables that causally influence Institutionalization and Democratization also influence the level of violence. These are perhaps best designated as "second-removed" effects to emphasize their lower status in the causal hierarchy.

Consider the case of Elite Electoral Accountability, which diminishes Repression and indirectly violence. *Since economic development, which is measured here by GNP per capita, facilitates democratization* (+.403), *it consequently tends to decrease the level of violence, although in a very indirect or "second-removed" way.* Gross National Product per capita (ln transformed) also appears with a positive path coefficient (+.524) in the equation for Institutionalization. Hence *the level of economic development indirectly diminishes violence by way of its effect on institutionalization as well.* Similarly, the Communist Regime Dummy variable appears with a sizable positive path coefficient (+.377) in the equation for institutionalization. This means that *regime type has indirect as well as direct negative influence on levels of political violence.* Lagged Internal War, however, manifests a significant negative effect on Institutionalization (-.237). By vitiating subsequent institutional development, it makes current Coups and Repression more likely and thereby increases the magnitude of current mass violence. *Not only does Internal War in the recent past have a second-removed positive influence on the current incidence of both kinds of domestic violence, but it also has a substantial direct impact on current Internal War.* This is sharply demonstrated by the large positive path coefficient (+.432) of Internal War D1 on Internal War D2.[19] It provides persuasive evidence

---

[19] There is probably some upward bias in this estimate. Compare the *supplementary* estimation results to the *primary* results for this variable in Tables 9.12 and A4.12.

that the "culture of violence" effect hypothesized by Gurr and others is operative for the Internal War dimension of violence.

Lagged Internal War is only one of a number of predetermined and exogenous variables in the model that directly or indirectly *increase* levels of mass political violence. Let us now examine the others. Consider first the remaining variables exerting causal influence on the extent of Elite Repression (ln Negative Sanctions D2). We have analyzed the direct effects of Elite Accountability and the Social Mobilization–Institutionalization interaction on Repression, as well as the indirect effects of variables such as Economic Development, Regime type, and lagged Internal War. Only one causal influence is left: ln Internal Security Forces per 1000 sq km It displays a moderately high and positive path coefficient of +.155. Although less important than the other immediate determinants of ln Negative Sanctions, it implies nevertheless that *where elites have large (spatially dense) coercive forces at their disposal, they more readily resort to Repression.* Thus, even though the Internal Security Forces variable was inferred to have no substantial direct (linear or curvilinear) effect on domestic violence, it does exert a nontrivial, indirect causal influence through its impact on elite inclination to apply "Negative Sanctions." The essentials of this indirect linkage are illustrated in Figure 9.10.

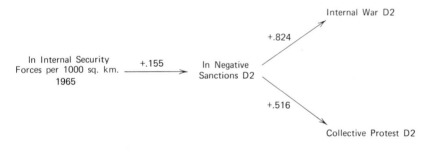

**Figure 9.10.**

The major determinants of ln Coups D2 have a similar causal role. The most important is lagged Coups with a path coefficient of +.468. This result strongly supports the earlier, tentative conclusion that *an "interventionist" history is likely to develop a tradition or "culture" that makes current interventions more likely than otherwise would be the case.* This outcome implies, then, that in nations where the military has frequently intervened in the past, "praetorian" seizures of power come to be viewed as a more or less normal (but not necessarily acceptable) feature of political life by substantial segments of the general and elite publics and by the military establishment itself. In this manner, lagged as well as current Coups indirectly promote mass political violence.

Another variable that influences the number of actual and attempted Coups is the proportion of government expenditures allocated to the defense establishment. Although this variable is treated as exogenous, it is undoubtedly influenced, like current Coups, by past military interventions. That is, we expect a military which has intervened in the recent past to have secured for itself a substantial share of the government budget. Hence, if the model was elaborated so that Defense Expenditures became endogenous, lagged Coups would surely appear in its equation. The point to be made here, however, is that *where Defense Expenditures are high (for whatever reasons), the military has a good deal at stake in domestic politics and as a result is more likely to play a "praetorian" or interventionist political role—if only to protect its privileged budgetary status. Moreover, in nations where the military's share of governmental resources is large relative to that of civilian agencies, the organizational capacity of the military for domestic political involvement is likely to be correspondingly great.*[30] It is not surprising, therefore, that Defense Expenditures has a positive coefficient (+.218) in a causal path to Coups. Figure 9.11 extracts from the complete model in Figure 9.3 the indirect, positive effects of Defense Expenditures and lagged Coups on each dimension of violence.

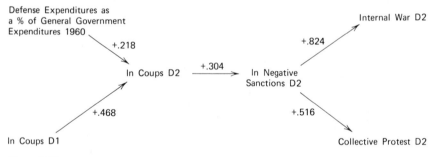

**Figure 9.11.**

Several predetermined endogenous variables that have not yet been discussed exert a more direct causal impact on Collective Protest and Internal War. The only remaining variable that directly influences Internal War is ln Political Separatism, which has a path coefficient of +.163. *It is not unexpected that Political Separatism, a phenomenon which poses a sharp challenge to the integrity of the nation itself, results in Internal War.* More revealing is the recursive causal sequence that generates Separatism and, indirectly, Internal War. It is one that was explored in some detail

[20] Previous interventions also increase the military's capabilities in the domestic politics sphere.

in Chapter 5. The most distinctive feature of the process underlying cross-national differences in Separatism is the powerful positive impact of the Social Mobilization–Ethnolinguistic Fractionalization multiplicative interaction. It eclipses entirely the significant bivariate relationship of Fractionalization and Separatism. The large path coefficient for this inter-action ($+.456$) clearly supports the proposition that *the conjunction of a socially mobilized and culturally differentiated population has severe consequences for national unity and domestic stability.* The importance of the mobilization–differentiation interaction effect is even more sharply illustrated by the finding that Mobilization alone *decreases* Separatism. This is demonstrated by the path coefficient of $-.378$ for the "main effect" of Mobilization on Separatism (Figure 9.3).

The Postwar Independence dummy variable also appears in the ln Political Separatism equation and, as hypothesized, has a positive parameter ($+.206$). This result indicates that *recently independent ex-colonies, whose national boundaries often were determined by European imperialists without regard for ethnolinguistic or cultural composition, have higher separatism than one would otherwise anticipate.*

Ethnolinguistic Fractionalization, or cultural differentiation, is also endogenous to the model; therefore, variables that appear in its equation provide what might be called "third-removed" causal influences on political violence. One of these is the Postwar Independence dummy variable, which has a path coefficient of $+.367$ in the Differentiation equation in addition to its positive parameter in the Separatism equation. The high cultural differentiation characteristic of the ex-colonial, "new" nations is a con-sequence of the imperial practice of arbitrarily establishing colonial areas, referred to above. What this suggests is that the *legacy of European imperial-ism has indirectly promoted Internal War through its effect on differentiation as well as through its impact on subsequent separatism.*

Another factor in the equation for Cultural Differentiation is ln Social Mobilization. Its relatively large negative path coefficient of $-.336$ implies that the modal cross-national pattern is for differentiated subgroups to become assimilated when mobilized into national life. This highlights the contrasting additive and interactive effects of the Social Mobilization variable. Additively, mobilization tends to diminish cultural differentiation and political separatism, and hence indirectly decrease the level of Internal War. Its interactive impact, however, is to promote violence, since it is precisely the nations that remain highly differentiated in spite of high mobilization that are most likely to have large separatist movements and, as a result, experience Internal War. The system of structural equations does not account for these important deviations from the modal pattern.

Although this surely is a topic that merits further investigation, it cannot readily be handled well with cross-national, aggregate data.

The remaining predetermined and exogenous influences in the model operate on Collective Protest. One of these, Group Discrimination, has a path coefficient of +.190 in the equation for Protest and is itself endogenous to the model and generated by the extent of Cultural Differentiation. Thus, whereas Separatism mediates the impact of Cultural Differentiation on Internal War, the evidence indicates that Group Discrimination mediates its effect on Collective Protest. This result is consistent with the theoretical discussion in Chapter 5. It supports the argument that *the consequence of discrimination, at least initially, is a "within the system" one of Protest. But although discrimination does not directly lead to the fundamentally "antisystem" response of Internal War, it clearly may escalate to this if the Protest which it does elicit is met with repression by political elites.*[21] This observation follows in a straightforward manner from our previous conclusion about the causal sequence linking Collective Protest to Internal War (Figure 9.5).

The last remaining predetermined influence on Protest is the (ln transformed) size of Communist Party Membership. Figure 9.3 indicates that this variable has a modest but positive path coefficient of +.169. *The finding that Communist parties promote Protest activity is not unanticipated. It squares with our observation in Chapter 7 that Communist parties are typically in the forefront of movements that militantly press working class demands.* What is more striking is that the size of such parties bears no systemic relationship to the incidence of Internal War. This suggests that *although large Communist parties may advocate revolutionary change, they nevertheless do not consistently engage in activities that seriously and directly threaten the structure of the existing political system.* This probably reflects the "parliamentary mentality" that characterizes, with some significant exceptions, large, mass-based parties on the radical left.

A number of exogenous variables indirectly influence the magnitude of Protest through their effects on Communist membership. For example, (ln) Social Mobilization has a positive impact (+.373) on Communist Party size and thereby indirectly increases Protest. This is yet another illustration of the contrasting effects of the Mobilization process. It was established earlier that Mobilization indirectly diminishes levels of violence by decreasing Cultural Differentiation and Political Separatism, although the same variable promotes violence through its interactive effects on Separatism and Repression. Here it is evident that *social mobilization*

---

[21] If we had systematic data on nonrepressive government responses to discrimination as well as separatism, the relationships could be much more precisely specified and the dynamic interpretations would be more than merely suggestive.

*increases Protest by facilitating Communist politicization and recruitment.* These contrasting effects, which we have been able to carefully specify on the basis of the empirical results, probably underlie the incongruities in the qualitative literature dealing with the consequences of mobilization, urbanization, and the like for domestic violence. Figure 9.12 illustrates the diverse, indirect linkages of mobilization to mass violence.

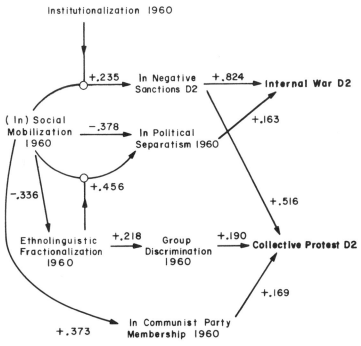

**Figure 9.12.**

Economic development also has differing indirect effects on levels of violence. We argued previously that by contributing to institutionalization and democratization, economic development diminished the severity of violence in a "second-removed" way. But the results here indicate that *economic development, which is measured by GNP per capita, bears a curvilinear relationship to Communist Party Membership.* That is, Communist party strength typically increases with advances in economic development but drops off at the highest levels.[22] Since Communist Membership has a

---

[22] We feel less confident of this inference than we do of all the others that have been made from the cross-sectional data base. The impact of technological change and economic development on mass support for the radical left clearly needs to be studied from a time-series perspective.

linear and positive causal influence on Protest, economic development indirectly produces greater Protest except at the higher levels, where its impact is to diminish this type of political violence. The contrasting effects of economic development on mass political violence are delineated in Figure 9.13.

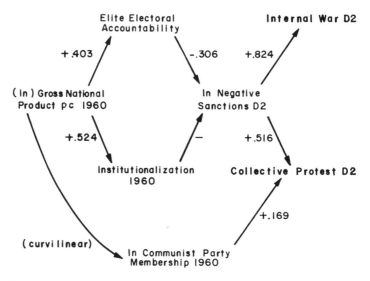

**Figure 9.13.**

## Conclusion

This concludes the evaluation of the structural equation causal model of mass political violence. In the process of analyzing the estimation results, we have pointed out which variables directly and indirectly influence the magnitude of each dimension of violence, in what contexts some variables exert contrasting causal effects, and where significant interactions are operative; we have also explored the most important feedback processes implicit in the model's structure. How well does the model perform? In many ways the answer to this question awaits future research and validation efforts—a point we take up briefly in the final chapter.

As things stand, we can further evaluate the final model from two perspectives. First, and most important, is the model *theoretically* sound? Great parts of the study have been devoted to arguing that it is. Throughout we have tried to avoid "rank empiricism" and thus have explored only relationships that had a solid theoretical foundation. The reader may judge for himself how successful we have been in incrementally developing a well-grounded causal structure.

Second, how well does the final model *fit the data* in the sample of available observations? Although most of the equations in the model have very respectable $R^2$'s, a few manifest very poor fits to the observed data. We are particularly dissatisfied with the $R^2$'s of the Group Discrimination and Elite Electoral Accountability equations. However, all the equations of central importance—those in the simultaneously interdependent $Y_m$ sector—display quite adequate fits.[23] Let us focus in particular on the most important simultaneously determined variables in the model: Collective Protest and Internal War. Examination of the residuals—the errors in prediction—for each of these variables can expose major flaws in the model.

The residuals, along with the actual and fitted values of Collective Protest and Internal War, appear in Tables A5.1 and A5.2. A careful analysis of these residuals uncovered no systematic patterns. The prediction errors are normally distributed about mean zero and are randomly arrayed around the fitted values of Collective Protest and Internal War, as well as across regions, development levels, and types of political systems. Hence the residuals appear to disclose nothing that invalidates the structure of the model or the assumptions of the analysis.[24] Of course it is possible to cite particular reasons for especially large positive or negative residuals for individual nations. The point to be emphasized, however, is that no pattern in the errors seems to emerge. This is not to say that we have incorporated everything we would have liked in the model, or that the variables we have included are without defects, or indeed that alternative research strategies might not prove superior. The model is hardly definitive.

The limitations as well as the strengths of the investigation are pursued more fully in the next and final chapter.

---

[23] Recall, however, that our principal objective in estimation was to obtain sharp and consistent parameter estimates and not to maximize $R^2$'s.

[24] Excellent treatments of residual analysis procedures are provided by N. R. Draper and H. Smith, *Applied Regression Analysis* (New York: John Wiley & Sons, Inc., 1966), Chapter 3; and F. Anscombe and J. Tukey, "The Examination and Analysis of Residuals," *Technometrics*, Vol. 5, 1963, pp. 141–160.

# CHAPTER TEN

# Problems and Prospects

In this final chapter we confront some of the principal problems with the model of mass political violence and briefly outline what seem to be the most productive lines for future research. The discussion centers around the issues of specification error, aggregation of data, and cross-sectional causal analysis.

## Specification Error

Misspecification of the structural equations of a causal model arises from a number of sources. Perhaps the most important is the omission of significant causal influences. Although we investigated as many potential causes of mass violence as the available data allowed, some important variables have undoubtedly been omitted from the causal system. In the previous chapter it was noted that the structural equations for Elite Electoral Accountability and Group Discrimination are particularly unsatisfactory. There certainly are significant causal influences that have been left out of these equations. But such variables would exert only indirect effects on political violence and so they are not crucial for this study. However, there is a class of variables that most likely does exert substantial direct effects on domestic violence. These omitted influences concern various aspects of inequality.

We would anticipate intuitively that the degree of inequality in the distribution of socioeconomic resources bears an important causal relation to mass political violence. Indeed, a considerable amount of evidence from the sizeable qualitative literature on the topic, as well as from the smaller number of quantitative studies, indicates this to be the case, although it is by no means clear that the linkages between mass violence and various kinds of inequality are linear or additive.[1] We did not evaluate the causal role of inequality because hard data on the distribution of land, income, or wealth are simply not available for a very large number of nations.[2] A useful future research effort would be to replicate this study for the relatively small number of nations for which some inequality data are available and to ascertain how much the model developed here is altered by incorporating inequality into the causal structure. Our results would be seriously modified only if inequality turned out to be strongly related to variables which we have already concluded exert a substantial direct causal impact on violence. This is a possibility, and its implications cannot be ignored. Previous quantitative research suggests that land and income inequality are causally influenced by the level of economic development (curvilinearly), and by democratization—to the extent that democratic regimes in fact promote the redistribution of social resources.[3] Economic development poses no difficulty because it has relatively low status in the causal hierarchy and its effects on violence are quite removed. More problematic are variables such as democratization (Elite Electoral Accountability), the size of Communist Parties, and perhaps even Communist Regime type. For example, democratization may have an indirect influence on mass violence by diminishing inequality, in addition to the impact it has by decreasing Elite Repression. Similarly, the size of Communist Party

---

[1] For the quantitative evidence, see Edward D. Mitchell, "Inequality and Insurgency: A Statistical Study of South Vietnam," *World Politics*, Vol. 20, April 1968, pp. 421–438; *idem.*, "Some Econometrics of the Huk Rebellion," *American Political Science Review*, Vol. 68, December 1969, pp. 1159–1171; Jeffrey M. Paige, "Inequality and Insurgency in Vietnam: A Re-analysis," *World Politics*, Vol. 23, October 1970, pp. 24–37; Bruce M. Russett, "Inequality and Instability: The Relation of Land Tenure to Politics," *World Politics*, Vol. 16, April 1964, pp. 442–438; Anthony J. Russo, Jr., "Economic and Social Correlates of Government Control in South Vietnam," in Ivo K. Feierabend et al. (eds.), *Anger, Violence and Politics: Theories and Research* (Englewood Cliffs, N.J.: Prentice-Hall Inc., 1972); and Raymond Tanter and Manus Midlarsky, "A Theory of Revolution," *Journal of Conflict Resolution*, Vol. 11, September 1967, pp. 264–280. Suggestive qualitative studies include Charles Tilly, *The Vendée* (Cambridge, Mass.: M.I.T. Press, 1964); Barrington Moore, Jr., *Social Origins of Dictatorship and Democracy: Lord and Peasant in the Making of the Modern World* (Boston: Beacon Press, 1966); and Eric R. Wolf, *Peasant Wars of the Twentieth Century* (New York: Harper & Row, 1969).
[2] Crude data on land and income distributions exist for no more than 50 nations. There is even less cross-national data on the distribution of other components of wealth (capital assets, etc.).
[3] See Phillips Cutright, "Inequality: A Cross-National Analysis," *American Sociological Review*, Vol. 32, No. 4, August 1967, pp. 562–578; Simon Kuznets, "Economic Growth and Income Inequality," *American Economic Review*, Vol. 45, No. 1, March 1955, pp. 1–28; *idem.*, *Modern Economic Growth* (New Haven: Yale University Press, 1966); and Gerhard Lenski, *Power and Privilege; A Theory of Social Stratification* (New York: McGraw-Hill Book Company, Inc., 1966).

Membership or the strength of the non-Communist Left may exert enough "left pressure" on the political system to produce policies that diminish inequality and thus violence. Or, the negative impact of Communist Regime type which has been attributed to the police-state, totalitarian character of Communist systems may in part reflect the more equalitarian income and wealth structure of such nations. None of these possibilities was explored in this study.

Another class of omitted variables that certainly has causal significance involves the extent to which nations suffer political penetration and economic exploitation by imperialist or "neocolonialist" powers. Rebellion and protest against foreign economic and political influence or control, although relatively infrequent, provide some of the most dramatic examples of domestic violence. Variables that accurately appraise foreign economic ownership and political manipulation have yet to be developed. This surely should have high priority in future investigations of mass political violence.

Violence itself may produce a diminution of foreign influence or compel elite concessions that decrease inequality and thus future violence. This would imply a lagged reciprocity with negative feedback between these variables. The whole question of the long-run consequences of violence remains to be systematically studied. Considerable work on indicator development and theoretical specification must be undertaken before these possibilities can be rigorously evaluated. It is not improbable, however, that if the relevant data were available, inequality and foreign penetration would turn out to be the core variables of additional sectors in our model and hence would elaborate on, but not fundamentally alter, the model's structure.

Another potential source of specification error is the method by which inferences were made throughout the model-building process. Although we analyzed only relationships that had a sound theoretical foundation, the choice of functional forms for the variables involved was determined by goodness of fits and significance of parameters, rather than by the theoretical implications of the various alternatives. The reason is, of course, that the qualitative theoretical work typically provides barely enough information about which variables should appear in which equations and, aside from occasionally suggesting interaction effects, usually specifies nothing further about functional form. It is possible, however, that the correct formulation is not the one that maximizes least-squares regression fits in a particular sample. Hence, one or more of the equations may suffer from specification error.

Moreover, since our research strategy was to incrementally develop a multiequation model by the exploratory analysis of single equation hypotheses and partial theories, it is possible that such specification errors are cumulative. This stems from the multicollinearity among independent variables that is present in our data and, indeed, plagues virtually all non-experimental research. For when variables are moderately to highly correlated, as they are here, then incorrect decisions made in the early stages of analysis (Part II) can critically influence what functional forms are inferred to be valid in the final stages (Part III). However, since we were unwilling to rely exclusively on any previous theory of mass political violence in developing the structural equation model, some specification error from this source is unavoidable.[4] Yet, it may be minimized if we undertake a theoretically constrained (if not completely defined) method of analysis that is geared to the determination of causal relations. And this is precisely how we have tried to conduct the investigation.

## Aggregation of Data

The aggregation issue is not a problem in the sense that specification error is, as long as it is realized that the research results derive from an aggregate data base and hence causal inferences are most securely made at the macro level of analysis. The "ecological fallacy" issue, which in the present context pertains to the validity of making inferences about relationships between subnational units (provinces, social strata, individuals) on the basis of data on national aggregates, is not germane for large parts of the model because Institutionalization, Democratization, rates of Economic Change and the like are intrinsically macro-level phenomena.[5] This is not entirely true, however, for variables such as Social Mobilization, Cultural Differentiation, Political Separatism, and Group Discrimination. Here we are inclined to draw conclusions about the behavior of groups of mobilized, differentiated, separatist, or discriminated-against individuals— as indeed we have done at various points in the book. Whether we have erred in so doing depends on how well the structural equations have been specified, and on how the data have been grouped with respect to the

---

[4] For a good discussion of this problem see Arthur S. Goldberger, *Topics in Regression Analysis* (New York: The Macmillan Co., 1968), Chapter 9, and Potluri Rao and Roger L. Miller, *Applied Econometrics* (Belmont, Calif: Wadsworth Publishing Co., 1971).

[5] Treatments of the "ecological fallacy" issue include: Otis D. Duncan et al., *Statistical Geography* (New York: The Free Press, 1961); Hubert M. Blalock, *Causal Inferences in Non-experimental Research* (Chapel Hill: University of North Carolina Press, 1964), pp. 95–114; and Hayward R. Alker, Jr., "A Typology of Ecological Fallacies," in Mattei Dogan and Stein Rokkan (eds.), *Quantitative Ecological Analysis in the Social Sciences* (Cambridge, Mass.: M.I.T. Press, 1969), pp. 69–86. A comprehensive review of the aggregation literature generally is provided by Michael T. Hannan, *Aggregation and Disaggregation in Sociology* (Lexington, Mass.: D.C. Heath and Co., 1971).

variables in question. In the case of cross-national aggregate data, the grouping is obviously by subnational units situated within national boundaries. If the consequence of this is to aggregate or group the data primarily according to the values of independent variables, it is not unreasonable to assume that regression coefficients, but not correlations, hold for subnational units. If, on the other hand, using national aggregates means that data are grouped principally by the values of dependent variables, then both regression and correlation coefficients will typically be larger in the aggregated analyses than they would be in analogous regressions with disaggregated data.[6] It is likely that nation-level aggregation results in data being grouped primarily by such independent variables as discrimination, separatism, and mobilization, and only derivatively by the core dependent variables—Collective Protest and Internal War. If this assumption is well-founded, the cross-national, aggregate causal inferences can properly be extended to subnational strata. Moreover, aggregation bias is known to be minimized when the structural equations are specified without great error.[7]

## Cross-Sectional Analysis

The final problem to be discussed concerns the use of cross-sectional data throughout the study. Although we have relied heavily on such data, the investigation has not been entirely "static." In the case of the core endogenous variables—Mass Violence, Elite Repression, and Coups—two time points were employed to incorporate into the model the lagged effects that prior theory indicated were operative. This helps preserve the dynamic

---

[6] These results were first derived from experimental trials with real data by Blalock, *Causal Inferences*, pp. 95–114. An exposition of the mathematics underlying Blalock's empirical results for both independent and dependent variables in the bivariate linear regression model is provided in Douglas A. Hibbs, Jr., "Ecological Fallacy: Grouping Observations in Regression Analysis," unpublished ms., M.I.T., 1971. Also see W. P. Shively, "Ecological Inference: The Use of Aggregate data to Study Individuals," *American Political Science Review*, Vol. 63, December 1969, pp. 1183–1196; S. J. Prais and J. Aitchison, "The Grouping of Observations in Regression Analysis," *Review of the International Statistical Institute*, 1954, pp. 1–22, and J. S. Cramer, "Efficient Grouping, Regression and Correlation in Engel Curve Analysis," *Journal of the American Statistical Association*, 1964, pp. 233–250. Note, however, that the results summarized in the text are known to hold exactly only for the bivariate regression case. Precise analytical results for the magnitude of aggregation bias in multivariate, cross-sectional models remain to be derived.

[7] See Eric A. Hanushek et al., "Model Specification, Use of Aggregate Data, and the Ecological Correlation Fallacy," unpublished Discussion Paper, Harvard Program on Quantitative Analysis in Political Science, January 1972.

validity of the parameter estimates.[8] Moreover, for urbanization and economic development, where the literature suggested that rates of change were important, the available data afforded an analysis of the impact of five- and ten-year growth rates. And, all the remaining variables except one (Internal Security Forces) had a 1960 time point which for the most part lags them vis à vis the simultaneously determined endogenous variables whose aggregation period is 1958 to 1967. This insures that exogenous and predetermined endogenous variables have prior temporal status in the model, which is essential for (nonsimultaneous) causal arguments.

Nevertheless, the investigation is fundamentally based on cross-sectional data from which we seek to make dynamic causal inferences. That is, we are not only interested in ascertaining relationships at one point (cross-section) in time but we also hope that the model has valid dynamic implications. What conditions are necessary for the results to apply to successive cross-sections? Coleman put it well:

"The cross-section analysis assumes, either implicitly or explicitly, that causal processes have resulted in an equilibrium state. That is, the implicit assumption in regression analysis is that this is a stable relationship, which would give the same values for the regression coefficients in a later cross-section unless an exogenous factor disturbed the situation."[9]

The only way to establish whether the assumption of aggregate equilibrium holds is to re-estimate the model with successive cross-sections and/or with long time series for a (preferably) heterogeneous group of nations. Validation of the model requires that these replications produce approximately the same parameter estimates and causal inferences as those reported here.

There is no reason, however, to be apologetic about having used cross-sectional data in this research. In many ways cross-section-based models are superior to those estimated against time-series data, since typical time series, especially those available to social scientists, are of relatively short duration. Short-duration time series simply cannot pick up the effects of such variables as regime type, levels of institutionalization, cultural differentiation, and democratization. These variables, which have important effects on levels of mass political violence, do not change much in the short run; and without variance, estimation precision and causal inference are not feasible. This is why careful studies of the utility of cross-sectional versus time-series analysis in economics indicate that " . . . cross-section

[8] See Dennis J. Aigner and Julian L. Simon, "A Specification Bias Interpretation of Cross-Section Vs. Time Series Parameter Estimates," *Western Economic Journal*, Vol. 8, No. 2, June 1970, pp. 144–161.
[9] James S. Coleman, "The Mathematical Study of Change," in H. M. Blalock and A. B. Blalock (eds.), *Methodology in Social Research* (New York: McGraw-Hill Book Company, Inc., 1968), p. 444.

data tend to measure long run and other effects that are not observable, for a number of reasons, in short period . . . time series variations . . . ."[10] And " . . . cross-sections typically will reflect long run adjustments whereas annual time series will tend to reflect shorter run reaction."[11] Since the principal purpose of this study, like that of most comparative research efforts in political science, has been to detect long run or developmental processes, it is precisely on "long run effects and adjustments" that our interest centers. Therefore, until data on the important variables in the model become available for long-duration time series which will make possible the dynamic analysis of long-run processes and effects, the cross-sectional approach we have employed, which includes lagged effects and rates of change, is perhaps the best way to have proceeded.

[10] Edwin Kuh and John R. Meyer, "How Extraneous are Extraneous Estimates," *The Review of Economics and Statistics*, Vol. 39, 1957, p. 381.

[11] Edwin Kuh, "The Validity of Cross-Sectionally Estimated Behavior Equations in Time Series Applications," *Econometrica*, Vol. 27, 1959, pp. 207–208.

APPENDIX ONE

# Nations in the Cross-National Sample

Table A1.1   Nations in the Cross-National Sample ($N = 108$)

| | | | |
|---|---|---|---|
| Afghanistan | El Salvador | Laos | Senegal |
| Albania | Ethiopia | Lebanon | Sierra Leone |
| Algeria | Finland | Liberia | Singapore |
| Argentina | France | Libya | Somalia |
| Australia | Germany, East | Madagascar | South Africa |
| Austria | Germany, West | Malawi | Spain |
| Belgium | Ghana | Malaysia | Sudan |
| Bolivia | Greece | Mali | Sweden |
| Brazil | Guatemala | Mexico | Switzerland |
| Bulgaria | Guinea | Morocco | Syria |
| Burma | Haiti | Netherlands | Taiwan |
| Cambodia | Honduras | New Zealand | Tanzania |
| Cameroon | Hong Kong | Nicaragua | Thailand |
| Canada | Hungary | Niger | Togoland |
| Central African Rep. | India | Nigeria | Tunisia |
| Ceylon | Indonesia | Norway | Turkey |
| Chad | Iran | Pakistan | Uganda |
| Chile | Iraq | Panama | United Arab Republic (Egypt) |
| Colombia | Ireland | Paraguay | USSR |
| Congo, Leopoldville | Israel | Peru | United Kingdom |
| Costa Rica | Italy | Philippines | United States |
| Cuba | Ivory Coast | Poland | Upper Volta |
| Czechoslovakia | Jamaica | Portugal | Uruguay |
| Dahomey | Japan | Puerto Rico | Venezuela |
| Denmark | Jordan | Rhodesia | Viet Nam, South |
| Dominican Republic | Kenya | Rumania | Yugoslavia |
| Ecuador | Korea, South | Saudi Arabia | Zambia |

203

APPENDIX TWO

# Variables in the Multiequation Model

Table A2    Variables in the Multiequation Model

| Variable Name | Denotation | Chapter First Introduced |
|---|---|---|
| Collective Protest D2 | $Y_1$ | 2 |
| Internal War D2 | $Y_2$ | 2 |
| ln Negative Sanctions D2 | $Y_3$ | 6 |
| ln Coups D2 | $Y_4$ | 6 |
| Average Annual % Change in Energy Consumption per capita 1955 to 1965 | $Y_5$ | 3 |
| Average Annual % Change in Gross National Product per capita 1955 to 1965 | $Y_6$ | 3 |
| Collective Protest D1 | $Y_1^*$ | 2 |
| Internal War D1 | $Y_2^*$ | 2 |
| ln Negative Sanctions D1 | $Y_3^*$ | 6 |
| ln Coups D1 | $Y_4^*$ | 6 |
| Group Discrimination 1960 | $X_1$ | 5 |
| ln Political Separatism 1960 | $X_2$ | 5 |
| Ethnolinguistic Fractionalization 1960 | $X_3$ | 5 |
| ln Communist Party Membership 1960 | $X_4$ | 7 |
| % Legislative Seats Held by the Non-Communist Left 1960 | $X_5$ | 7 |
| Elite Electoral Accountability | $X_6$ | 6 |
| ln Nondefense General Government Expenditures as a % of the Gross Domestic Product 1960 | $X_7$ | 4 |
| Social Welfare 1960 | $X_8$ | 4 |

## Table A2    Variables in the Multiequation Model (continued)

| Variable Name | Denotation | Chapter First Introduced |
|---|---|---|
| ln Social Welfare 1960 | $X_8^*$ | 4 |
| Institutionalization 1960 | $X_9$ | 6 |
| ln Institutionalization 1960 | $X_9^*$ | 6 |
| Average Annual % Change in Population 1955 to 1965 | $X_{10}$ | 3 |
| ln Population 1960 | $Z_1$ | 3 |
| Social Mobilization 1960 | $Z_2$ | 4 |
| ln Social Mobilization 1960 | $Z_2^*$ | 4 |
| Communist Regime Dummy | $Z_3$ | 7 |
| Communist Party Legal Status Dummy | $Z_4$ | 8 |
| Postwar Independence Dummy | $Z_5$ | 5 |
| ln Energy Consumption per capita 1960 | $Z_6$ | 3 |
| (ln Energy Consumption per capita 1960)$^2$ | $Z_6^*$ | 3 |
| ln GNP per capita 1960 | $Z_7$ | 3 |
| Gross Fixed Domestic Capital Formation as a % of GNP 1960 | $Z_8$ | 8 |
| ln Internal Security Forces per 1000 sq km 1965 | $Z_9$ | 6 |
| Defense Expenditures as a % of General Government Expenditures 1960 | $Z_{10}$ | 6 |
| Social Mobilization 1960/Institutionalization 1960 | $Z_{11}$ | 6 |
| Social Mobilization 1960/Social Welfare 1960 | $Z_{12}$ | 4 |
| Ethnolinguistic Fractionalization 1960* Social Mobilization 1960 | $Z_{13}$ | 5 |
| Population in Cities of 100,000 or More Residents per 1000 Population 1965 | $Z_{14}$ | 4 |

# Estimation and Identification of
# Multiequation Causal Models

In this appendix we develop the procedures by which the structural equations of the multiequation model may be consistently estimated. Structural estimation is not possible, however, unless sufficient a priori information is either implied by the model itself or assumed by the theorist concerning the equations to be estimated. This brings us to a discussion in the latter part of the appendix of what is known as the "identification problem." The material that follows is thus essential for understanding what is required for consistent estimation of both the simultaneous and recursive causal relations in the (block recursive) multiequation model of mass political violence.[1]

## Consistency and Ordinary Least Squares

Let us define precisely what is meant by a "consistent" estimator: $\hat{\beta}$ is a consistent estimator of the true parameter $\beta$, if[2]

$$\text{plim } \hat{\beta} = \beta$$

[1] The topics surveyed in this appendix are treated at varying levels of sophistication and completeness in the following sources: Carl F. Christ, *Econometric Models and Methods* (New York: John Wiley & Sons, Inc., 1966); Franklin M. Fisher, *The Identification Problem in Econometrics* (New York: McGraw-Hill Book Co., Inc., 1966); Arthur S. Goldberger, *Econometric Theory* (New York: John Wiley & Sons, Inc., 1964); John J. Johnston, *Econometric Methods*, 2nd edition (New York: McGraw-Hill Book Co., Inc., 1972); E. Malinvaud, *Statistical Methods of Econometrics* (Chicago: Rand McNally & Co., 1966); Henri Theil, *Principles of Econometrics* (New York: John Wiley & Sons, Inc., 1971); and R. J. Wonnacott and T. H. Wonnacott, *Econometrics* (New York: John Wiley & Sons, Inc., 1970).

Consistency is, then, a minimum criterion, since an inconsistent estimator would not converge to the true parameter even if an infinite number of empirical observations were available to the researcher.

Ordinary Least Squares (OLS) produces inconsistent estimates when independent or right-hand side variables are correlated with the disturbances of the model. This is the crux of the simultaneous equations estimation problem, but it is no less troublesome in single equation models or multiequation, recursive models. The point is most easily illustrated in the single equation case. Consider a linear regression model of the form

$$(A3.1) \qquad Y_i = \alpha + \beta X_i + \varepsilon_i$$

Without loss of generality, $Y$ and $X$ may be deviated from their respective means to create $x_i$ and $y_i$. Equation A3.1 may then be expressed as

$$(A3.2) \qquad y_i = \beta x_i + \varepsilon_i$$

Ordinary Least Squares uses the independent variable $x$ as its own "instrument"; multiplying (A3.2) through by $x$ and taking covariances yields[3]

$$(A3.3) \qquad m_{xy} = \beta m_{xx} + m_{x\varepsilon}$$

In order to estimate $\beta$, divide (A3.3) through by $m_{xx}$. This produces

$$(A3.4) \qquad \frac{m_{xy}}{m_{xx}} = \beta + \frac{m_{x\varepsilon}}{m_{xx}}$$

Recall that the left-hand side of (A3.4), $m_{xy}/m_{xx}$, is the conventional OLS estimator of $\beta$. If in the probability limit the covariance of $x$ and $\varepsilon$ is zero or at least small enough to ignore, then the OLS estimator of $\beta$, which is denoted as $\hat{\beta}$, will consistently estimate the true parameter. That is:

$$(A3.5) \qquad \text{if} \quad \text{plim}\, m_{x\varepsilon} = 0 \quad \text{then} \quad \text{plim}\, \frac{m_{xy}}{m_{xx}} = \hat{\beta} = \beta$$

If plim $m_{x\varepsilon}$ is not zero or nearly so, then $\hat{\beta}$ estimates not $\beta$, but

---

[2] "plim" denotes "in the probability limit." An alternative formulation of consistency is "consistency in mean-square":

$$E(\hat{\beta} - \beta)^2 \to 0 \quad \text{as} \quad N \to \infty$$

Hence a consistent estimator is one whose bias and variance converge to zero as sample size becomes infinite. Thus it provides a perfect point estimate of the target parameter in the probability limit.

[3] Here $m$ designates the "moment of." Note that $m_{xy}$ equals the covariance of $X$ and $Y$. Similarly, $m_{xx}$ equals the variance of $X$, and so on.

(A3.6)                          $$\beta + \frac{m_{x\varepsilon}}{m_{xx}}$$

And this is true regardless of how many observations are used in the calculations.

In Chapters 3 through 7 we emphasized the tentativeness of the regression results, since particular independent variables $X_i$ were considered in isolation from other $X_i$ that also causally influenced the dimensions of mass political violence ($Y_i$). Hence the omitted $X_i$ would appear in the disturbance terms ($\varepsilon_i$). To the extent that these omitted $X_i$ were correlated with the independent variable(s) being analyzed in a particular equation (included $X_i$), $m_{x\varepsilon}$ would not equal zero, and thus the OLS estimate(s) $\hat{\beta}_k$ would be inconsistent. However, the single equation results in those chapters did provide the information necessary to reject some hypotheses, provisionally retain others, and reformulate others as partial, multiequation causal systems. We noted that consistent estimates, or more nearly consistent estimates, could then be obtained by examining a fully specified model of mass violence; that is, one incorporating all the tentatively established causal influences.

## Instrumental Variables

Now let us consider the inconsistency problem in (A3.2) from another perspective which will prove useful in dealing with the simultaneous equations estimation problem. If $m_{x\varepsilon} \neq 0$, a solution for estimation inconsistency in models such as (A3.2) is to find an *instrumental variable*, $Z$, such that[4]

    1. $z$ and $\varepsilon$ are uncorrelated, or nearly so; that is
$$\text{plim } m_{z\varepsilon} = 0$$

and

    2. $z$ and $x$ are correlated, preferably highly; so that
$$\text{plim } m_{zx} \neq 0$$

The instrumental variable $Z$ can then be used to consistently estimate the true parameter $\beta$ by least-squares regression. Multiplying (A3.2) through by $z$ and taking covariances yields

(A3.7)                     $$m_{zy} = \beta m_{zx} + m_{z\varepsilon}$$

Dividing through by $m_{zx}$ gives

---

[4] In the following, $z$ denotes $Z$ deviated from its mean, as $x$ and $y$ denote $X$ and $Y$ deviated from their respective means.

(A3.8)
$$\frac{m_{zy}}{m_{zx}} = \beta + \frac{m_{z\varepsilon}}{m_{zx}}$$

Since plim $m_{z\varepsilon} = 0$, a consistent estimate of $\beta$ is now obtained:[5]

(A3.9)
$$\text{plim}\,\frac{m_{zy}}{m_{zx}} = \hat{\beta} = \beta$$

The argument is easily generalized using matrix notation to the multivariate case. Consider the multivariate linear regression model

(A3.10)
$$Y = X\mathbf{B} + \mathbf{E}$$

where $Y$ is an $N \times 1$ vector of observations on the dependent or left-hand side variable;

$X$ is an $N \times K$ matrix of observations on independent or right-hand side variables;

$\mathbf{B}$ is the $K \times 1$ vector of parameters to be estimated;

$\mathbf{E}$ is the $N \times 1$ vector of disturbances in the model;

all variables are mean deviates;

If plim $(X'\mathbf{E}/N) \neq 0$, then the conventional OLS estimator of $\mathbf{B}, \hat{\mathbf{B}} = (X'X)^{-1}X'Y$, renders inconsistent estimates. However, consistent estimation is possible if there are sufficient instrumental variables $Z$ that satisfy the

$$\text{plim}\left(\frac{Z'\mathbf{E}}{N}\right) = 0 \quad \text{and} \quad \text{plim}\left(\frac{Z'X}{N}\right) \neq 0$$

where vectors in $Z$ and $X$ are linearly independent.

To secure consistent estimates of the elements in $\mathbf{B}$ we proceed as before applying all instruments to (A3.10) by premultiplying by $Z'$:

(A3.11)
$$Z'Y = (Z'X)\mathbf{B} + Z'\mathbf{E}$$

Since plim $\left(\dfrac{Z'\mathbf{E}}{N}\right) = 0$, least-squares estimation of (A3.11) produces the consistent estimator $\hat{\mathbf{B}}$. Hence, premultiplying (A3.11) by $(Z'X)^{-1}$ yields

(A3.12)
$$(Z'X)^{-1}Z'Y = \hat{\mathbf{B}} = \mathbf{B}$$

---

[5] The *efficiency* of this consistent estimator of $\beta$, depends on how highly correlated $Z$ and $X$ are in the sample. An efficient estimator is one that has small variance and therefore concentrates on the target parameter. "The" efficient estimator is the one with the smallest variance of all the acceptable estimators. Hence an instrumental variables estimation procedure may yield consistent estimates that are very inefficient; that is, the estimate obtained is on target in the probability limit but is quite sloppy in a particular sample. On the other hand, $Z$ and $X$ cannot be too highly correlated, since $m_{z\varepsilon}$ is not likely to be zero if they are.

## Simultaneous Equations and Instrumental Variables: Two Stage Least Squares

The solution for inconsistency developed thus far in the context of single equation models provides the basis for an analogous Instrumental Variables–Two Stage Least Squares (IV-2SLS) solution for the simultaneous equations estimation problem.[6] The nature of the problem in the simultaneous equations case is illustrated by the following two-equation system:

(A3.13)
$$y_1 = \alpha_1 \, y_2 + \sum \beta_k \, z_k + \varepsilon_1$$

(A3.14)
$$y_2 = \alpha_2 \, y_1 + \sum \beta_j \, z_j + \varepsilon_2$$

where $z_k$ and $z_j$ are predetermined or exogenous (instrumental) variables uncorrelated with the equation disturbances $\varepsilon_1$, $\varepsilon_2$; $z_k$, $z_j$ may have common terms;
all variables are mean deviates.

The jointly dependent or simultaneous relationship of the endogenous variables $y_1$ and $y_2$ means that these variables are correlated with the disturbances of each of the equations. For example, to see the nonzero covariance of $\varepsilon_1$ and the right-hand side endogenous variable in (A3.13), $y_2$, multiply the equation for $y_2$ through by $\varepsilon_1$ and take covariances. This produces

(A3.15)
$$m_{\varepsilon_1 y_2} = \alpha_2 \left( m_{\varepsilon_1 y_1} \right) + \sum \beta_j \left( m_{\varepsilon_1 z_j} \right) + m_{\varepsilon_1 \varepsilon_2}$$

---

[6] There are quite a number of estimation methods for simultaneous equations causal systems. We discuss and employ the leading Limited Information estimation procedure—2SLS. Its main advantages over Full Information procedures such as Three Stage Least Squares are (a) it is less sensitive to multicollinearity and (b) it does not spread specification error in a particular equation throughout the causal system. Simultaneous equations estimators are surveyed in some detail and the advantages of 2SLS elaborated in Franklin M. Fisher, "Dynamic Structure and Estimation in Economy-Wide Econometric Models," in J. Duesenberry et al., _The Brookings Quarterly Econometric Model of the United States_ (Chicago: Rand McNally & Co., 1965), pp. 588–635; and _idem._, "Simultaneous Equations Estimation: The State of the Art," Working paper, Department of Economics, M.I.T., July, 1970. We develop 2SLS from an Instrumental Variables perspective for heuristic reasons.

The exposition to follow is again framed in terms of consistency rather than bias. All simultaneous equations estimators—Ordinary Least Squares as well as its "consistent" alternatives—are biased in the sample. Indeed, in some small sample situations OLS estimation of simultaneous equations has much to recommend it. However, in samples as large as ours, two stage least squares is clearly superior.

Since $m_{\varepsilon_1 z_j} = 0$ by the assumption that the $z_j$ are predetermined or exogenous variables, (A3.15) reduces to

(A3.16) $\qquad m_{\varepsilon_1 y_2} = \alpha_2 (m_{\varepsilon_1 y_1}) + m_{\varepsilon_1 \varepsilon_2}$

The (nonzero) covariance of $\varepsilon_2$ and $y_1$ can be similarly derived. Multiplying the equation for $y_1$ through by $\varepsilon_2$ and taking covariances renders

(A3.17) $\qquad m_{\varepsilon_2 y_1} = \alpha_1 (m_{\varepsilon_2 y_2}) + \sum \beta_k (m_{\varepsilon_2 z_k}) + m_{\varepsilon_2 \varepsilon_1}$

Again, given the assumptions about the $z_k$, this becomes

(A3.18) $\qquad m_{\varepsilon_2 y_1} = \alpha_1 (m_{\varepsilon_2 y_2}) + m_{\varepsilon_2 \varepsilon_1}$

Clearly, $\varepsilon_1$ and $y_2$, and $\varepsilon_2$ and $y_1$ will be correlated unless $\alpha_1$ and/or $\alpha_2$ are zero, which would make plausible the assumption that $m_{\varepsilon_1 \varepsilon_2}$ is also zero or nearly so. However, if $\alpha_1$ or $\alpha_2$ or both are zero, the system is of course no longer simultaneous. As we demonstrated in the single equation example earlier, OLS regression will not yield consistent estimates for equations such as (A3.13) and (A3.14), where right-hand side variables are correlated with the disturbances.

The consistency problem in simultaneous systems is resolved in a way analogous to that employed in the previous single equation case by using an IV-2SLS estimation procedure. In the "first stage" the "systematic part" of the jointly determined $y_i$ are generated by regressing each of these variables on *all* the predetermined and exogenous $z_{kj}$ "instrumental" variables in the model. That is, we perform the regression

(A3.19) $\qquad y_i = \sum \lambda_{kj} z_{kj} + v_i$

where $z_{kj}$ denotes all the $z_k$, $z_j$ in (A3.13) and (A3.14)
$\lambda_{kj}$ are the coefficients of the instrumental variables; $z_k$, $z_j$
$v_i$ are the error terms in the first stage regressions

Hence the "systematic part" of each of the $y_i$, which is designated as $\hat{y}_i$, is

(A3.20) $\qquad \hat{y}_i = y_i - v_i = \sum \hat{\lambda}_{kj} z_{kj}$

In the "second stage" regressions the structural parameters of the original model are consistently estimated by replacing $y_1$ and $y_2$ in (A3.13) and (A3.14) with their "purified" counterparts $\hat{y}_1$ and $\hat{y}_2$. The second stage equations are:

second stage equations are:[7]

(A3.21)                    $$y_1 = \alpha_1 \hat{y}_2 + \sum \beta_k z_k + \omega_1$$

(A3.22)                    $$y_2 = \alpha_2 \hat{y}_1 + \sum \beta_j z_j + \omega_2$$

where                      $$\omega_i = \varepsilon_i + \sum \hat{\alpha}_i \hat{v}_i$$

Since all variables are now (asymptotically) uncorrelated with the composite disturbances $\omega_i$, the IV-2SLS procedure will produce consistent estimates of the structural parameters in the model. This is assured because the $z_k$ and $z_j$ are uncorrelated in the probability limit with the $\varepsilon_i$ by assumption and in the sample with the $v_i$ by construction. Because the $\hat{y}_i$ are generated from linear functions of the $z_{kj}$, they too are asymptotically uncorrelated with the composite disturbances $\omega_i$. Hence consistent estimates can now be secured.

Although the second stage regressions render the desired estimates of the structural parameters in the simultaneous system, they do not yield appropriate computations of residual variance, $R^2$'s, $t$ statistics, and so on. These are obtained by applying the consistent second stage parameter estimates to the original data and model. In the example at hand, this means that the second stage coefficient estimates $(\hat{\alpha}_1, \hat{\alpha}_2, \hat{\beta}_k, \hat{\beta}_j)$ are plugged into the original model—(A3.13) and (A3.14)—and then goodness of fit and significance statistics are calculated in the usual manner.

These results may readily be generalized to the case of an $M$-equation simultaneous system by using matrix notation. Consider a model with $M$ simultaneously determined $Y_m$; the *first* structural equation is

(A3.23)                    $$y_1 = Y_1 A_1 + Z_1 B_1 + E_1$$

In partitioned matrix notation this is written

(A3.24)                    $$y_1 = [Y_1, Z_1] \begin{bmatrix} A_1 \\ B_1 \end{bmatrix} + E_1$$

where  $y_1$ is an $N \times 1$ vector of observations on the endogenous variable determined by the first equation—a column of $Y$;

$Y_1$ is a matrix of observations for endogenous variables appearing in the equation for $y_1$—$Y_1$ can be as large as $N \times (M - 1)$;

$A_1$ is a vector of parameters to be estimated for the right-hand side endogenous variables;

---

[7] Note that here we actually *replace* the $y_i$ with the "purified" $\hat{y}_i$ rather than multiplying through each equation by the $\hat{y}_i$, $z_{kj}$ instrumental variables. Both procedures yield the same structural parameter estimates and are mathematically equivalent. We return to the latter method in the matrix exposition below.

$Z_1$ is a matrix of observations for the predetermined or exogenous instrumental variables appearing in the equation for $y_1$—columns of $Z$;

$B_1$ is a vector of parameters to be estimated for the predetermined and exogenous variables;

$E_1$ is an $N \times 1$ vector of disturbances for the equation—a column of $E$.

Consistent estimates of the parameters in (A3.24) may be obtained as follows. Form the "systematic part" of every column (variable) in $Y_1$ by regressing each on $Z$ in the first stage regressions. That is, estimate

$$(A3.25) \qquad Y_1 = Z\Lambda_1 + N_1$$

where  $Z$ is a matrix of observations on all the predetermined and exo-genous (instrumental) variables in the $M$-equation system;

$\Lambda$  is a vector of parameters for the instrumental variables, $Z$;

$N_1$ is a vector of error terms in the first stage regressions;

Then generate

$$(A3.26) \qquad \hat{Y}_1 = Z\hat{\Lambda}_1$$

where $\hat{\Lambda}_1 = (Z'Z)^{-1} Z'Y$ is the estimate of $\Lambda_1$.

In the second stage regressions, $\hat{Y}_1$ and $Z_1$ serve as instrumental variables to secure consistent estimates of $A_1$ and $B_1$. Premultiplying (A3.24) by $(\hat{Y}_1, Z_1)'$ yields

$$(A3.27) \quad (\hat{Y}_1, Z_1)' \, y_1 = [(\hat{Y}_1, Z_1)' \, (Y_1, Z_1)] \begin{bmatrix} A_1 \\ B_1 \end{bmatrix} + (\hat{Y}_1, Z_1)' \, E_1$$

To solve for the parameters premultiply (A3.27) by $[(\hat{Y}_1, Z_1)'(Y_1, Z_1)]^{-1}$. This produces (in the probability limit)

$$(A3.28) \quad [(\hat{Y}_1, Z_1)' \, (Y_1, Z_1)]^{-1} \, (\hat{Y}_1, Z_1)' \, y_1 = \begin{bmatrix} \hat{A}_1 \\ \hat{B}_1 \end{bmatrix} = \begin{bmatrix} A_1 \\ B_1 \end{bmatrix}$$

$$\text{since}^8 \qquad \text{plim} \begin{bmatrix} (\hat{Y}_1, Z_1)' \, E_1 \\ N \end{bmatrix} = 0$$

---

[8] This may be shown as follows: plim $(Z_1' \, {}_1/N) = 0$ by the assumption that vectors in $Z_1$ are genuine instrumental variables. Thus it need only be demonstrated that plim $(Y_1' \, {}_1/N) = 0$. Recall that $\hat{Y}_1 = Z\hat{\Lambda}_1$.

Hence $\left(\dfrac{\hat{Y}_1' \, E_1}{N}\right) = \left[\dfrac{(Z\hat{\Lambda}_1)' \, E_1}{N}\right] = \left[\dfrac{\hat{\Lambda}_1' \, (Z' \, E_1)}{N}\right]$

Since plim $Z'E_1/N = 0$ by the original assumption, then plim $\hat{Y}'E_1/N = (\hat{\Lambda}'0) = 0$.

Hence the IV-2SLS estimates $\begin{bmatrix} \hat{\mathbf{A}}_1 \\ \hat{\mathbf{B}}_1 \end{bmatrix}$ are consistent estimates of the true

parameter vectors $\begin{bmatrix} \mathbf{A}_1 \\ \mathbf{B}_1 \end{bmatrix}$. *Consistent estimates of the parameters in each of the remaining equations of the system $y_2, \ldots, y_m$ are obtained in exactly the same way.*

This establishes the procedure by which it is possible to consistently estimate the structural parameters of the simultaneously determined $Y_m$ variables in the multiequation model of mass political violence. But all that has been developed so far is a method. We have ignored the question of whether we have sufficient information to allow structural estimation at all: Does the model specify enough apriori restrictions and instrumental variables in the block of equations for the jointly dependent $Y_m$ to make the parameters estimable? We must also deal with the status of the lagged endogenous variables $Y_m^*$ in the equations. Are they validly used as predetermined instruments or are they more properly treated as endogenous? Finally, we have only hinted about the estimation of recursive causal relations in the model and have not yet developed the implications of the model's overall block recursive structure. This brings us to a discussion of the identification problem.

## The Identification Problem[9]

Identification is one of the central issues in the specification and estimation of multiequation causal models. The crux of the problem is this: A given equation in a system of structural equations which articulates mathematically a theoretically postulated model cannot necessarily be distinguished from linear combinations of other equations of the same form (or scalar multiples thereof) by observational data alone. For example, consider the following simple two-equation system:

(A3.29)          $y_1 + \alpha_{12} y_2 + \beta_{11} z_1 + \beta_{12} z_2 = \varepsilon_1$

(A3.30)          $\alpha_{21} y_1 + y_2 + \beta_{21} z_1 = \varepsilon_2$

where $z_1$, $z_2$ are predetermined or exogenous (instrumental) variables uncorrelated with the equation disturbances;

---

[9] The exposition of the identification problem in this section is taken, with some modifications, from Franklin M. Fisher, *The Identification Problem in Econometrics* (New York: McGraw-Hill Book Company, Inc., 1966). See this definitive source for elaboration and rigorous proofs of all points covered here, as well as treatment of many other facets of the issue.

the system has been subjected to a normalization rule such that left-hand side endogenous variables have an implicit coefficient of unity and all terms except disturbances appear on the left-hand side for heuristic purposes;
all variables are mean deviates.

If the two equations are added, we have

$$(A3.31) \quad (1 + \alpha_{21})y_1 + (1 + \alpha_{12})y_2 + (\beta_{11} + \beta_{21})z_1 + \beta_{12}z_2 = (\varepsilon_1 + \varepsilon_2)$$

Clearly (A3.31)—a linear combination of (A3.29) and (A3.30)—is indistinguishable from (A3.29). Both the "fake" equation and the "real" equation of the original model are admissible by the data and model—(A3.29) *is underidentified*.

Another way to view the problem is to note what would happen if we attempted to estimate (A3.29) ignoring the identification issue. In the first stage $\hat{y}_2$ could successfully be created in the usual way via the regression of $y_2$ on all the $z_k$ in the system, in this case $z_1$ and $z_2$. However, in the second stage, which involves regressing $y_1$ on $\hat{y}_2$ and the $z_k$ in (A3.29), the structural coefficients would *not* be estimable because $y_2$ would be an *exact* linear function of $z_1$ and $z_2$. In the context of the earlier matrix exposition of IV-2SLS estimation, the bracketed expression on the left-hand side of (A3.28) would be singular and not invertible, and therefore parameter estimates could not be obtained. In this way estimation, identification, and prior theoretical specification are intimately bound together. Estimation of the structural parameters is not possible unless equations are identified, and identifiability hinges on the causal system including the required a priori theoretical information.

Thus an equation is identifiable only if some combination of prior and posterior information enables the investigator to distinguish its parameters from those of any other equation of the same form. More specifically, an equation is defined to be:

1. *Underidentified*, if there is no way to distinguish it from others of the same form.
2. *Just Identified*, if there is only one way to distinguish it from others of the same form.
3. *Overidentified*, if there is more than one way to distinguish it from others of the same form.

Just how much information is required to insure identification? This is best answered by introducing some formal rules by which an equation's identifiability can be assessed. Consider the following simple system:

(A3.32)                $y_1 + \alpha_{12}y_2 + \beta_{11}z_1 \qquad = \varepsilon_1$

(A3.33)                $\alpha_{21}y_1 + \quad y_2 \qquad + \beta_{21}z_2 = \varepsilon_2$

where       all conditions are as in (A3.29) and (A3.30).

The matrix of coefficients for this system is denoted $A$ and is written[10]

$$A = \begin{bmatrix} 1 & \alpha_{12} & \beta_{11} & 0 \\ \alpha_{21} & 1 & 0 & \beta_{21} \end{bmatrix}$$

Let $\phi^i$ denote a column vector that summarizes all prior theoretical information we have on the $i$th row in the matrix $A$, such that 0's are entered where there are no restrictions, and 1's are entered where there are restrictions. Thus $\phi = \begin{bmatrix} 0 \\ 0 \\ 0 \\ 1 \end{bmatrix}$ where the 1 entry signifies that in (A3.32),

the first row of $A$, $z_2$ has been specified with an implicit coefficient of zero. Similarly, $\phi^2 = \begin{bmatrix} 0 \\ 0 \\ 1 \\ 0 \end{bmatrix}$ where the 1 entry corresponds to the restriction

that $z_1$ does not appear in (A3.33), represented by the second row of $A$. Note that $A_1\phi^1 = 0$ and likewise $A_2\phi^2 = 0$, and that, in general, $A_i\phi^i = 0$ will be true. The rules for identification—the "order" and "rank" conditions—can now be stated. At this point we deal only with coefficient restrictions, or what are known as "exclusion" criteria.

1. *Order Condition.* A necessary (but not sufficient) condition for the identification of the $i$th equation of a model is that $\boxed{\rho(\phi^i) \geq M - 1}$; where $M$ equals the number of equations or endogenous variables in the system and $\rho$ denotes "the rank of." It is referred to as the "order" condition because it specifies the order of magnitude of the required information. In the coefficient restriction case it simply means that for the $i$th equation to be identified, a necessary condition is that at least $M - 1$ variables be excluded from that equation on the basis of prior theoretical knowledge. Note that both (A3.32) and (A3.33) satisfy the order condition

---

[10] It is assumed throughout that the rank of $A = M$, where $M$ is the number of equations in the system—the number of endogenous variables. That is, we assume that the systems are mathematically complete, and focus only on the identification problem of having enough information to estimate the parameters.

for just identification, since $\rho(\phi^1) = 1$, and $\rho(\phi^2) = 1$, where $M - 1 = 1$. Equation (A3.29) fails the order condition, however, since $\rho(\phi)$ for that equation is zero, which obviously is less than $M - 1 = 1$.

2. *Rank Condition.* A necessary *and* sufficient condition for the identification of the $i$th equation of a model under exclusion restrictions is that $\boxed{\rho(A\phi^i) = M - 1}$. An equivalent statement of this condition is that it must be possible to form at least one nonvanishing determinant of order $M - 1$ from the columns of $A$ corresponding to the variables excluded a priori from the $i$th equation. Let us apply the rank condition rule to the system in (A3.32) and (A3.33). For the first equation, we have

$$\rho(A\phi^1) = \begin{bmatrix} 1 & \alpha_{12} & \beta_{11} & 0 \\ \\ \alpha_{21} & 1 & 0 & \beta_{21} \end{bmatrix} \begin{bmatrix} 0 \\ 0 \\ 0 \\ 1 \end{bmatrix}$$

$$= \begin{bmatrix} 0 \\ \beta_{21} \end{bmatrix}$$

Assuming $\beta_{21} \neq 0$, this result has a rank of $1 = M - 1$. Equation (A3.32) is identified.

Similarly, we have for the second equation

$$\rho(A\phi^2) = \begin{bmatrix} 1 & \alpha_{12} & \beta_{11} & 0 \\ \\ \alpha_{21} & 1 & 0 & \beta_{21} \end{bmatrix} \begin{bmatrix} 0 \\ 0 \\ 1 \\ 0 \end{bmatrix}$$

$$= \begin{bmatrix} \beta_{11} \\ 0 \end{bmatrix}$$

Assuming $\beta_{11} \neq 0$, this result also has a rank of $1 = M - 1$, and hence (A3.33) is identified.

The hypothetical causal system of (A3.32)–(A3.33) fulfills both the rank and order conditions for identification and therefore its structural coefficients are estimable. The order condition specifies the minimum number of independent restrictions that must be available from prior theory if an equation is to be distinguished from others in the model. It is not a sufficient condition, however, because restrictions obeyed by all equations in a model *give no help whatever* in identifying a particular equation. This point is illustrated by the following two-equation system:

(A3.34) $\qquad\qquad y_1 + \alpha_{12}y_2 + \beta_{11}z_1 + \beta_{12}z_2 = \varepsilon_1$

(A3.35) $\qquad \alpha_{21}y_1 + \quad y_2 + \beta_{21}z_1 \qquad = \varepsilon_2$

where      all conditions are as in (A3.29) and (A3.30).

Application of the order condition rule would demonstrate that (A3.34) is not identified. Now suppose we exclude $z_2$ from (A3.34) by setting $\beta_{12}$ equal to zero. The matrix of coefficients in the system is then

$$A = \begin{bmatrix} 1 & \alpha_{12} & \beta_{11} & 0 \\ \alpha_{21} & 1 & \beta_{21} & 0 \end{bmatrix}$$

The order condition would now be satisfied by (A3.34) as well as by (A3.35), since $\rho(\phi^1) = 1$, and $\rho(\phi^2) = 1$. Yet in each case the rank condition would fail: $\rho(A\phi^1) = 0$, and $\rho(A\phi^2) = 0$. This is obvious in a simple two-equation system, but it is often less clear in very large models— hence the need for the rank condition to insure identifiability. It is also clear that a given equation can be identified (distinguished) vis à vis some particular equation(s) in a large causal system but not identified with respect to others and thus the model as a whole. The extension of the rank and order conditions to this case is straightforward but is not developed here.[11]

One extension of the rank and order conditions must be developed because of its importance for the identification and estimation of causal models such as ours, which specify undirectional and noncircular relationships within and between blocks of equations. It is an extension in which restrictions are imposed on the *covariances of the disturbance terms*. Recall that the disturbances, denoted throughout as $\varepsilon_i$, may be thought of as representing the net effects of numerous unobserved and hopefully minor influences omitted from the structural part of the equations. All that has been assumed about the $\varepsilon_i$ so far is that they are uncorrelated in the probability limit with the predetermined and exogenous variables. Any other assumption would have been untenable, since in models with simultaneous reciprocities the disturbances are correlated *across* equations by definition.

To illustrate the discussion to follow, let us consider a "hierarchical" model, where all causal influences are unidirectional and noncircular, of the form

(A3.36) $\qquad y_1 \qquad\qquad\quad = \beta_{11}z_1 + \varepsilon_1$

(A3.37) $\qquad \alpha_{21}y_1 + \quad y_2 \qquad\quad = \beta_{21}z_1 + \varepsilon_2$

(A3.38) $\qquad \alpha_{31}y_1 + \alpha_{32}y_2 + y_3 = \beta_{31}z_1 + \varepsilon_3$

where  $z_1$ is a predetermined or exogenous variable uncorrelated with the equation disturbances;

---

[11] See Fisher, *The Identification Problem in Econometrics*, Chapter 3. We deal with the implications of an overidentified system in a following section of the appendix.

the system has been subjected to a normalization rule such that left-hand side endogenous variables have an implicit coefficient of unity; all endogenous variables are shown on the left-hand-side; and all exogenous variables and disturbances are shown on the right-hand side for heuristic purposes;
all variables are mean deviates.

The coefficient matrix for this system of equations is

$$A = \begin{bmatrix} 1 & 0 & 0 & \beta_{11} \\ \alpha_{21} & 1 & 0 & \beta_{21} \\ \alpha_{31} & \alpha_{32} & 1 & \beta_{31} \end{bmatrix}$$

In the above causal system, (A3.36) is identified by coefficient restrictions alone, since $\rho(\phi^1) = 2 = M - 1$, and $\rho(A\phi^1) = 2 = M - 1$. This follows from the exclusion of $y_2$ and $y_3$ from the first equation in the model providing the required $M - 1$ independent restrictions. However, Application of the rank and order condition rules—or, in such an elementary system, mere visual inspection—reveals that (A3.37) and (A3.38) are *not* identified. This is true generally for *all equations after the first* in "hierarchical" models where the coefficients for the endogenous variables, the $\alpha_i$, form a triangular matrix (hereafter denoted as $A^*$). Equations beyond the first in models of this type are identifiable only if the investigator is willing to introduce additional restrictions which should have a sound theoretical foundation.

One possibility is that prior information on the system is such that variables endogenous to the whole system may be considered to be *predetermined with respect to a given equation* in the sense of being uncorrelated with the disturbance of that equation. These variables may then be used to gain information on the equation in question and to aid in its identification. A variable is predetermined with respect to a particular equation, then, if and only if it is uncorrelated with the disturbance of that equation. Recall that in the causal system of (A3.36) through (A3.38), $y_2$ does not appear in the equation for $y_1$ and $y_3$ does not appear in the equation for $y_2$; that is, causal influence only flows from $y_1$ to $y_2$, and from $y_1$ and $y_2$ to $y_3$, in hierarchical fashion. This of course is implied by the triangularity of $A^*$. Now if it is also possible to specify that the disturbances of these equations are uncorrelated in the probability limit, so that the *cross-equation* covariance matrix of the $\varepsilon_i$ (hereafter denoted as $E^*$) is diagonal, then $y_1$ can be considered to be predetermined with respect to $y_2$, and $y_1$ and $y_2$ can be considered to be predetermined with respect to $y_3$. This additional information will serve to identify (A3.37) and (A3.38). Moreover, each equation in the system can now be consistently estimated, equation by equation, by *Ordinary Least Squares* regression.

This can be seen intuitively by noting that although $y_2$ does not appear in the equation for $y_1$, if $\varepsilon_1$ and $\varepsilon_2$ are correlated, a "pip" or movement in $\varepsilon_2$ would be associated with a similar movement in $\varepsilon_1$ and therefore in $y_1$. Consequently, if some of the influences omitted from (A3.36) and represented by $\varepsilon_1$ are also present in $\varepsilon_2$, their joint effect on $\varepsilon_2$ and $y_1$ means that $y_1$ cannot be considered to be predetermined vis à vis (A3.37) and this equation remains underidentified. Hence the need for the additional restriction that the covariance of $\varepsilon_2$, $\varepsilon_1$ is zero.

This comes out clearly in the algebra. The dependence of $y_1$ and $\varepsilon_2$ is established by multiplying the equation for $y_1$ (A3.36), through by $\varepsilon_2$ and taking covariances:

$$(A3.39) \quad m_{\varepsilon_2 y_1} = \beta_{11} m_{\varepsilon_2 z_1} + m_{\varepsilon_2 \varepsilon_1}$$

The first term on the right-hand side of (A3.39) is zero by the original assumption that $z_1$ is an exogenous variable; that is, plim $m_{z_1 \varepsilon_i} = 0$.

Thus in the probability limit (A3.39) becomes

$$(A3.40) \quad m_{\varepsilon_2 y_1} = m_{\varepsilon_2 \varepsilon_1}$$

It should now be obvious that for $y_1$ to be considered predetermined in the equation for $y_2$ (uncorrelated with the disturbance of $y_2$), the covariance of $\varepsilon_1$ and $\varepsilon_2$ must be zero or nearly so. Analogous conditions must be hold to insure the identification and consistent estimation of all equations beyond the first in such hierarchical models.

We sum up this section with a general rule and a definition:

*In all models where $A^*$ is triangular, the matrix of cross-equation disturbance covariances, denoted as $E^*$, must be diagonal to insure the identification of any equation after the first. Systems that have these properties—$A^*$ triangular and $E^*$ diagonal—are defined as "recursive." Every equation of a recursive system is identified and can be consistently estimated by OLS regression.*[12]

[12] There is an important qualification of this general rule. It is possible to have a causal system that specifies only unidirectional and noncircular relationships between variables (i.e., $A^*$ is triangular). In such systems, however, there may be a sufficient number of exogenous variables ($z_k$) included in some equations and excluded from others and/or endogenous variables ($y_i$) excluded from some equations (all entries in $A^*$ below the diagonal are not nonzero, although all entries above the diagonal are zero) so that the system satisfies the order and rank conditions for identification *without* imposing additional restrictions on the *cross-equation* covariances of disturbances. We deal with this possibility in a following section in the context of a discussion of overidentified models. Although such systems are identified without covariance restrictions on the disturbances, they cannot be consistently estimated by OLS regression.

## Identification in Block Recursive Models

The previous discussion indicates that our use of the term "recursive" throughout the book in reference to models or "partial" models with unidirectional and noncircular causal relationships was not strictly correct. Recursive systems require the additional specification that disturbances be uncorrelated in the probability limit across equations. This amounts to saying that we have not omitted any (important) influences that causally affect more than one endogenous variable. Since all relationships within sectors for the $X_k$ variables were hypothesized to be unidirectional and noncircular [Equations (8.7)−(8.16)], the additional assumption that cross-equation disturbances are uncorrelated allows us to estimate these relationships by OLS regression—*provided* that sectors can be separately analyzed when they are embedded in a larger causal structure. Are the sectors or blocks for the $X_k$ isolable for estimation purposes? And what are the implications for identification and estimation of the relationships between the $X_k$ sectors and the block of equations of the simultaneously determined $Y_m$?

These questions pose no difficulty if the complete causal system is truly block recursive. Again, this denotation was used rather loosely when referring to the multiequation model in Chapter 8.

### A block recursive system must satisfy two conditions:

1. Relationships between sectors or blocks (but not necessarily within them) must be unidirectional and without simultaneous circularities or feedback loops. Hence, if the matrix of endogenous variable coefficients for the complete model is partitioned into its component blocks, the resulting (partitioned) matrix must be block–triangular just as $A^*$ was in the earlier illustration of "simple" recursive systems.

2. Disturbances between blocks (but not necessarily within them) must be uncorrelated in the probability limit. Hence, if the cross-equation matrix of disturbance covariances for the complete model is partitioned into its component blocks, the resulting (partitioned) matrix must be block–diagonal just as $E^*$ was in the case of "simple" recursive systems.

It is not necessary to actually present a partitioned matrix of endogenous variable coefficients to establish that condition 1 holds for the multiequation model. Inspection of Figure 8.2 verifies that all relationships between blocks are unidirectional and simultaneously noncircular. In order to satisfy the second condition—and hence to be able to estimate equations for the $X_k$ variables, sector by sector, by OLS *and* to consider the $X_k$ as predetermined in the IV-2SLS estimation of the simultaneously determined $Y_m$—we must assume that the disturbances are uncorrelated across functionally related blocks. Thus consistent estimation hinges on the inclusion of all variables that exert (substantial) causal influence in two or more sectors that are functionally related to one another. Again, this drives home the importance of sound prior theoretical specification of the model.

So far we have established that the block of equations for the simultaneously determined $Y_m$, which is embedded in a larger causal system, may be estimated by IV-2SLS using the $X_k$ as predetermined instruments along with the exogenous $Z_i$, *if* it is assumed that disturbances are not correlated across blocks. Similarly, we may then proceed "backward" in the complete causal system and estimate the equations for the $X_k$ variables sector by sector, using OLS regression. Consistency is insured if disturbances within as well as between sectors are uncorrelated in the probability limit.

One issue that was raised at the outset has not yet been confronted: the status of the lagged endogenous variables $Y_m^*$ for the identification and estimation of the structural equations.

## Lagged Endogenous Variables and Estimation Strategies

We are concerned in this section with the status of the $Y_m^*$ vis a vis their simultaneously determined counterparts the $Y_m$ [ Equations (8.1)–(8.6) of the complete model in Chapter 8]. The question at issue is: Are the $Y_m^*$ validly used as predetermined instruments for estimating causal relations among the $Y_m$? The answer—in general, no—follows in a straightforward manner from the previous analysis of the $X_k$. In order to use the $X_k$ as predetermined, it is necessary to assume that the disturbances of the equations generating these variables are uncorrelated with the disturbances of the equations for the $Y_m$. This assumption is not implausible, since it is only seriously violated when one or more causally important variables influence *both* the $X_k$ and the corresponding $Y_m$. Indeed, we invested a great deal of effort in preliminary hypothesis testing, model reformulation, and final specification precisely to avoid this pitfall.

Treating the $Y_m^*$ as predetermined requires exactly the same assumption: The disturbances of the (implicit) equations generating the $Y_m^*$ must be uncorrelated in the probability limit with the disturbances of the (explicit) equations for the $Y_m$. For example, to consider ln Coups D1 as predetermined with respect to ln Coups D2 [see Equation (8.4)], the disturbance of the (implicit) ln Coups D1 equation must be uncorrelated with the disturbance of the ln Coups D2 equation. Since the former equation is merely a lagged version of the latter, this is equivalent to assuming that the disturbances are not *autocorrelated*. To see this, note that current endogenous variables are obviously correlated with current disturbances; hence lagged endogenous variables are correlated with lagged disturbances.

Therefore, if current and lagged disturbances are correlated, then current disturbances and lagged endogenous variables will also be correlated. As a result, the latter cannot be treated as predetermined for identification and estimation purposes.

The assumption of no disturbance autocorrelation is clearly less tenable than the analogous supposition in the case of the $X_k$. It is tantamount to assuming that no significant variable, itself autocorrelated, has been omitted from any of the $Y_m$ equations that incorporate corresponding $Y_m^*$'s.[13] This is certainly a more difficult leap than assuming, as we did for the $X_k$, that there is no important omitted variable that causally affects *two* or more functionally related sectors or predetermined endogenous variables. Moreover, these considerations apply not only to the $Y_m^*$ and their corresponding $Y_m$, but to the $Y_m^*$ and *all* the $Y_m$. This follows directly from the specification that the $Y_m$ are simultaneously interdependent. For example, the simultaneous relationship between Internal War D2 and ln Negative Sanctions D2 in Equations (8.2) and (8.3) of the $Y_m$ block means that ln Negative Sanctions D2 is correlated with the disturbance of Internal War D2, and conversely. Hence if the current and lagged ln Negative Sanctions disturbances are correlated (autocorrelation), which is likely, it follows that lagged ln Negative Sanctions (D1) will be correlated with the current disturbance of Internal War D2. Consequently, lagged ln Negative Sanctions (D1) cannot properly be considered to be predetermined with respect to Internal War D2.

How then are the lagged endogenous $Y_m^*$ best treated? There are at least three options:[14]

1. Eliminate the lagged endogenous variables from the model entirely and accept specification error as a result. The seriousness of such error

---

[13] The most common source of disturbance autocorrelation is the omission of a serially correlated variable from the equation. Thus if a causal variable omitted from the equation of a particular $Y_m$ is correlated with itself through time *and* if it causally influences $Y_m^*$, it will appear in the disturbances of $Y_m$ and $Y_m^*$, which as a consequence will be auto-correlated. Hence $Y_m^*$ will be correlated with the disturbance of its own subsequent value $Y_m$ and it cannot therefore be considered to be predetermined if consistency is to be preserved. For a technical treatment of this problem see Douglas A. Hibbs, Jr. "Problems of Statistical Estimation and Causal Inference in Dynamic, Time-Series Regression Models," in Herbert Costner, ed., *Sociological Methodology*, 1973 (San Francisco: Jossey-Bass Inc., 1973).

[14] There is a fourth option which we do not consider here because it requires specific assumptions about the structure and (in the cross-sectional case) prior knowledge of the coefficients of the disturbance interdependence. It involves a combination of the Generalized Least Squares estimation method that is conventionally used to handle disturbance autocorrelation in single equation models with the IV-2SLS estimation procedure for simultaneous systems. See Ray C. Fair, "The Estimation of Simultaneous Equation Models with Lagged Endogenous Variables and First Order Serially Correlated Errors," *Econometrica*, Vol. 38, May 1970, pp. 507–516.

will depend on the magnitude of the true causal influence of the omitted variables and the extent to which they are intercorrelated with the remaining explanatory variables.

2. Assume the "worst" and treat the lagged endogenous variables as *endogenous* rather than as predetermined. This requires that sufficient variables, $X_k$ and $Z_i$, be available to identify an $(M + N^*)$ equation system—where $M$ equals the number of equations for the current endogenous $Y_m$ (six in our case), and $N^*$ equals the number of lagged endogenous variables to be treated as endogenous (four in our case). Thus it is now necessary to satisfy an order condition of the form $\rho(\phi^i) \geqslant (M + N^*) - 1$, as opposed to the general order condition $\rho(\phi^i) \geqslant M - 1$. Ideally, lagged $X_k$ and $Z_i$ should be introduced as instruments for the lagged endogenous $Y_m^*$, however, these are *not* available in the 108-nation cross-section. Instead we must rely exclusively on current $X_k$ and $Z_i$ as surrogates. This procedure is robust against all forms of disturbance autocorrelation and it insures consistency; however, it is likely to produce great *inefficiency*.

3. Finally, we may assume the "best" and regard the $Y_m^*$ as predetermined along with the $X_k$ and the exogenous $Z_i$. This approach produces inconsistency proportionate to the magnitude of the disturbance autocorrelation in the equations for the $Y_m$, but it does have the advantage of greater efficiency.

The first alternative is clearly the least desirable. The lagged endogenous variables were not casually entered into the structural equations for the $Y_m$—they appear for good theoretical reasons. Omitting them would surely result in greater distortions of estimation results and causal inferences than either of the other options. The second alternative, treating the $Y_m^*$ as endogenous, has great merit in situations where autocorrelation is serious and good instruments are available. Neither seems to be true in this case. There is no way of ascertaining the form or the magnitude of the autocorrelation in cross-sectional data with but one set of lagged $Y_m$ observations. Autocorrelation is not likely to be severe, however, since the lags between the $Y_m$ and the corresponding $Y_m^*$ are not very short.[15] Moreover, alternative 2 necessitates using current $X_k$ and $Z_i$ as instruments (assuming we are sufficiently rich in such variables; see below) which as we have already noted is likely to yield very inefficient, albeit consistent, estimates. *If the inefficiency produced by alternative 2 is very large in relation to the inconsistency that will result from regarding the $Y_m^*$ as predetermined (alternative*

---

[15] Autocorrelation of variables and hence disturbances (cf. the discussion in footnote 14) is usually high in data with short time lags, for example, monthly or quarterly series. It typically becomes less serious as the lag between observation periods grows larger. A de-

3), *then the latter is the optimum way to proceed.* Since the magnitude of the disturbance autocorrelation is *not likely* to be very large given the lag structure of the model, and the inefficiency attendant to alternative 2 *is likely* to be large given the available instruments, the most desirable solution is to accept a (probably) small degree of inconsistency and estimate, as alternative 3 suggests.

Thus our *primary estimation strategy* employs the lagged endogenous $Y_m^*$ as predetermined. However, if sufficient instrumental variables are available, Equations 8.1 through 8.6 can also be estimated treating the $Y_m^*$ as endogenous. This *supplementary estimation method* allows us to compare the coefficient estimates from a somewhat inconsistent but relatively efficient procedure with those rendered by a consistent but comparatively inefficient procedure. Considered jointly, these estimates should yield a sharper picture of the true causal effects of the lagged endogenous $Y_m^*$ in the block of equations for the simultaneously determined $Y_m$.

## Identification of the Multiequation Model

We conclude this appendix by establishing that our fully specified multiequation model presented in Chapter 8 is in fact identified. Consider first the simultaneously determined $Y_m$ block—presented in Equations (8.1) through (8.6). Table A3.1 displays the coefficient matrix for this crucial block of equations. Note that the rows of the matrix in the table correspond to the equations, and the columns correspond to the variables.[16] Since there are six equations or current endogenous variables $Y_m$ in this block, $M$ is 6. Four lagged endogenous variables ($Y_m^*$) appear in the equations, and so $N^*$ is 4.

In order to employ the primary estimation strategy, where the lagged endogenous $Y_m^*$ are considered predetermined, the order condition that must be met is

$$\rho(\phi^i) \geqslant 5 = M - 1$$

The supplementary estimation procedure, where the lagged endogenous variables are regarded as endogenous, involves a more demanding order condition:

$$\rho(\phi^i) \geqslant 9 = (M + N^*) - 1$$

The rank condition to be satisfied is the same for both estimation

---

[16] The coefficients in Table A3.1 derive from a normalized version of (8.1) to (8.6) such that left-hand side endogenous variables have a coefficient of unity and all endogenous, predetermined, and exogenous variables appear on the left-hand side.

strategies :[17]

$$\rho(A\phi^i) = 5 = M - 1$$

Application of the order and rank condition rules to each equation of the $Y_m$ block (or row of Table A3.1) produces the following results:

*Equation 8.1—$Y_1$*

Order condition:     $\rho(\phi^1) = 15 > M - 1$ and $(M + N^*) - 1$

Rank condition:

$\rho(A \phi^1) =$

$$\begin{array}{ll}
(1) & \left[ \begin{array}{l} 0 \\ \alpha_{23} + \alpha_{26} + \alpha_{22}^* + \alpha_{23}^* + \beta_{22} + \beta_{28}^* \\ \alpha_{32} + \beta_{36} + \beta_{39} + \gamma_{39} + \gamma_{3,11} \\ \alpha_{42} + \alpha_{44}^* + \gamma_{4,10} \\ \gamma_{56} + \gamma_{58} \\ \alpha_{62} + 1 + \alpha_{62}^* + \gamma_{67} + \gamma_{68} \end{array} \right]
\end{array}$$

$$\rho(A \phi^1) = 5 = M - 1$$

Equation 8.1 is overidentified regardless of how the lagged endogenous variables are treated.

*Equation 8.2—$Y_2$*

Order condition:     $\rho(\phi^2) = 18 > M - 1$ and $(M + N^*) - 1$

Rank condition:

$\rho(A \phi^2) =$

$$\begin{array}{ll}
(1) & \left[ \begin{array}{l} 1 + \alpha_{15} + \alpha_{11}^* + \beta_{14} + \beta_{15} + \beta_{18} + \beta_{19} + \gamma_{12} + \gamma_{1,12} \\ 0 \\ \alpha_{31} + \beta_{35} + \beta_{36} + \beta_{39} + \gamma_{32} + \gamma_{39} + \gamma_{3,11} \end{array} \right]
\end{array}$$

---

[17] The rank condition is the same because there are no explicit equations for the $Y_m^*$—they are merely lagged versions of $Y_m$ equations. In the general time-series case, where lagged exogenous $Z_t$ $(Z_{t-\theta}$'s) would be used in our supplementary estimation method as instrumental variables for the lagged endogenous $Y_m^*$ $(Y_{t-1}$'s), the rank condition is more complicated. In particular, the current exogenous $Z_t$ must be linearly independent of certain linear functions of the past exogenous $Z_{t-\theta}$'s. This is necessary to insure that enough elements of $\hat{Y}_{t-1}$ and $Z_t$ are not connected by linear identities. See Franklin M. Fisher, *The identification Problem in Econometrics* (New York: McGraw-Hill Book Company, Inc., 1966), Chapter 6.

(4) $\begin{bmatrix} \alpha_{41} + \alpha_{44}^* + \beta_{49}^* + \gamma_{4,10} \end{bmatrix}$

(5) $\alpha_{51} + 1 + \alpha_{51}^* + \gamma_{56} + \gamma_{58}$

(6) $\gamma_{67} + \gamma_{68}$

$\rho(A\,\phi^2) = 5 = M - 1$

Equation 8.2 is overidentified regardless of how the lagged endogenous variables are treated.

*Equation 8.3—$Y_3$*

Order condition:    $\rho(\phi^3) = 20 > M - 1$    and    $(M + N^*) - 1$

Rank condition:

$\rho(A\,\phi^3) =$

(1) $\begin{bmatrix} \alpha_{15} + \alpha_{11}^* + \beta_{11} + \beta_{14} + \beta_{17} + \beta_{18} + \beta_{19}^* + \\ \beta_{1,10} + \gamma_{13} + \gamma_{1,12} \end{bmatrix}$

(2) $\alpha_{26} + \alpha_{22}^* + \alpha_{23}^* + \beta_{21} + \beta_{22} + \beta_{27} + \beta_{28}^* + \\ \beta_{29}^* + \beta_{2,10} + \gamma_{23}$

(3) $0$

(4) $\alpha_{44}^* + \beta_{49}^* + \gamma_{4,10}$

(5) $1 + \alpha_{51}^* + \beta_{5,10} + \gamma_{56} + \gamma_{58}$

(6) $1 + \alpha_{62}^* + \beta_{6,10} + \gamma_{67} + \gamma_{68}$

$\rho(A\,\phi^3) = 5 = M - 1$

Equation 8.3 is overidentified regardless of how the lagged endogenous variables are treated.

*Equation 8.4—$Y_4$*

Order condition:    $\rho(\phi^4) = 25 > M - 1$ and $(M + N^*) - 1$

Rank condition:

$\rho(A\,\phi^4) =$

(1) $\begin{bmatrix} \alpha_{13} + \alpha_{15} + \alpha_{11}^* + \beta_{11} + \beta_{14} + \beta_{15} + \beta_{17} + \\ \beta_{18} + \beta_{1,10} + \gamma_{11} + \gamma_{12} + \gamma_{13} + \gamma_{1,12} \end{bmatrix}$

(2) $\alpha_{23} + \alpha_{26} + \alpha_{22}^* + \beta_{21} + \beta_{22} + \beta_{27} + \beta_{28}^* + \\ \beta_{2,10} + \gamma_{21} + \gamma_{23}$

(3) $1 + \beta_{35} + \beta_{36} + \beta_{39} + \gamma_{31} + \gamma_{32} + \gamma_{39} + \\ \gamma_{3,11}$

$$
\begin{array}{ll}
(4) \\
(5) \\
(6)
\end{array}
\left[
\begin{array}{l}
0 \\
1 + \alpha_{51}^* + \beta_{5,10} + \gamma_{56} + \gamma_{58} \\
1 + \alpha_{62}^* + \beta_{6,10} + \gamma_{67} + \gamma_{68}
\end{array}
\right]
$$

$$\rho(A \ \phi^4) = 5 = M - 1$$

Equation 8.4 is overidentified regardless of how the lagged endogenous variables are treated.

*Equation 8.5—$Y_5$*

Order condition:     $\rho(\phi^5) = 25 > M - 1$ and $(M + N^*) - 1$

Rank condition:

$\rho(A \ \phi^5) =$

$$
\begin{array}{ll}
(1) \\
\\
(2) \\
\\
(3) \\
\\
(4) \\
(5) \\
(6)
\end{array}
\left[
\begin{array}{l}
\alpha_{13} + \alpha_{14} + \beta_{11} + \beta_{14} + \beta_{15} + \beta_{17} + \beta_{18} + \\
\beta_{19}^* + \gamma_{11} + \gamma_{12} + \gamma_{13} + \gamma_{1,12} \\
1 + \alpha_{23} + \alpha_{24} + \alpha_{26} + \alpha_{22}^* + \alpha_{23}^* + \beta_{21} + \\
\beta_{22} + \beta_{27} + \beta_{28}^* + \beta_{29}^* + \gamma_{21} + \gamma_{23} \\
\alpha_{32} + 1 + \alpha_{34} + \beta_{35} + \beta_{36} + \beta_{39} + \gamma_{31} + \\
\gamma_{32} + \gamma_{39} + \gamma_{3,11} \\
\alpha_{42} + 1 + \alpha_{44}^* + \beta_{49}^* + \gamma_{4,10} \\
0 \\
\alpha_{62} + 1 + \alpha_{62}^* + \gamma_{67}
\end{array}
\right]
$$

$$\rho(A \ \phi^5) = 5 = M - 1$$

Equation 8.5 is overidentified regardless of how the lagged endogenous variables are treated.

*Equation 8.6—$Y_6$*

Order condition:     $\rho(\phi^6) = 25 > M - 1$ and $(M + N^*) - 1$

Rank condition:

$\rho(A \ \phi^6) =$

$$
\begin{array}{ll}
(1) \\
\\
(2) \\
\\
\end{array}
\left[
\begin{array}{l}
1 + \alpha_{13} + \alpha_{14} + \alpha_{15} + \alpha_{11}^* + \beta_{11} + \beta_{14} + \beta_{15} + \\
\beta_{17} + \beta_{18} + \beta_{19}^* + \gamma_{11} + \gamma_{12} +, \gamma_{13} + \gamma_{1,12} \\
\alpha_{23} + \alpha_{24} + \alpha_{23}^* + \beta_{21} + \beta_{22} + \beta_{27} + \beta_{28}^* + \\
\beta_{29}^* + \gamma_{21} + \gamma_{23}
\end{array}
\right]
$$

$$
\begin{array}{ll}
(3) & \left[\begin{array}{l} \alpha_{31} + 1 + \alpha_{34} + \beta_{35} + \beta_{36} + \beta_{39} + \gamma_{31} + \gamma_{32} + \\ \gamma_{39} + \gamma_{3,11} \end{array}\right. \\
(4) & \alpha_{41} + 1 + \alpha_{44}^* + \beta_{49}^* + \gamma_{4,10} \\
(5) & \alpha_{51} + 1 + \alpha_{51}^* + \gamma_{56} \\
(6) & \left. 0 \right]
\end{array}
$$

$$\rho(A\,\phi^6) = 5 = M - 1$$

Equation 8.6 is overidentified regardless of how the lagged endogenous variables are treated.

The preceding results demonstrate that each equation in the $Y_m$ block more than satisfies the order and rank conditions for identification: each is overidentified. And this is true whether the lagged endogenous $Y_m^*$ variables are regarded as predetermined, where we operate on an $M$-equation system, or as endogenous, where we operate on an (implicit) $M + N^*$ equation system.

What are the implications for estimation of an overidentified system? An overidentified equation has already been defined as one that can be distinguished in more than one way from others of the same functional form. Thus if the "reduced form" of the system is generated by rewriting each equation as a function only of predetermined and exogenous variables, there would be more than one way to deduce the structural parameters from the reduced form parameters. Of course asymptotically the same "on-target" structural parameter estimates would be obtained from every admissible combination of reduced form parameters. However, in a particular sample this is seldom true. Two Stage Least Squares handles the "excess" reduced form information by using a weighted combination of the (more than sufficient) instrumental variables when creating the "systematic parts" of the simultaneously determined $Y_m$. The weights correspond to the coefficients in the first stage regressions, that is, the elements in the coefficient vector denoted $\hat{\mathbf{\Lambda}}_1$ in the matrix formulation of IV-2SLS that was developed earlier in the appendix [see (A3.25) and (A3.26)]. Hence overidentification poses no difficulty for the estimation of relationships among the $Y_m$—indeed it facilitates sharper estimation of the true causal parameters.

Equations within sectors for the predetermined $X_k$ variables of the model are similarly overidentified. Inspection of Figure 8.2 and/or Equations (8.7) to (8.16) makes this clear. Therefore, it is not necessary to impose on all these equations the additional restriction that cross-equation disturbances are uncorrelated, since many exogenous variables are included in some equations but excluded from others, and not all the endogenous $X_k$

## Table A3.1  Coefficient Matrix for (8.1) through (8.6)

| Equation | $Y_1$ | $Y_2$ | $Y_3$ | $Y_4$ | $Y_5$ | $Y_6$ | $Y^*_1$ | $Y^*_2$ | $Y^*_3$ | $Y^*_4$ | $X_1$ | $X_2$ | $X_4$ | $X_5$ | $X_6$ | $X_7$ | $X_8$ | $X^*_8$ | $X_9$ | $X^*_9$ | $X_{10}$ | $Z_1$ | $Z_2$ | $Z_3$ | $Z_6$ | $Z_7$ | $Z_8$ | $Z_9$ | $Z_{10}$ | $Z_{11}$ | $Z_{12}$ |
|---|---|---|---|---|---|---|---|---|---|---|---|---|---|---|---|---|---|---|---|---|---|---|---|---|---|---|---|---|---|---|---|
| (8.1) | 1 | 0 | $\alpha_{13}$ | $\alpha_{14}$ | $\alpha_{15}$ | 0 | $\alpha^*_{11}$ | 0 | 0 | 0 | $\beta_{11}$ | 0 | $\beta_{14}$ | $\beta_{15}$ | 0 | $\beta_{17}$ | $\beta_{18}$ | 0 | 0 | $\beta^*_{19}$ | $\beta_{1,10}$ | $\gamma_{11}$ | $\gamma_{12}$ | $\gamma_{13}$ | 0 | 0 | 0 | 0 | 0 | 0 | $\gamma_{1,12}$ |
| (8.2) | 0 | 1 | $\alpha_{23}$ | $\alpha_{24}$ | 0 | $\alpha_{26}$ | 0 | $\alpha^*_{22}$ | $\alpha^*_{23}$ | 0 | $\beta_{21}$ | $\beta_{22}$ | 0 | 0 | 0 | $\beta_{27}$ | 0 | $\beta^*_{28}$ | 0 | $\beta^*_{29}$ | $\beta_{2,10}$ | $\gamma_{21}$ | 0 | $\gamma_{23}$ | 0 | 0 | 0 | 0 | 0 | 0 | 0 |
| (8.3) | $\alpha_{31}$ | $\alpha_{32}$ | 1 | $\alpha_{34}$ | 0 | 0 | 0 | 0 | 0 | 0 | 0 | 0 | 0 | $\beta_{35}$ | $\beta_{36}$ | 0 | 0 | 0 | $\beta_{39}$ | 0 | 0 | 0 | 0 | 0 | 0 | 0 | 0 | $\gamma_{39}$ | 0 | $\gamma_{3,11}$ | 0 |
| (8.4) | $\alpha_{41}$ | $\alpha_{42}$ | 0 | 1 | 0 | 0 | 0 | 0 | 0 | $\alpha^*_{44}$ | 0 | 0 | 0 | 0 | 0 | 0 | 0 | 0 | 0 | $\beta^*_{49}$ | 0 | 0 | 0 | 0 | 0 | 0 | 0 | 0 | $\gamma_{4,10}$ | 0 | 0 |
| (8.5) | $\alpha_{51}$ | 0 | 0 | 0 | 1 | 0 | $\alpha^*_{51}$ | 0 | 0 | 0 | 0 | 0 | 0 | 0 | 0 | 0 | 0 | 0 | 0 | 0 | $\beta_{5,10}$ | 0 | 0 | 0 | $\gamma_{56}$ | 0 | $\gamma_{58}$ | 0 | 0 | 0 | 0 |
| (8.6) | 0 | $\alpha_{62}$ | 0 | 0 | 0 | 1 | 0 | $\alpha^*_{62}$ | 0 | 0 | 0 | 0 | 0 | 0 | 0 | 0 | 0 | 0 | 0 | 0 | $\beta_{6,10}$ | 0 | 0 | 0 | 0 | $\gamma_{67}$ | $\gamma_{68}$ | 0 | 0 | 0 | 0 |

variables are (hierarchically) related to others. Hence we could accept the possibility that some of the right-hand side $X_k$ in these equations are correlated with the disturbances and rely upon Instrumental Variable estimation here as well as within the $Y_m$ block. This estimation strategy would yield consistency but also great inefficiency. *Given the non-simultaneous structure of causality in these equations, and our efforts to include as many of the theoretically relevant causal influences as possible, the most reasonable procedure is to assume that disturbances are uncorrelated across equations ($E^*$ diagonal) and to estimate by Ordinary Least Squares where the $X_k$ serve as their own instruments.*

# Supplementary Instrumental Variables—Two Stage Least Squares Estimation Results

Table A 4.1   Equation for Collective Protest D2 ($Y_1$)
(Lagged Endogenous Variables Treated as Endogenous)

| Independent Variable | Parameter Estimate | $t$ Statistic |
|---|---|---|
| ln Negative Sanctions D2 | 0.582 | 1.06 |
| ln Coups D2 | −0.280 | −0.38 |
| Average Annual % Change in Energy Consumption per capita, 1955–1965 | −0.146 | −1.43 |
| Collective Protest D1 | 0.586 | 1.21 |
| Group Discrimination 1960 | 0.014 | 2.11 |
| ln Communist Party Membership 1960 | −0.020 | −0.19 |
| ln Nondefense General Government Expenditures as a % of GDP 1960 | −0.259 | −0.57 |
| ln Institutionalization 1960 | 0.629 | 1.01 |
| % Legislative Seats Held by Non-Communist Left 1960 | −0.004 | −0.74 |
| Average Annual % Change in Population 1955–1965 | −0.072 | −0.37 |
| Social Welfare 1960 | −0.002 | −0.54 |
| Social Mobilization 1960 | 0.003 | 0.42 |
| Social Mobilization/Social Welfare | −3.170 | −0.82 |
| ln Population 1960 | 0.013 | 0.06 |
| Communist Regime Dummy | −2.310 | −2.08 |
| Constant | 0.406 | 0.13 |

| $R^2$ | Regression Standard Error | $F$ |
|---|---|---|
| .482 | 1.38 | 15,92   5.7 |

Table A 4.2 Equation for Internal War D2 ($Y_2$)
(Lagged Endogenous Variables Treated as Endogenous)

| Independent Variable | Parameter Estimate | $t$ Statistic |
|---|---|---|
| ln Negative Sanctions D2 | 1.540 | 3.21 |
| ln Coups D2 | 0.471 | 0.88 |
| Average Annual % Change in GNP per capita 1955–1965 | −0.034 | 0.15 |
| Internal War D1 | 0.424 | 1.69 |
| ln Negative Sanctions D1 | −0.745 | −1.91 |
| Group Discrimination 1960 | 0.004 | 0.65 |
| ln Political Separatism 1960 | 0.341 | 2.28 |
| ln Nondefense General Government Expenditures as a % of GDP 1960 | −0.088 | −0.16 |
| ln Social Welfare 1960 | 0.134 | 0.14 |
| ln Institutionalization 1960 | 0.275 | 0.49 |
| Average Annual % Change in Population 1955–1965 | −0.145 | −0.72 |
| ln Population 1960 | 0.061 | 0.28 |
| Communist Regime Dummy | −2.850 | −3.48 |
| Constant | −3.070 | −0.51 |

| $R^2$ | Regression Standard Error | $F$ |
|---|---|---|
| .713 | 1.65 | 13,94  18.0 |

Table A 4.3 Equation for ln Negative Sanctions D2 ($Y_3$)
(Lagged Endogenous Variables Treated as Endogenous)

| Independent Variable | Parameter Estimate | $t$ Statistic |
|---|---|---|
| Collective Protest D2 | 0.310 | 2.15 |
| Internal War D2 | 0.119 | 1.00 |
| ln Coups D2 | 0.386 | 1.68 |
| % Legislative Seats Held by Non-Communist Left 1960 | 0.0006 | 0.27 |
| Elite Electoral Accountability | −0.632 | −4.72 |
| Institutionalization 1960 | 0.021 | 1.55 |
| Social Mobilization 1960 | −0.0007 | −0.72 |
| Social Mobilization/Institutionalization | 0.044 | 2.19 |
| ln Population 1960 | 0.221 | 3.05 |
| ln Internal Security Forces per 1000 sq km 1965 | 0.134 | 2.59 |
| Constant | 0.324 | 0.44 |

| $R^2$ | Regression Standard Error | $F$ |
|---|---|---|
| .769 | 0.69 | 10,97  32.3 |

Table A 4.4   Equation for ln Coups D2 ($Y_4$)
(Lagged Endogenous Variables Treated as Endogenous)

| Independent Variable | Parameter Estimate | $t$ Statistic |
|---|---|---|
| Collective Protest D2 | −0.111 | −1.05 |
| Internal War D2 | 0.147 | 1.85 |
| ln Coups D1 | 0.640 | 5.22 |
| ln Institutionalization 1960 | −0.110 | −0.65 |
| Defense Expenditures as a % of | | |
| General Government Expenditures 1960 | 0.011 | 1.36 |
| Constant | 0.207 | 0.36 |

| $R^2$ | Regression Standard Error | $F$ |
|---|---|---|
| .458 | 0.69 | 5,102   17.3 |

Table A 4.5   Equation for Average Annual Percentage Change in Energy
Consumption Per Capita 1955–1965 ($Y_5$)
(Lagged Endogenous Variables Treated as Endogenous)

| Independent Variable | Parameter Estimate | $t$ Statistic |
|---|---|---|
| Collective Protest D2 | −0.265 | −0.64 |
| Collective Protest D1 | 0.039 | 0.08 |
| Average Annual % Change in | | |
| Population 1955–1965 | −0.113 | −0.34 |
| ln Energy Consumption | | |
| per capita 1960 | −0.529 | −1.74 |
| Gross Fixed Domestic Capital | | |
| Formation as a % of GNP 1960 | 0.078 | 0.76 |
| Constant | 5.763 | 2.46 |

| $R^2$ | Regression Standard Error | $F$ |
|---|---|---|
| .071 | 3.73 | 5,102   1.57 |

Table A4.6  Equation for Average Annual Percentage Change in Gross National Product Per Capita 1955–1965 ($Y_6$)
(Lagged Endogenous Variables Treated as Endogenous)

| Independent Variable | Parameter Estimate | $t$ Statistic |
|---|---|---|
| Internal War D2 | −0.044 | −0.27 |
| Internal War D1 | −0.217 | −1.40 |
| Average Annual % Change in Population 1955–1965 | 0.362 | 1.66 |
| ln GNP per capita 1960 (in thousands of 1965 U.S. dollars) | 0.094 | 0.31 |
| Gross Fixed Domestic Capital Formation as a % of GNP 1960 | 0.101 | 1.39 |
| Constant | −0.578 | −0.27 |

| $R^2$ | Regression Standard Error | $F$ |
|---|---|---|
| .079 | 2.51 | 5,102  1.7 |


Table A4.7  First Revised Equation for Collective Protest D2 ($Y_1$)
(Lagged Endogenous Variables Treated as Endogenous)

| Independent Variable | Parameter Estimate | $t$ Statistic |
|---|---|---|
| ln Negative Sanctions D2 | 0.649 | 4.61 |
| Average Annual % Change in Energy Consumption per capita 1955–1965 | −0.071 | −2.46 |
| Group Discrimination 1960 | 0.012 | 2.67 |
| ln Communist Party Membership 1960 | 0.063 | 2.04 |
| % Legislative Seats Held by Non-Communist Left 1960 | −0.003 | −0.86 |
| ln Population 1960 | 0.259 | 2.31 |
| Communist Regime Dummy | −2.489 | −5.61 |
| Constant | −1.828 | −2.09 |

| $R^2$ | Regression Standard Error | $F$ |
|---|---|---|
| .658 | 1.08 | 7,100  27.5 |

235

Table A 4.8 First Revised Equation for Internal War D2 ($Y_2$)
(Lagged Endogenous Variables Treated as Endogenous)

| Independent Variable | Parameter Estimate | $t$ Statistic |
|---|---|---|
| ln Negative Sanctions D2 | 1.570 | 3.76 |
| ln Coups D2 | 0.371 | 0.77 |
| Internal War D1 | 0.330 | 2.00 |
| ln Negative Sanctions D1 | −0.671 | −3.23 |
| Group Discrimination 1960 | 0.003 | 0.53 |
| ln Political Separatism 1960 | 0.288 | 2.45 |
| ln Population 1960 | 0.149 | 0.72 |
| Communist Regime Dummy | −2.652 | −3.67 |
| Constant | −2.712 | −1.94 |

| $R^2$ | Regression Standard Error | $F$ |
|---|---|---|
| .700 | 1.64 | 8,99   28.8 |

Table A 4.9 First Revised Equation for ln Negative Sanctions D2 ($Y_3$)
(Lagged Endogenous Variables Treated as Endogenous)

| Independent Variable | Parameter Estimate | $t$ Statistic |
|---|---|---|
| Collective Protest D2 | 0.306 | 2.14 |
| Internal War D2 | 0.149 | 1.26 |
| ln Coups D2 | 0.366 | 1.62 |
| Elite Electoral Accountability | −0.633 | −4.79 |
| Institutionalization 1960 | 0.021 | 1.55 |
| Social Mobilization 1960 | −.0007 | −0.71 |
| Social Mobilization/Institutionalization | 0.044 | 2.22 |
| ln Population 1960 | 0.219 | 3.06 |
| ln Internal Security Forces per 1000 sq km 1965 | 0.127 | 2.72 |
| Constant | 0.446 | 0.59 |

| $R^2$ | Regression Standard Error | $F$ |
|---|---|---|
| .771 | 0.68 | 9,98   36.8 |

Table A 4.10 First Revised Equation for ln Coups D2 $(Y_4)$
(Lagged Endogenous Variables Treated as Endogenous)

| Independent Variable | Parameter Estimate | $t$ Statistic |
|---|---|---|
| Internal War D2 | 0.074 | 1.96 |
| ln Coups D1 | 0.634 | 5.39 |
| ln Institutionalization 1960 | −0.195 | −1.51 |
| Defense Expenditures as a % of General Government Expenditures 1960 | 0.015 | 2.20 |
| Constant | 0.360 | 0.74 |

| $R^2$ | Regression Standard Error | $F$ |
|---|---|---|
| .498 | 0.66 | 4,103   25.6 |

Table A 4.11 Second Revised Equation for Collective Protest D2 $(Y_1)$
(Lagged Endogenous Variables Treated as Endogenous)

| Independent Variable | Parameter Estimate | $t$ Statistic |
|---|---|---|
| ln Negative Sanctions D2 | 0.672 | 4.90 |
| Average Annual % Change in Energy Consumption per capita 1955–1965 | −0.070 | −2.41 |
| Group Discrimination 1960 | 0.012 | 2.84 |
| ln Communist Party Membership 1960 | 0.061 | 2.00 |
| ln Population 1960 | 0.261 | 2.34 |
| Communist Regime Dummy | −2.414 | −5.59 |
| Constant | −2.029 | −2.42 |

| $R^2$ | Regression Standard Error | $F$ |
|---|---|---|
| .658 | 1.07 | 6,101   32.5 |

Table A 4.12  Second Revised Equation for Internal War D2 $(Y_2)$
(Lagged Endogenous Variables Treated as Endogenous)

| Independent Variable | Parameter Estimate | $t$ Statistic |
|---|---|---|
| ln Negative Sanctions D2 | 1.816 | 5.60 |
| Internal War D1 | 0.378 | 2.42 |
| ln Negative Sanctions D1 | −0.745 | −3.80 |
| ln Political Separatism | 0.276 | 2.30 |
| ln Population 1960 | 0.038 | 0.22 |
| Communist Regime Dummy | −2.848 | −4.06 |
| Constant | −2.304 | −1.69 |

| $R^2$ | Regression Standard Error | $F$ |
|---|---|---|
| .671 | 1.71 | 6,101   34.3 |

# Values of Collective Protest D2 and Internal War D2

Table A5.1  Actual, Fitted, and Residual Values of Collective Protest D2

| Nation | Actual | Fitted | Residual |
|---|---|---|---|
| Afghanistan | 3.045 | 1.972 | 1.073 |
| Albania | 0.0 | 0.164 | −0.164 |
| Algeria | 5.075 | 4.444 | 0.631 |
| Argentina | 5.268 | 5.265 | 0.003 |
| Australia | 1.099 | 1.289 | −0.190 |
| Austria | 3.258 | 2.873 | 0.385 |
| Belgium | 4.511 | 2.961 | 1.550 |
| Bolivia | 5.416 | 4.612 | 0.804 |
| Brazil | 5.308 | 5.284 | 0.024 |
| Bulgaria | 1.609 | 1.142 | 0.467 |
| Burma | 3.178 | 4.165 | −0.987 |
| Cambodia | 1.792 | 1.979 | −0.187 |
| Cameroon | 1.792 | 1.829 | −0.037 |
| Canada | 3.738 | 3.697 | 0.041 |
| Central African Rep. | 0.0 | 0.535 | −0.535 |
| Ceylon | 4.317 | 4.058 | 0.259 |
| Chad | 3.045 | 1.796 | 1.249 |
| Chile | 4.533 | 3.701 | 0.832 |
| Colombia | 5.215 | 4.232 | 0.983 |
| Congo, Leopoldville | 5.176 | 4.246 | 0.930 |
| Costa Rica | 2.303 | 2.516 | −0.213 |
| Cuba | 4.304 | 5.130 | −0.826 |
| Czechoslovakia | 2.773 | 1.954 | 0.819 |
| Dahomey | 3.912 | 2.024 | 1.888 |
| Denmark | 2.773 | 2.061 | 0.712 |
| Dominican Republic | 5.198 | 4.920 | 0.278 |

| Nation | Actual | Fitted | Residual |
|---|---|---|---|
| Ecuador | 5.063 | 4.358 | 0.705 |
| El Salvador | 3.611 | 3.674 | −0.063 |
| Ethiopia | 2.197 | 2.577 | −0.380 |
| Finland | 1.946 | 2.149 | −0.203 |
| France | 5.209 | 5.265 | −0.056 |
| Germany, East | 2.639 | 2.794 | −0.155 |
| Germany, West | 4.466 | 5.060 | −0.594 |
| Ghana | 2.639 | 3.565 | −0.926 |
| Greece | 4.078 | 3.359 | 0.719 |
| Guatemala | 4.533 | 4.613 | −0.080 |
| Guinea | 2.833 | 2.093 | 0.740 |
| Haiti | 3.219 | 4.000 | −0.781 |
| Honduras | 2.944 | 3.338 | −0.394 |
| Hong Kong | 0.0 | 2.889 | −2.889 |
| Hungary | 1.386 | 2.501 | −1.115 |
| India | 7.331 | 5.450 | 1.881 |
| Indonesia | 4.025 | 5.839 | −1.814 |
| Iran | 4.920 | 4.548 | 0.372 |
| Iraq | 4.454 | 3.894 | 0.560 |
| Ireland | 1.386 | 1.587 | −0.201 |
| Israel | 4.263 | 3.393 | 0.870 |
| Italy | 4.934 | 4.159 | 0.775 |
| Ivory Coast | 0.0 | 1.800 | −1.800 |
| Jamaica | 1.946 | 1.260 | 0.686 |
| Japan | 5.142 | 3.823 | 1.319 |
| Jordan | 3.555 | 3.254 | 0.301 |
| Kenya | 4.585 | 4.730 | −0.145 |
| Korea, South | 5.561 | 3.761 | 1.800 |
| Laos | 0.693 | 1.727 | −1.034 |
| Lebanon | 4.575 | 4.408 | 0.167 |
| Liberia | 1.386 | 1.105 | 0.281 |
| Libya | 3.219 | 1.282 | 1.937 |
| Madagascar | 0.0 | 0.529 | −0.529 |
| Malawi | 4.745 | 4.109 | 0.636 |
| Malaysia | 3.951 | 4.259 | −0.308 |
| Mali | 2.398 | 1.287 | 1.111 |
| Mexico | 5.043 | 4.527 | 0.516 |
| Morocco | 3.932 | 4.141 | −0.209 |
| Netherlands | 1.099 | 2.824 | −1.725 |
| New Zealand | 0.0 | 1.082 | −1.082 |
| Nicaragua | 3.932 | 3.441 | 0.491 |
| Niger | 0.0 | 1.370 | −1.370 |
| Nigeria | 4.682 | 3.951 | 0.731 |
| Norway | 1.099 | 1.797 | −0.698 |

Table A5.1  Actual, Fitted, and Residual Values of Collective
Protest D2 (Continued)

| Nation | Actual | Fitted | Residual |
|---|---|---|---|
| Pakistan | 5.075 | 4.662 | 0.413 |
| Panama | 4.710 | 3.763 | 0.947 |
| Paraguay | 3.219 | 4.198 | −0.979 |
| Peru | 4.554 | 4.346 | 0.208 |
| Philippines | 1.609 | 3.267 | −1.658 |
| Poland | 3.401 | 2.486 | 0.915 |
| Portugal | 4.564 | 4.314 | 0.250 |
| Puerto Rico | 2.944 | 1.462 | 1.482 |
| Rhodesia | 5.273 | 4.684 | 0.589 |
| Rumania | 1.386 | 1.710 | −0.324 |
| Saudi Arabia | 0.0 | 2.082 | −2.082 |
| Senegal | 3.584 | 2.134 | 1.450 |
| Sierra Leone | 0.693 | 1.473 | −0.780 |
| Singapore | 2.197 | 2.701 | −0.504 |
| Somalia | 2.773 | 1.969 | 0.804 |
| South Africa | 5.384 | 5.983 | −0.599 |
| Spain | 4.111 | 4.792 | −0.681 |
| Sudan | 4.394 | 3.901 | 0.493 |
| Sweden | 1.792 | 2.551 | −0.759 |
| Switzerland | 1.609 | 2.549 | −0.940 |
| Syria | 4.920 | 4.520 | 0.400 |
| Taiwan | 0.693 | 2.604 | −1.911 |
| Tanzania | 1.386 | 2.882 | −1.496 |
| Thailand | 0.0 | 3.887 | −3.887 |
| Togoland | 0.693 | 1.842 | −1.149 |
| Tunisia | 2.303 | 3.306 | −1.003 |
| Turkey | 4.575 | 4.869 | −0.294 |
| Uganda | 4.804 | 3.994 | 0.810 |
| United Arab Republic (Egypt) | 2.079 | 4.229 | −2.150 |
| USSR | 3.850 | 4.016 | −0.166 |
| United Kingdom | 5.088 | 4.528 | 0.560 |
| United States | 7.116 | 6.137 | 0.979 |
| Upper Volta | 0.693 | 1.014 | −0.321 |
| Uruguay | 4.248 | 2.762 | 1.486 |
| Venezuela | 5.663 | 5.132 | 0.531 |
| Vietnam, South | 5.318 | 4.957 | 0.361 |
| Yugoslavia | 1.609 | 1.885 | −0.276 |
| Zambia | 5.366 | 3.914 | 1.452 |

Table A 5.2   Actual, Fitted and Residual Values of Internal
                War D2

| Nation | Actual | Fitted | Residual |
|---|---|---|---|
| Afghanistan | 5.011 | 1.871 | 3.140 |
| Albania | 0.0 | 0.212 | −0.212 |
| Algeria | 9.970 | 8.406 | 1.564 |
| Argentina | 6.198 | 7.391 | −1.193 |
| Australia | 1.946 | −3.072 | 5.018 |
| Austria | 2.079 | 1.134 | 0.945 |
| Belgium | 6.326 | 3.616 | 2.710 |
| Bolivia | 7.060 | 5.958 | 1.102 |
| Brazil | 5.370 | 5.759 | −0.388 |
| Bulgaria | 0.693 | −0.266 | 0.959 |
| Burma | 6.361 | 7.260 | −0.899 |
| Cambodia | 1.386 | 4.988 | −3.602 |
| Cameroon | 11.166 | 4.687 | 6.479 |
| Canada | 4.682 | 3.764 | 0.918 |
| Central African Rep. | 1.609 | 0.394 | 1.214 |
| Ceylon | 5.846 | 5.832 | 0.014 |
| Chad | 2.996 | 4.080 | −1.084 |
| Chile | 3.871 | 3.179 | 0.692 |
| Colombia | 8.761 | 6.006 | 2.755 |
| Congo, Leopoldville | 9.693 | 8.578 | 1.116 |
| Costa Rica | 1.946 | 3.267 | −1.321 |
| Cuba | 9.047 | 8.352 | 0.695 |
| Czechoslovakia | 0.0 | 1.369 | −1.369 |
| Dahomey | 3.689 | 4.783 | −1.094 |
| Denmark | 0.0 | 0.782 | −0.782 |
| Dominican Republic | 8.074 | 6.931 | 1.143 |
| Ecuador | 5.568 | 5.265 | 0.303 |
| El Salvador | 3.850 | 3.737 | 0.113 |
| Ethiopia | 6.402 | 4.518 | 1.884 |
| Finland | 1.609 | 0.305 | 1.304 |
| France | 6.380 | 6.121 | 0.259 |
| Germany, East | 3.850 | 2.981 | 0.869 |
| Germany, West | 2.833 | 4.773 | −1.940 |
| Ghana | 3.892 | 6.755 | −2.863 |
| Greece | 2.833 | 5.048 | −2.215 |
| Guatemala | 5.986 | 5.973 | 0.013 |
| Guinea | 1.609 | 3.647 | −2.038 |
| Haiti | 6.378 | 6.656 | −0.278 |
| Honduras | 5.829 | 3.799 | 2.030 |
| Hong Kong | 0.0 | 2.137 | −2.137 |
| Hungary | 3.219 | 3.665 | −0.446 |
| India | 7.689 | 7.241 | 0.448 |
| Indonesia | 9.931 | 10.163 | −0.232 |
| Iran | 6.229 | 7.421 | −1.192 |

Table A 5.2    Actual, Fitted and Residual Values of Internal
War D2 (Continued)

| Nation | Actual | Fitted | Residual |
|---|---|---|---|
| Iraq | 9.274 | 7.075 | 2.199 |
| Ireland | 2.773 | 1.452 | 1.321 |
| Israel | 3.091 | 3.324 | −0.233 |
| Italy | 5.182 | 3.225 | 1.957 |
| Ivory Coast | 0.693 | 3.008 | −2.315 |
| Jamaica | 3.045 | 1.082 | 1.963 |
| Japan | 2.197 | 2.408 | −0.211 |
| Jordan | 4.110 | 6.090 | −1.979 |
| Kenya | 7.160 | 8.443 | −1.283 |
| Korea, South | 6.321 | 7.373 | −1.052 |
| Laos | 7.871 | 7.577 | 0.294 |
| Lebanon | 7.033 | 6.858 | 0.175 |
| Liberia | 0.0 | 1.036 | −1.036 |
| Libya | 3.135 | 2.247 | 0.888 |
| Madagascar | 0.0 | −0.806 | 0.806 |
| Malawi | 4.736 | 5.914 | −1.178 |
| Malaysia | 8.272 | 6.537 | 1.735 |
| Mali | 2.565 | 1.892 | 0.673 |
| Mexico | 5.727 | 6.310 | −0.583 |
| Morocco | 5.781 | 6.992 | −1.211 |
| Netherlands | 0.0 | −0.182 | 0.182 |
| New Zealand | 0.0 | −0.296 | 0.296 |
| Nicaragua | 6.111 | 5.291 | 0.820 |
| Niger | 3.526 | 3.136 | 0.390 |
| Nigeria | 7.550 | 7.651 | −0.101 |
| Norway | 0.0 | −0.128 | 0.128 |
| Pakistan | 7.796 | 7.266 | 0.530 |
| Panama | 4.682 | 4.382 | 0.300 |
| Paraguay | 5.142 | 5.746 | −0.604 |
| Peru | 6.326 | 5.889 | 0.437 |
| Philippines | 5.434 | 4.575 | 0.859 |
| Poland | 2.639 | 2.621 | 0.018 |
| Portugal | 4.111 | 4.903 | −0.792 |
| Puerto Rico | 2.639 | 2.362 | 0.277 |
| Rhodesia | 5.226 | 7.432 | −2.206 |
| Rumania | 0.0 | 0.218 | −0.218 |
| Saudi Arabia | 0.0 | 0.983 | −0.983 |
| Senegal | 3.367 | 3.895 | −0.528 |
| Sierra Leone | 1.792 | 2.304 | −0.512 |
| Singapore | 0.0 | 3.214 | −3.214 |
| Somalia | 4.522 | 6.673 | −2.151 |
| South Africa | 6.567 | 8.276 | −1.709 |
| Spain | 4.663 | 6.644 | −1.981 |
| Sudan | 7.024 | 6.528 | 0.496 |

Table A 5.2    Actual, Fitted and Residual Values of Internal
War D2 (Continued)

| Nation | Actual | Fitted | Residual |
|---|---|---|---|
| Sweden | 0.0 | 0.157 | −0.157 |
| Switzerland | 0.693 | 1.659 | −0.966 |
| Syria | 7.231 | 7.910 | −0.679 |
| Taiwan | 6.762 | 4.603 | 2.159 |
| Tanzania | 3.434 | 4.282 | −0.848 |
| Thailand | 4.078 | 4.272 | −0.194 |
| Togoland | 2.485 | 3.506 | −1.021 |
| Tunisia | 7.946 | 4.868 | 3.078 |
| Turkey | 4.331 | 5.891 | −1.560 |
| Uganda | 6.356 | 4.638 | 1.718 |
| United Arab Republic (Egypt) | 1.946 | 4.976 | −3.030 |
| USSR | 5.796 | 4.296 | 1.500 |
| United Kingdom | 2.833 | 4.775 | −1.942 |
| United States | 6.454 | 8.656 | −2.202 |
| Upper Volta | 0.0 | 1.932 | −1.932 |
| Uruguay | 2.639 | 2.877 | −0.238 |
| Venezuela | 7.691 | 6.966 | 0.725 |
| Vietnam, South | 11.167 | 9.548 | 1.620 |
| Yugoslavia | 0.0 | 1.100 | −1.100 |
| Zambia | 6.891 | 4.889 | 2.002 |

# Index

Achievement, aspiration and imbalance between, 45n5
Affluence, growth of, 22
  post-industrial, 21-28 *passim*
Aggregation of data, 199-200
Aigner, Dennis J., 200n8
Aitchison, J., 200n6
Ake, Claude, 82, 82n2
Alienation, 43, 45
  of the intellectuals, 48n11
Alker, Hayward R. Jr., 3n1, 4n4, 11n10, 35, 35n35, 36, 199n5
Almond, Gabriel A., 55n18, 125n11
Anomic violence, 11, 36n36, 84
  definition of, 9
  factor scores for, 35
Anscombe, F. J., 10n7, 195n23
Antigovernment demonstrations, *see* Demonstrations, antigovernment
Armed attacks, *see* Attacks
Aspiration, achievement and imbalance between, 45n5
  education, 46
  urban-generated, 51-54 *passim*
Assassinations, 7, 8n2, 9, 11, 11n10, 15, 16. *See also* Internal War
Assimilated population, violence and, 67
Assimilation, 72
Attacks, armed, 8-16 *passim* ⇒ *see also* Internal war
Autocorrelation, 222-225
  bias and, 107n47

Benjamin, Roger W., 149, 149n13, 176
Berkowitz, Leonard, 43n1
Bernd, J. L., 3n1
Bias, statistical, 108-109
Binder, Leonard, 65n1

Blalock, Hubert M., 3n1, 4n3, 180n11, 199n5, 200n6
Block recursive models, defined, 221
  identification and, 221-222
  multiequation model, 135-153 *passim*
Bohrnstedt, George W., 158n2, 179n10, 180n11
Bolivia, Communist Party in, 125
Borgatta, Edgar F., 158n2, 179n10, 180n11
Briggs, F. E. A., 25n11
Brinton, Crane, 32n22, 48n11
Bwy, Douglas P., 8n11, 11, 14n11, 22n2, 35n36, 36n36, 84, 84n7

Canada, French separatism in, 65
Capital Formation, 137-146 *passim*
  in equations, 139, 156-161 *passim*
Causal effects, relative path coefficients and, 179
Causality, simultaneous, 139, 141
Causal systems, nonrecursive, 135
  recursive, 135
Center for Research on Conflict Resolution, 6, 8n2
Christ, Carl F., 206n1
Class conflict, 22
Class warfare, 22
Class, working, 22
Cnudde, Charles F., 118, 118n5, 149, 149n12
Cohen, Jacob, 10n5, 78n19
Coleman, James S., 45, 45n6, 46n7, 201, 201n9
Collective Protest, 14, 16, 25, 32, 36n36, 47
  aggregation of data and, 200
  communist party membership and, 125-131 *passim*, 192-194
  tables on, 126, 129
  communist regimes and, 122-131